D0615415

On Becoming a Leadership Coach

On Becoming a Leadership Coach

A Holistic Approach to Coaching Excellence

Edited by
Christine Wahl, Clarice Scriber,
and Beth Bloomfield

ON BECOMING A LEADERSHIP COACH

First published in 2008 by
PALGRAVE MACMILLAN®
in the US—a division of St. Martin's Press LLC,
175 Fifth Avenue, New York, NY 10010.

Where this book is distributed in the UK, Europe and the rest of the world,
this is by Palgrave Macmillan, a division of Macmillan Publishers Limited,
registered in England, company number 785998, of Houndmills,
Basingstoke, Hampshire RG21 6XS.

Palgrave Macmillan is the global academic imprint of the above companies
and has companies and representatives throughout the world.

Palgrave® and Macmillan® are registered trademarks in the United States,
the United Kingdom, Europe and other countries.

ISBN-13: 978–0–230–60678–4
ISBN-10: 0–230–60678–4

Library of Congress Cataloging-in-Publication Data

On becoming a leadership coach : a holistic approach to
coaching excellence / edited by : Christine Wahl, Clarice Scriber, and Beth
Bloomfield.
    p. cm.
Includes bibliographical references and index.
ISBN 0–230–60678–4
    1. Executives—Training of. 2. Executive coaching. 3. Leadership.
4. Employees—Coaching of. I. Wahl, Christine. II. Scriber, Clarice.
III. Bloomfield, Beth.

HD30.4.O5 2008
658.4'092—dc22   2008000544

A catalogue record for this book is available from the British Library.

Design by Newgen Imaging Systems (P) Ltd., Chennai, India.

First edition: August 2008

10 9 8 7 6 5 4 3 2 1

Transferred to Digital Printing in 2012

*To our students over the years in the
Georgetown University Leadership Coaching Program,
who have found their own unique leadership coaching
voices through mastery and improvisation.*

Contents

Part III   Using

Figures

Tables

Templates

Introduction

Christine M. Wahl

> One way or another, we all have to find what best fosters the flowering of
> our humanity in this contemporary life, and dedicate ourselves to that.
> —Joseph Campbell

Possibility. Sustainability. Agility. Reality. Opportunity. Quality. Authenticity. Ability. Capacity. Stability. Productivity. Curiosity. Rationality. Emotionality. Dignity. Humanity.

The meanings associated with this word list have tremendous connection to the work we do as leadership coaches. Coaching leaders is a heart-and-soul, mind-and-body endeavor. Such an endeavor focuses on results and requires clients to step on the challenging path of moving beyond one's current boundaries. Such work is uncomfortable, emboldening, freeing, and grounding. For surely, it brings leaders back to a person they know well—themselves.

So much of coaching leaders is about helping them remember their best version of "self." We call this authenticity. We need more of it from our leaders.

The chapters in *On Becoming a Leadership Coach: A Holistic Approach to Coaching Excellence* are written by coaches and educators who have been on the faculty of the Leadership Coaching Certificate Program at Georgetown University. The writings cover topics that reflect heart and soul, mind and body. Our intention in writing this book, divided into major sections of "Being," "Doing," and "Using," is to share our current thinking in multiple domains of leadership coaching. While aimed primarily at helping coaches stay in their own development and giving coaches concepts and tools to work with, this book speaks also to leaders, managers, educators, consultants, psychologists, clergy, and entrepreneurs. The concepts presented here apply to development and thereby help anyone wishing to understand themselves better find greater fulfillment in their personal lives and create more productive work lives.

In this book, you will find chapters on what it means to "be" a coach, what coaches "do," and tools that coaches "use." The act of coaching leaders is aimed at supporting them in producing sustainable results in the most humane way. Leaders create the future, they affect business, economics, global productivity, efficiency, and sustainability, and they do this through the "who" that they embody daily. Their "who" touches and influences all the people in their orbit, both near and far. It is from their "who" that their actions flow, and from their actions, they work to achieve results that will benefit the whole—their organizations and, ultimately, the larger systems within which they live.

As coaches, we have been influenced by many who came before us and wish to thank each of the big thinkers we have learned from. While there are too many to mention here, we are grateful to all of those teachers who have been in our lives, either by reading their work or experiencing their teaching in real-time, who have challenged our thinking and supported our humanness in ways big and small. We are grateful to all of our students, who over the past seven years, have stimulated fantastic conversations and helped us to continually refine our own processes. We are grateful to the deans and administrators who have known and supported us at Georgetown University. Lastly, we are grateful to our families, whose precious and generous support surely allows us to focus on our passion of creating more joy and life within organizations, through the courage of the leaders with whom we work.

As you read the following chapters, we hope you find inspiration and validation, and that your passion for excellence finds a new spark that continues to motivate. Every coach is an ambassador for bringing generosity, openness, curiosity, and kindness into the world of achieving in the workplace; coaching leaders brings these qualities of humanity to the foundation of doing business in today's world, with the mission of creating more and more ambassadors. May you be graced with time to reflect, support to engage in personal and professional renewal, and resolve to continue to make a difference in the lives—the "being alive"—of those you influence.

> I don't believe people are looking for the meaning of life as much as they are looking for the experience of being alive.
>
> —Joseph Campbell

PART I

Being

CHAPTER 1

On Becoming a Leadership Coach

Neil Stroul and Christine M. Wahl

There are two ways to live your life—one is as though nothing is a miracle, the other is as though everything is a miracle.

—Albert Einstein

The operative word in the title of this chapter is "becoming." Human beings always become something. Those who like to learn set their intention to becoming a new and learned version of their self. Those who are mindful find ways to learn from the multiple events, surprises, and disappointments that comprise daily life; they also know they will never really "arrive" at a place of achieving "becoming"—like a river that continues to flow, the lessons are too numerous, our time is too short.

A model we wrote about for the inaugural edition of *Choice*,[1] a publication devoted to the blossoming field of professional coaching, serves us here. We explored coaching through three distinct perspectives—Being versus Doing versus Using. In this chapter, we take the model in a new direction, exploring the three perspectives in the question of how one *becomes* a leadership coach.

Before moving into the model, we want to emphasize that becoming a leadership coach demands certain knowledge in addition to knowing the fundamentals of coaching. Leaders today are challenged to the max. Stakes are high. Competition in the marketplace is a fast-paced game. The spotlight is constant, and it is sometimes hot. The business world seems to require that leaders be beyond human, demanding 24/7 accessibility, perfection, up-to-the-minute knowledge, vision, stamina, emotional agility, and people savvy. Leadership coaches must have experience in organizations, systems, and change and must possess business acumen to have any credibility with leaders in today's organizations. Leadership coaches must understand and know how to work with pressured leaders in today's complicated systems and, as such, have highly developed distinctions of their own about what it means to be a leader.

The original conception of "becoming" was introduced in 1955 by Gordon Allport,[2] who found the then-prevalent conceptions of adult personality development to be lacking. Although Allport's framework is beyond the scope of this article, we do want to acknowledge his ideas that we humans continue to evolve and develop across the span of our lives, that each of us represents a unique self, continually integrating new experiences that are reflected in who we "be." Regardless of what might be apparently stable traits, we are continually *becoming*. The "who" that we "be" has the possibility of continued growth and development.

First, we believe that coaches need to develop their own voice, rigor, and conception of coaching, by blending what they learn from the experts in the field through training and experience with their own way of applying what they learn. As teachers in the field of coaching, we expose our students to many different formulations about coaching, and from their learning, we ask them to extract and integrate for themselves those ideas that are resonant with who they are as unique individuals. Coaches have a professional obligation to aspire to become masters of their own discipline and to engage in continual self-development. Our becoming reflects our being. Our being informs our doing. The tools and techniques we use are an extension of our being. *Being* is the cornerstone.

On Becoming a Coach: Being

> The real magic of discovery lies not in seeking new landscapes, but in having new eyes.
>
> —Marcel Proust

Although we encourage our student coaches to formulate a highly personalized understanding of coaching, that is not to say that we don't subscribe to several key principles. Coaching is a personalized vehicle for supporting clients in "stepping up and into" their own development. Development involves transformations based on increasing one's awareness. Through coaching, clients discover possibilities that were previously unavailable to them, given the way they had constructed their world; the clients' current state of awareness constrained the range of possibilities available to them. Awareness is not the same as insight. Awareness is dynamic. In the moment, what are we able to notice? Expanding awareness involves the capacity to shift what we notice and how we think so that we see our possibilities through new eyes.

Emerging awareness, seeing new perspectives, and noticing how and what we notice—these threads collectively generate a living tapestry we call *being*. To help aspiring coaches explore their being, we rely on several conceptual tools.

Bodies of Distinction

The first concept is "body of distinctions," which is a widely used concept in coach training. A body of distinctions equates to highly personalized frames of reference, or mental models, that serve as heuristics that determine what a person is able to notice. The idea that each of us possesses a highly personalized body of distinctions has been applied in music, cultural anthropology, philosophy, and now coaching. The idea of distinctions is best understood through illustrations.

Imagine standing on a bluff overlooking a desert landscape. Imagine allowing your gaze to slowly scan your surroundings. What might you notice? Sand? Vastness? Scrub vegetation? Blowing winds alternating with silence? Then, imagine being joined by a Saharan tribesman. What might the tribesman notice? Not only would he notice features of the landscape that escaped your notice, but he might also employ a dramatically different vocabulary to express what he notices. Much of what he is able to notice is informed by his body of distinctions. The tribesman would see the patterns in the sand, take clues from the vegetation. These might tell him of recent visitors to the area, or upcoming weather. He would be able to tell a story about the landscape that you would not be able to tell, based on the differences in your knowledge, or bodies of distinction.

Two individuals stand before a third person. We ask each individual, "What do you notice?" Would their descriptions be similar? If one individual is a fashion consultant and the other is a fitness trainer, might they focus on different features and express themselves through different vocabularies? Our bodies of distinctions will often draw our attention to different features of what we observe.

Are the words "red" and "green" in your vocabulary? If we show you two identical items, except one is painted red and the other green, would you be able to distinguish one from the other on the basis of color? If so, you have the distinction of red versus green. Similarly, we could ask someone who suffers from red-green color blindness the same question, and although such a person's vocabulary may have the words red and green, the person doesn't truly operate with the red-green distinction.

Generally, our bodies of distinction work in the background, operating implicitly. Yet, as we said in our introduction, all of us are unique individuals with unique histories and, therefore, unique bodies of distinction. Unless we consciously choose to make these distinctions explicit, we may never recognize that we may "see" yet not truly notice. Generally, we are inclined to attach significance to what we notice only to the degree that the significance meets one of these conditions: One, it is already present in our preexisting body of distinctions, or, two, we are engaged in some form of learning that is intended to expand or modify our current body of distinctions. The immense implication is that, as often as not, our experiences are determined not only by features of events in real time, but also by preconceptions and conditioned tendencies that shape our experience.

For all of us, our "structural determinism" is at work. The idea of structural determinism was initially proposed by the research biologists Humberto Maturana and Francisco Varela.[3] Structural determinism represents that experience involves an interaction, and that experience is not "pure." Rather, our experience is to some degree determined by both the nature of our biological/physical structure, and the recognition that prior experience shapes what we are able to experience in the present. We are all Pavlov's dog, creatures of habit, repositories of our individual conditioning histories, reflexively salivating to our own wide, highly personalized array of tones and bells. If we are able to learn to notice how we notice, we will also be able to reclaim greater control of our experience. How do we learn to explicitly recognize our body of distinctions?

> Reality is merely an illusion, albeit a very persistent one.
>
> —Albert Einstein

Our bodies of distinction operate implicitly. We don't experience our distinctions directly, or with awareness, though we do experience the effects of them. Part of the early work of becoming a coach is to learn how to bring our bodies of distinction to the surface, to make them explicit. To help aspiring coaches expose their distinctions, we work with the concept of "stories."

We experience our lives as extending through time, as a subjective narrative. Said a different way, your life is a story. The idea of story suggests the creative nature of our experience of our lives. We do not necessarily choose the circumstances of our lives, but we can choose the stories regarding how we "hold" and interpret those experiences. We not only live life, we also explain it. We communicate our lives to others through the stories that we tell. We are meaning making creatures. Subjectively, the various events and experiences of life are connected to each other through time and through a series of linkages of causes and effects. At the most basic level, a story is nothing more than our account of the relationship between some effect or result that we notice, and what we perceive as the cause. The stories you live and the stories you tell are a window into your body of distinctions.

For all of us, the common factor in our stories is we ourselves. We are the recurring character—the hero. We are the constant thread. Initiating the process of examining our own stories, becoming genuinely curious about who we are and how we conduct ourselves, and shifting away from relating to our stories as journalistic reports of news to seeing them as expressions of our creative self allow us to examine the dynamic way we as storytellers create our story. Coaches must be able to distinguish their stories! The intent at this stage is to raise awareness rather than to generate insight.

As a coach, as we achieve a better grasp of our way of being in our stories, we are able to see that we are both author and actor. For any adult, seeing oneself as both author and actor constitutes a major step into one's own development, being able to make meaning from the viewpoint of a curious observer, where the self becomes both subject and object. To do this, a coach must become genuinely curious about their self and learn to tolerate discomfort, as aspects of self that had previously been hidden from view are now available for personal scrutiny and learning. Later, when a coach engages with clients, this same curiosity becomes part of the coaching relationship in service of clients, helping them to explore their stories and how their stories inform their thinking, feelings, decisions, and actions.

> The most beautiful thing we can experience is the mysterious. It is the source of all true art and all science. He to whom this emotion is a stranger, who can no longer pause to wonder and stand rapt in awe, is as good as dead: his eyes are closed.
>
> —Albert Einstein

For aspiring coaches, learning how your stories reveal your body of distinctions represents an accessible framework for perceiving "who you be" and for creating new awareness. This new level of awareness is the beginning of a walk into infinity in terms of the possibility for personal learning. In other words, once the awareness muscle is exposed and consciously used, it is regenerative ad infinitum.

From an examined state of being and an ability to be present, coaches have the ability to choose from a wider array of responses and actions to benefit their clients. Lacking this level of engagement internally, which comes from being able to be aware of stories and their impact on how a coach sees and makes sense of the world, the coach runs the risk of having the story in charge versus being in charge of the story.

> Not everything that can be counted counts, and not everything that counts can be counted.
>
> —Albert Einstein

On Becoming a Coach: Doing

Coaching is a highly personalized process for development in which the coach, as the instrument of coaching, plays a critical role. Development, in our view, is an "inside out" process. For both the client and the coach, "who you be" is the bedrock on which "what you do" rests. Our premise is that for coaches to share in this journey with a client, it must be a journey on which they themselves have already embarked and with which they are fully engaged. The coach's personal journey into greater self-awareness informs how the coach works with a client who is on a similar path. Still, being is only one part of the coach's craft; without it, the coach ends up relying on tools and techniques that don't work well on human beings. The coach has to learn and accept his human-being-ness to be able to move beyond the use of simplistic tools and techniques.

Coaches engage with clients primarily through conversation. Yet not all conversations are created equal. The first distinction that we address is that coaching conversations, although they might be interesting, must be purposeful. A simply "interesting" conversation does not constitute a coaching conversation. To be purposeful, coaching conversations focus dialogue on the client's development. To do this, the coach must be *present to the client*. In other words, when a coach enters into a conversation with a client, the coach must have already cleared his mind of distractions and attained a quiet-minded stance, thereby being open and engaged in the moment—or being present, with the client. Being present helps the coach to keep the purpose of the conversation front and center.

Boundaries are critical in a coaching relationship. Being in condition to coach by having worked on one's own awareness steers the coach to be able to listen for the client's struggles and successes, and it keeps the coach from overidentifying or imagining that the client's struggles are solved by sharing "solutions" from the coach's own life. We often see new coaches "doing" too much! It is easy for them to fall into the trap of believing that their worth comes only if they resolve the client's struggles. Au contraire. Developing good boundaries begins with the coach believing that the client is already capable of resolving issues, once the client is able to open up to a wider lens view of the challenge. Only in this way will the client learn and develop from the "inside-out"—therefore, while keeping the conversation purposeful, the coach also needs to keep the conversation focused on what the client is aware of, perceiving, thinking, and feeling, to expand the client's field of view.

To be good at this, a coach must have highly developed listening skills—listening for meaning, for the story, for the commitment in the story, for the values in the story, for the emotion, for the somatic messages, and, of course, for what is not being said. Such a tall order can only be achieved from a state of "being" that is evolved and quiet. The less noise inside the coach, the better the listening.

The kind of listening to which we are referring integrates boundary awareness and genuine curiosity. By boundary awareness, we mean that the coach stays separate while being connected to the client. The coach knows where his or her story starts and stops, and how the coach's story is *not* the client's experience. The client has his or her own experience for the coach to witness. The intent is to listen to clients' stories and manage our boundary awareness in service of clients. Are we able to grasp how their structural determinism shapes the array of possibilities that they are able to notice? The coach doesn't simply point out new or different possibilities by virtue of a different structural determinism and body of distinctions. Rather, the coach, through asking "powerful questions," evokes from the client "the opening of new eyes." Listening and evoking represent the key combination of doing and invite the client to explore what and how they notice. Later, the coach and the client will be able to see the client's story as a story and then determine options for restructuring the story.

We have often found the saying "Name, Claim, Reframe" to be very apropos in working with coaching clients. Assigning a "name" to the story helps clients see their story as a story. Many stories represent repeatable themes that show up in several domains of clients' lives. For example, the story name might be "That's my *'I have too much on my plate'* story," or "That's my *'going small when I could play big'* story." When the client and coach name the client's story, they also create the possibility that the client will claim the story as the client's creation. *The client is the author.* Once the client can recognize and claim authorship, then a new possibility becomes available: Reframing. Reframing is learning to assemble the factual elements of the story into a new interpretation, one in which the clients reclaims the power of authorship and choice.

A person starts to live when he can live outside himself.

—Albert Einstein

On Becoming a Coach: Using

The coach's craft extends beyond *being* and *doing*. The third element, equally significant, is *using*. Using as a concept refers to the tools, techniques, and frameworks that the coach employs in service of the client. We will devote a limited amount of time to the concept of using, as many of the applications that coaches use are addressed in subsequent chapters of this book.

Yet a few thoughts are valuable here. First, tools, techniques, and frameworks are good and useful only to the extent that they serve the client and expand the client's field of view, or lens, and range of action. We encourage coaches to be creative in applying these tools and not to be overreliant on any tools. Being creative with tools not only keeps the coach active in imagining how to help the client move in the desired direction, but it also mitigates a one-size-fits-all mentality. New coaches can fall into the trap of thinking that an exercise they love, such as a certain meditation exercise, is right for every client, or that every client needs to do a values exercise. However, this is not so. As coaches, meeting the client where they are builds a trusting relationship where much good work can be accomplished. Leaders are interested in accomplishing goals, and a coach must be focused on the best ways to do that.

Second, a coach whose listening skills are superb will be able to detect and creatively "use" frameworks from the client's own life and thereby develop experiments and practices that will fit the client's ability and desire to stretch. For instance, a stressed executive confided that years ago, creating music was his way of relaxing. The coach asked the client to imagine bringing music back into his life. She then asked whether he could commit to doing one activity a week that had to do with music, where he would be engaged with music, versus passively listening to it. What this assignment did was to reopen the client's love of composition and recording; six months later, the client handed the coach a self-published CD of his writing and playing. Relaxing back into music had a parallel consequence for the client at work. The client began to see more clearly. Stories that he had been wedded to about how the world at work should unfold started to lose their power. He started to see how stress had affected his thinking, and his every moment, and shifted his story about how to be engaged at work and how work should engage with him. The point here is that in a truly dynamic and alive coaching relationship, the coach is never "doing to"—and coaches, both new and seasoned, need to remember that applying tools to a coaching situation is more than using the same tools repeatedly. This is the art of coaching, using the craft in masterful ways.

Tools and frameworks represent a two-edged sword, offering both the possibility of expanding and limiting options. Most coaches and consultants are familiar with various personality instruments, from the MBTI®,[4] to the DISC®,[5] to Personalysis®,[6] to name a few. The distinctions from each of these represent useful and powerful descriptive frameworks for exploring individual differences. Yet many individuals operate as if their type defines who they are. They begin to explain their behavior (create a story) from the perspective of the type's rationale (i.e., "I don't participate in the meeting because I'm so introverted," or, "I am 'very red' when I am at my best, and so I can't really do planning"). The "type" itself becomes a story from which individuals choose options. Of course, this is limiting. The point here is to neither criticize any of these tools, as they are all brilliant and useful, nor discourage assessment tools in the practice of coaching. Rather, coaches need to be clear about their intentions when they use tools and frameworks, listen for the story the client may be creating, and keep working to keep the client from limiting thought patterns.

The coach's body of distinctions, when made explicit and used with awareness, is a set of tools that clients can benefit from. In leadership coaching, for example, the coach's distinctions about leadership become invaluable in helping the clients learn their own distinctions about leadership. Later chapters in this book point to distinctions that are used in leadership coaching.

The greater question in bringing tools into coaching involves "In service of what?" Coaching embraces many objectives, not the least of which is to help clients expand the array of choices available to them. It is imperative that coaches continually deploy tools and frameworks creatively in service of helping clients explore their choices, from a stance of curiosity.

> Try not to become a man of success, but rather to become a man of value.
>
> —Albert Einstein

In summary, coaches have an obligation to be in and stay in their own development. We have covered three broad ways of thinking about what it takes to *become a coach* and encourage all coaches, seasoned or not, to revisit their roots, their stories, their automatic actions, and the tools they are using. In the absence of such reflection, coaches run the risk of dousing their spark, creating unexamined habits and burning out. We take the process of "becoming" very seriously, and we ask coaches to periodically ask themselves these questions:

- What am I learning about myself?
- What story am I living in?
- How is that story empowering me or limiting me?
- What do I need to pay more attention to?
- What clients am I attracting?
- How does being in my own development help me serve my clients?
- Who am I in the process of becoming?

> Every day I remind myself that my inner and outer life are based on the labors of other men, living and dead, and that I must exert myself in order to give in the same measure as I have received and am still receiving.
>
> —Albert Einstein

Notes

1. Neil Stroul and Christine Wahl, "Being, Doing, Using: A Way to Understanding Coaching," *Choice,* Fall 2003, 43–45.
2. Gordon W. Allport, *Becoming: Basic Considerations for a Psychology of Personality* (New Haven, CT: Yale University Press, 1963).
3. Humberto Maturana and Francisco Varela, "Structural Determinism," *The Tree of Knowledge* (Boston: Shambhala Publications, 1987).
4. Myers-Briggs Type Indicator® (Consulting Psychologists Press), www.cpp.com.
5. DISC® Personality Profile, www.discprofile.com.
6. Personalysis® Questionnaire, www.personalysis.com.

CHAPTER 2

Sacred Space: Where Possibilities Abound and Change Is Engendered

Julie K. Shows and Clarice L. Scriber

Your sacred space is where you can find yourself again and again.
—Joseph Campbell

Early morning—at dawn—I find my rhythm, my mind quiets, and I am completely at peace. The house is quiet. I am connected with spirit, known to myself and the universe. It is a time full of grace, a time when I am connected to my center and open to what is calling me. My dreams whisper to me. The answers to the questions I pose are revealed. I trust what I hear. This is for me sacred space. (Clarice L. Scriber)

At the start of another day, I focus my mind on the stillness and feeling of calmness. I push away my thoughts of things to do and obligations to others—this is a sacred time that is mine alone. I breathe deeply and release the worries and concerns. I breathe deeply and connect to the wisdom of my spirit. It is in this space that I can pause and set my intentions for the day, reflect on what is important to me, and connect to what inspires me. From this sacred space, I start my day with a feeling of purpose and presence. I am ready for another day. (Julie K. Shows)

We begin this article with the premise that "each human being has a wellspring of innate intelligence from which deep qualities like presence, wisdom, common sense, resiliency, and peace of mind emerge." To access that innate intelligence, we coaches learn to create a space for ourselves and for the leaders we coach. We call this *sacred space*.

The coaching hour provides the opportunity so that men and women who are called to "do" can learn to "be." It's a space where leaders reconnect with their values, shift into possibility, and explore future options. As leadership coaches, we cocreate *sacred space* with leaders to help them fashion strategies that bring positive action in service to the organizations they lead. It allows our clients to leave ego out of the conversation and to connect with their greater wisdom and authenticity. It is the space for conversations about learning and growth, intentions and desires, and values and purpose. From this space, leaders can move forward with clarity of intention, foresight, and balance.

How does the practice of creating sacred space influence our ability to be masterful leadership coaches? What qualities allow the coach to be present—to listen with the "third ear," intuitively and deeply, for what is spoken and not said? How do coaches facilitate moments of grace in which leaders learn and grow?

Qualities That Embody Sacred Space

We had our own ideas and, at the same time, we wondered what other leadership coaches believe about creating sacred space. With that question in mind, we distributed an online survey to 100 coaches. Those coaches were selected for gender diversity, variety in training venues, number of years of experience, and geographical differences. We received a 50 percent response rate from the survey. Subsequently, we followed up with interviews of twenty coaches to gain additional insight into the question of sacred space.

We began by identifying attributes that we believe coaches embody when they create sacred space (table 2.1). We asked coaches to select the top five qualities that a leadership coach should embody to create sacred space. In a companion survey, we asked the same questions of coaching clients to see if what coaches think and experience matches what clients observe and experience. Although not quantitatively valid, the survey and follow-up interviews yielded rich data culled from the experience of the coach respondents and clients.

The coach respondents selected and thereby validated the qualities that we deem most important to the coaching relationship. The qualities both the coach respondents and we selected were as follows:

- Ability to connect
- Trust
- Presence
- Self-awareness
- Wisdom

Ability to Connect

"The essence of communication is connection."[1] The ability to connect was the quality most identified by coaches and leaders alike. What makes that quality so important? For the coach and the client, it is the catalyst for the genesis of the partnership, and it recurs throughout the course of the alliance. It is not static; it deepens as trust grows.

This ability is fed by the leaders who reveal themselves, warts and all, as the coach reciprocates with regard and respect and compassion. Both leader and coach become more open and thereby vulnerable.

Table 2.1 Leadership coaching survey: Qualities

Please select the top five qualities a leadership coach should embody to create sacred space. Then, rank your selections in order of importance with 1 being the most important and 5 being the least important.

1.	Ability to connect
2.	Commitment to others
3.	Confidence
4.	Congruence
5.	Comfortable
6.	Equanimity
7.	Grace
8.	Heart
9.	Humor
10.	Intelligence
11.	Inspiration
12.	Motivation
13.	Openness
14.	Political savvy
15.	Presence
16.	Self-awareness
17.	Spirit
18.	Trust
19.	Warmth
20.	Wisdom

If there are other qualities that you believe are important to a leadership coach, please list them:

_____

_____

_____

_____

_____

_____

The coach is open to the client; the leader feels safe to disclose, to try on new behaviors, to wade and perhaps later plunge into uncharted water, to be courageous in the face of uncertainty. There is a dance—an exchange of energy—as the client and coach garner trust to challenge, to hold accountability for new actions. During this exchange, it becomes even more likely leaders will "act" into the future they imagine.

If you don't connect, then the coachees are less likely to open up when they don't feel the connection. When people do connect, [there is] more of a free flow of dialogue, said a manager in a global law firm who worked with her coach for a year.[2]

Therefore, how the connection is established sets the tone for the coaching relationship. As in many relationships, a decision to work together occurs quickly. Is the coach someone who makes it easy to engage? Can leaders see themselves in partnership with their coaches? Is the coach able to create the space for discernment to occur—for them both to choose to relate and to form a relationship?

Trust

If the ability to connect is the catalyst to forming the relationship, then trust is the glue that cements the coaching alliance. Trust is what allows the clients to be truthful and to fully reveal their challenges, concerns, dreams, and strengths. In other words, they can be vulnerable and not be judged. Trust is a two-way street, a complementary process.

The coach enters the coaching alliance with the premise that the client is whole and competent, and the coach helps to establish trust by partnering with the client to create the parameters for the coaching engagement.

In large organizations, the coaching hour may be the only place a leader can fully reveal what it is like to sit in the leadership seat or to be held accountable by someone whose purpose is to hold an agenda. In this setting, the leader-clients are able to root for themselves and to act as their best selves for personal change and growth as individuals and as leaders. One consultant (who is also trained as a coach) we interviewed put it this way:

> For any work relationship, a level of trust between people that is comparable to the level of vulnerability and power that people have over one another [must] be very high for the coach. If it's a good coaching relationship, the clients will share information that puts them in a very vulnerable situation. If they don't open up, that [lack] will hurt the coaching relationship.[3]

To that end, contracting around confidentiality is a crucial element. A frank discussion of the terms of confidentiality—what the coach won't and what the coach is obliged to reveal can help make the process trustworthy and transparent. Throughout the engagement, the coach holds the client's agenda, listens deeply, and fosters both reflection and self-examination. As time elapses, both the client and coach can move into that sacred space comfortably with each other and can trust the process.

Presence

Presence is the quality that affects the coach's capacity to hold the space. It is the essence of the individual, and presence manifests itself both physically and spiritually. It is the embodiment of the individual.

In the context of coaching, we view this presence as a positive force, as the ability to manifest compelling energy that is confident without being cocky and is open without crossing boundaries. Spirit abounds. It contributes to the chemistry of coaching.

The coach's presence helps us to attract the clients for whom we can contribute. Presence fosters credibility with the leader. When the coach is congruent, centered, relaxed, and fully aware of herself and is in tune with the client and the environs, the clients are freer to access their own willingness and intuition.

The coaches' presence (i.e., their way of being) can engender positive energy that is conducive to openings for new possibilities.

Presence also supports the connection that the coach makes with the leader. For all of us, when we are in tune with our values, our beliefs, and ourselves, it shows. And it allows us to engage confidently, welcomingly, empathically, and powerfully.

The coach's full presence needs to be there, observed a coach. "[That presence] is to provide a big enough container to take everything in." [The client] needs to know that there's a spine there, not just a friendly, nice, empathetic energy, but one that can question, push back—a clear gravitas to the coach.[4]

Self-Awareness

Now we come to the quality of self-awareness. The self-aware coaches do the internal work to understand their boundaries, triggers, gifts, and limitations. In this way, the coaches are able to enter the coaching space authentically and confidently.

How do we increase self-awareness and thereby enhance the safety of the coaching alliance? Very simply, it is by following many of the tenets we propose for our clients. Consistent self-care—the day-to-day activities that engender health and well-being; self-observations and practices that encourage reflection; willingness to examine our successes and our mistakes, and the ability to learn from them are factors that foster self-awareness. Beyond these basic practices, we find coaches regularly include many other activities in their daily routines to support their work. These range from yoga to morning poetry readings. Later in this chapter, we address in more detail the practices coaches use to get themselves into shape mentally, physically, and spiritually that in turn foster greater self-awareness.

We want to point out that self-awareness alone does not lead to action. From careful self-observation, we learn what we want to change as we show up and behave differently. Self-awareness is a catalyst for new thinking, new possibilities, new behaviors, and new outcomes.

Wisdom

The fifth quality or characteristic that our respondents identified was wisdom. The word *wisdom* means more than knowledge. It is accessing the wisdom of a greater intelligence, the wisdom of the ages. It is using all the senses to listen. It is cognitive—and more. Wisdom embraces the domains of body, emotion, and spirit. It is being able to tap into an inner knowing for both the client and the coach.

Such wisdom is possible only through the creation of sacred space that is built on connection, self-awareness, trust, and presence. The access to wisdom is the internal process for a coach and a leader; the external process comes from inquiry. By asking questions from a place of curiosity and by being in service to the highest potential of our clients, we coaches allow the leaders to connect to their own authenticity. Then the insights and answers will emerge.

The wise coach knows when to be silent; when to challenge; when to observe as the client moves into space and behavior that might derail; and when to intervene with humor, a story, a poem, or a practice. Coaches who call on their wisdom will tap into their knowledge of human nature, organizations, and the universe. In this sense, wisdom is bigger than both coach and client. It is capturing and practicing lessons of time immemorial. It is best used to know ourselves as coaches in service to client-leaders who join with us in their own development to become more humane, more competent leaders.

Does the coach create sacred space with every client? Absolutely not! We all have our off days—coach and leader alike. There are times when we are distracted and when the client is distracted or when conditions are too hectic to engage. There are times when the coach is grabbed by the leader's story and loses perspective. Occasionally, trust erodes. When such conditions show up—on either side of the relationship—we maintain that it is the coach who is called on to return to center and to seek discernment around the commitment to the relationship. If the client disengages, we coaches should seek to understand why and should endeavor to re-enroll. When we as coaches are harried, we should return to the practices that generate the capacity for creating sacred space.

Ways for Coaches to Get in Shape

This discussion leads us to the second part of the chapter: how does the coach get in shape for creating sacred space?

In our brief online survey, we asked leadership coaches about the practices they engage in to support their work. The list ranged from walking, journaling, meditating, practicing yoga, and praying—the more popular practices—to weight lifting, horseback riding, and practicing Reiki (table 2.2).

A common thread among all coaches who talked with us was that they engaged in those practices not only to create their own sacred space but also as a method of getting in condition to coach. If we believe that as coaches our work is about our own growth, then the practices that allow us to create our own sacred space so that we can access our own wisdom will become one of the foundations of our work. If as coaches we can create our own sacred space, then we can genuinely invite our clients to create that space for themselves.

It takes discipline to maintain such practices, and life gets in the way. As coaches and humans, we face the challenges of leading busy lives, being tired, or having too many commitments and daily interruptions—just as our clients do. It is also by creating the discipline to do those practices that we can understand the struggle that our clients go through in their busy lives as they try to create new ways of doing things. We can more consistently stay grounded and be present with our

Table 2.2 Leadership coaching survey: Practices

Please check all of the practices in which you regularly engage (at least 3 times per week) and include the number of hours each week you engage in those practices.

Practice

1.	Journaling
2.	Sitting meditation (30 minutes or more)
3.	Yoga
4.	Stopping
5.	Prayer
6.	Tai Chi
7.	Aikido
8.	Poetry or inspirational readings
9.	Walking (30 minutes or more)
10.	Running
11.	Visualization

What other practices do you regularly commit to (i.e., massage, Rolfing, Reiki), and how often do you engage in those practices?

_____

_____

_____

_____

_____

_____

clients as they walk their journey when we have taken the time to be centered in our own day.

The most popular practices mentioned by the coaches interviewed were these:

- Praying
- Walking
- Reading poetry or inspirational writings
- Journaling
- Stopping

Praying

Prayer—a conversation with a greater wisdom—was named as the number one practice that coaches engaged in as a daily practice. Prayer is used as a practice for centering, as a time for reflection, and as a time for gratitude. Prayer is the connection between the sacred and the present moment.

Walking

Used as exercise, as a way of being in nature, or as a meditation, walking was the next practice that coaches mentioned. Taking the time to be connected with nature regularly and walking as a moving meditation provide a structure for pausing in our lives and connecting to our own sacred space.

Reading Poetry or Inspirational Writings

Both poetry and inspirational readings can be used in reflective practices, as well as being offered to the leaders we coach. Starting a meditation period with a poem often sparks new learning or observations about one's self and gives food for thought for journaling or self-observation.

Journaling

As we record our inner thoughts and use reflective learning, journaling lends itself to slowing down. It allows us to speak from our hearts, to connect to the joy of learning, and the wonder of being a beginner. It gives us a place to be ourselves without the fear of judgment. It allows us to solve problems and to clear our mind for the day so that we can be present with our clients and ourselves.

Stopping

By taking time out from our busy schedules as we stop or pause, that respite helps us to come back to ourselves, to rediscover day in and day out our sacred space. We stop, recover, and reconnect to our inner sense of ourselves. At Georgetown University, an important component of the leadership coach training program is for our students to take on a new practice in a domain where they want to build capacity, as well as learn a practice that allows them to stop and to pause from the busyness of the day. We ask students to write in a journal so they enhance their self-awareness. For some students, the journal is a welcome developmental tool that allows them to learn about themselves and to discover entrenched beliefs that hinder growth. For others, journaling is a tedious practice and is difficult to begin, much less maintain. That revelation in itself provides a conversation for the coach and the leader in the hour of sacred coaching space. Laura Divine and Joanne Hunt speak about such a stop in their article titled "The Power of Pause":

> There are certain words associated with pausing that we do not hold as positive within our culture. Words such as delay, hesitate, or doubt give us some insight into how pausing can be held as something that delays action, forward movement, or success. Pausing can be interpreted as a lack of decisiveness or a sense of being unsure. As coaches, we need to take into consideration both what frightens people about slowing down . . . as well as how our culture holds this construct. Together these two forces create resistance in our ability to value and build this competency as an individual or as a society. (Hunt and Devine)[5]

By experiencing the resistance as well as the joy of pausing and reflective learning, the coach will better use those practices in their own lives before introducing them to the clients they serve. We want to emphasize, as well, that pausing or finding sacred time in one's routine is an important concept not only for the coach, but also for leaders, many of whom rarely come up for air during the grueling work day. When practiced consistently, the pause is generative and refreshing.

When we interviewed coaches, we learned that what seems to matter most is the consistency of the practice. Like the leaders who have competing commitments, our respondents acknowledged the challenge of keeping the intention and commitment of practice. How did those coaches bring consistency into the relentless demands of day-to-day living? For most, it required another rigor: scheduling the time. When they put the practice on their calendar, they found it easier to stick to their commitment. One coach we surveyed said, "When I get too busy with clients, secular space gets in the way. Being unfocused, my own resistance gets in the way of connecting, [of] being congruent."[6]

The coach-respondent also remarked, "Practices are patterns of attitude and habits. [Because] we experience and understand it, [we're] in the position to help others to create patterns for the way they want to be."[7]

Jim Loehr and Tony Schwartz more fully describe this practice of brief periods of stopping for renewal and its applicability for leaders in their article, "The Making of the Corporate Athlete,"[8] which appears in the January 2001 issue of the "Harvard Business Review." In their research, Schwartz and Loehr found that world-class athletes and top executives engage in a cycle of work and renewal to foster excellent performance over time. By incorporating downtime in a busy day and thereby managing their energy, the authors posit that top leaders will reap multiple benefits.

So again, as we coaches build in the practice of stopping, we want to ask leaders how they can schedule time to walk, to write in a journal, simply to breathe, to go to a gym, to eat lunch regularly, or to attend a yoga class. We should ask this question: what will leaders do to fulfill their intentions to themselves and to build a capacity for future "right" action (as they define it)?

Conclusion

As coaches, we do the following:

- Connect to build and sustain relationship.
- Engender trust to allow the client's truth to emerge.
- Self-observe and take on practices to generate self-awareness.
- Demonstrate presence that is open, grounded, and optimistic.
- Access wisdom to serve the client's agenda for a more effective and generative leadership stance.

To be sure, other ingredients can help the coach facilitate a safe, supportive environment, but we feel the ones we've discussed in this article are integral. By practicing those tenets, coaches create environments of self-examination and of learning for future success. By introducing leaders to the practice of creating time for reflecting; by accessing their wisdom and their capacity for growth and action; and by using the tools of self-care—be it through prayer, meditation, exercise, or a pauses—coaches can more fully engage and hold a *sacred space* for the leaders whom we coach.

Notes

1. Strozzi-Heckler, Richard, Being Human at Work: Bringing Somatic Intelligence into Your Professional Life (Berkeley, CA: North Atlantic Books, 2003).
2. Jacqueline Wilson Cranford, in discussion with Clarice Scriber, May 9, 2005.
3. Beatriz Boccalandro, in discussion with Clarice Scriber, May 13, 2005.
4. Ibid.
5. Joanne Hunt and Laura Divine, "The Power of Pause," Integral Institute of Canada, 2002.
6. Zayd Abdul-Karim, in discussion with Clarice Scriber, March 17, 2005.
7. Ibid.
8. Loehr, Jim and Tony Schwartz, "The Making of the Corporate Athlete," *Harvard Business Review*, January 2001.

CHAPTER 3

Eastern Influence on Coaching

Randy Chittum

The truth must dazzle gradually, or all the world be blind.

—Emily Dickinson

This chapter is not meant to be a scholarly treatment of the topic, but instead an effort to build awareness that coaching principles, philosophy, and practice are heavily influenced by, or at least related to, the diverse notion of "Eastern thinking." It is my hope that it may inspire further thinking and exploration on the part of the reader.

Writing requires linearity and reductionism, both of which are at least partly contradictory to the philosophy of Eastern thought. Know that all the parts are connected to all the other parts. There is a line in *The Tao* that essentially says, "He who speaks of the Tao, knows not the Tao." That which is most important may be well beyond the words we use to express it. It is with this full awareness that we forge ahead!

For this writing, I have reduced Eastern thinking into its parts, as suggested in Table 3.1, which is a somewhat generalized and simplified version.

Being

You must be the change you wish to see in the world.

—Mahatma Gandhi

The first, and perhaps most, significant way in which Eastern thought appears to influence or be aligned with coaching is in the domain of "being versus doing." Eastern thought takes the position that we are more than our actions, more than what we do. What matters most is who we are in the process of being, and in some cases, becoming. What we do is merely the reflection of who we are being.

Table 3.1 Eastern/Western thinking

Eastern thinking	Western thinking
I am who I am	I am what I do
I am connected	I am isolated
Nonattachment	Attached to beliefs and possessions
Wholeness	Parts
Lightness	Seriousness
Journey	Destination
Simplicity	Complexity
Mindful and Present	Distracted

Coaches similarly believe that the leverage in creating sustainable change is in changing the person, not the behavior. The behavior is an extension or symptom of who we are. Who we are is the core. As you might suspect, questions such as those that follow are deep, personal, and rewarding. A willingness to delve deeply into questions like these is one door into the sustainable and transformative change that most coaches seek.

Consider, who am I? When you sift away the roles, the history, the descriptors, who am I? If I am not my job, and not my relationships, then who am I? If I am not my body, then who am I? Who am I beyond personality, desires, and dreams? There are those who believe that a life's work is involved in answering and subsequently dealing with the implications of those answers. I believe that this is a conversation that coaches can and should have with leaders. Certainly not all leaders are interested or ready for this, but on average I think we sell many of our leaders short in this regard. I find that many of the leaders I coach are craving purpose and greater understanding. I am not shy about introducing questions in an attempt to get closer to the core. In an attempt to enter this domain I might ask questions like these. What do you imagine your enduring legacy to be? Who are you at your core and what do you stand for in the world? What matters to you? I have pondered, considered, meditated, and discussed such questions for more than 20 years and they still provide me new awareness and possibility.

I once had a teacher who told me that I could choose to either follow conventional wisdom and "don't just sit there, do something," or follow another path expressed in "don't just do something, sit there." Eastern thinking values the promise of stillness, whether manifested through meditation or truly simply doing nothing. One of my favorite Zen sayings expresses this—"sitting here quietly doing nothing, spring comes and the grass grows by itself." Many leaders are caught in a cycle of "deliverables" and doing. More rarely seen is the person who takes the time to be still, or pause. That person reaps the reward of a calm mind and presence, enlightened perspective, and lightness. Ample research points to the significance of our physical presence in leadership, the importance of healthy perspective, and the relationship of daily stress to our effectiveness and creativity. We have quickly forgotten the lessons of "sharpen your saw." It is not uncommon for a coach to work with leaders to help them practice pausing as a way to stay more centered. I have asked leaders to develop a practice of being quiet (internally and externally) for a few minutes several times a day. I have asked leaders to learn and practice basic breathing and meditation exercises. I have asked leaders to participate in a yoga class that I offer for leaders who I think are ready to benefit from a program. I have asked leaders to take a walk for fifteen minutes each workday and practice noticing. Any activity request is obviously specific to the leader and his/her needs and abilities. The significant point I think is to risk where appropriate to invite leaders into this domain of experience.

Connection and Wholeness

Peace comes with the souls of men
When they realize their oneness with the universe.

—Black Elk

Another way in which Eastern thought and coaching are aligned is in the significance of dealing with the whole as more than the sum of its parts. Simply stated, Eastern thought has maintained its focus on understanding the universe in its entirety where the Western approach has been to use science to break it into its parts in an attempt to understand it. It is fascinating to note that through the understandings afforded us from quantum physics and other "new sciences," that both schools of thought appear now to be arriving at the same place. This sense of wholeness extends beyond the "I." As the earlier quote so beautifully expresses, the wholeness extends to the universe. In this way, we are universally whole. In practical terms, leaders who can see beyond the needs of their team or department represent a form of wholeness. Leaders who can see beyond the needs of their organization to the greater needs of the community represent at a higher level. In a personal way, leaders who understand that they are connected to others through an invisible web are likely to be more thoughtful in how they behave and therefore how they impact others.

Being part of a whole raises issues of self that are present in both Eastern thinking as well as coaching. The "self" is, in most Eastern thinking, an illusion—but one in which we dearly believe. The "self" is home to the ego and pride, to name a few inhabitants.

Coaches are often faced with the challenge of working with leaders who think that if she can just learn how to present more powerfully, or be more assertive, or listen more, then all will be well. Particularly in high-pressure business environments, our mostly successful clients are taught to identify and then solve problems.

Coaching, with its emphasis on sustainable change and development, will likely push beyond the limits of the "parts" approach identified earlier. Instead, the coach will be interested in the entire experience of the client who wants to be more assertive. What belief systems does she hold that interfere with her performance? How does she explain things to herself? What emotions does she carry before and during an opportunity to be more assertive? What "shows up" in her body in terms of stress, and how does she hold her body to enable or interfere with her desired goal of more assertive behavior? Finally, what skills or information might be missing that would enable her? In short, the coach is interested in the whole person.

Another way in which coaches coach the whole person is that we may not be exclusively focused on the person at work. We understand and honor that she is more than an employee or a leader. Who is she as a person and how does that support or challenge her in achieving her stated goal?

One of the most commonly expressed interests for leaders in coaching is in achieving balance. For many, the world of work has taken a disproportionate place in our lives. We have neglected our families, our health, our communities, and our spirits for too long. Those being coached often come with this awareness but with little understanding of how to make changes. Eastern thinkers have had a lot to say about balance. Perhaps the most insightful antidote to an unbalanced life is presence. The notion of "being where you are" is profound and challenging for most of us. The simple act of attending and "not-doing" can be a significant life challenge. Similarly powerful is the notion of being wholehearted in our lives. To do everything wholeheartedly is another path to presence and balance.

In general, I believe that the leaders I have encountered over the past twenty years prove the point. The leaders I have known who are most powerful exhibit the qualities of wholeheartedness, balance, wholeness, and an understanding of their connection to others. The leaders I have known who are least powerful do not often demonstrate those same qualities. One person always stands out to me. He is a very senior executive in a large company. This company is the market leader in their industry. If you were to ask 100 people in this company, who is the best pure leader in the company, at least 90 would come back with his name. What is the source of this influence? He is completely present when he is with you. He separates from his desk, phone, computer, Blackberry, and so on and actually makes you feel as if you matter to him. He is vigorous and wholehearted. He demonstrates outstanding and consistent energy. In part his energy level is a result of a balanced and healthy life, but it is also a result of uncompromising belief in the importance of the purpose. I have heard him talk compellingly about the importance of going home and then being home to hundreds of his leaders. He is compelling in this case because he believes it. Finally, I notice how simply he lives by a set of self-authored principles. You rarely have to guess how he might respond to something because you so clearly know where he stands.

Attachment

The source of all suffering is attachment.

—Buddha

Letting go is often a fertile area for coaches and is one of the most profound ideas to come from Eastern thinking. Our inability to let go is the source of enormous suffering for many. Think about all the things to which you are attached—relationships, work, friends, possessions, status, pride, ideas, and opinions? The list is unending. The rise in popularity of emotional intelligence has put this issue into the conversation in some organizations. As a coach, I find that the source of suffering is very often an attachment, as the Buddha suggested. Beyond needless suffering, the consequence of attachment is limited possibility. Coaches then, are often in the conversation that creates the possibility of "letting go." As you might imagine, it is an area that is fraught with fear and uncertainty.

Similarly, one of the biggest attachments I see is to my sense of who I am. Sometimes, a coach is working to get a client to let go of their attachment to their very identity. Few things are more frightening than truly "reinventing" oneself as reinvention requires a letting go of "who you were" to become "who you wish to be." The ability to consciously choose who to be is the pinnacle of living a masterful and purposeful life—precisely because the risk of letting go seems so high.

The attachment to sense of self is arguably in part a developmental issue and therefore not everyone is developmentally ready to discuss concepts like true self-authoring. For those leaders who are ready, their coach has to also be ready and ideally have begun the journey. This is another of those areas where the coach would benefit from having a coach.

Related to letting go is the concept of acceptance. Acceptance is different from settling or giving up. Acceptance comes in that graceful space where one is able to release themselves from the hold of emotion that is limiting them. In the world of leaders, acceptance often comes after a huge effort to change or achieve something. After the effort, there can be a place where the client accepts whatever outcome awaits. I find that leaders often struggle to be unattached to outcomes. A degree of attachment to outcomes can serve a leader, up to a point. It eventually becomes unhealthy for the leader that can never let go of the outcome.

Lightness

> God writes a lot of comedy...the trouble is, he's stuck with so many bad actors who don't know how to play funny.
>
> —Garrison Keillor

What naturally flows from a sense of acceptance and letting go? I believe a sense of perspective and lightness. In this case, think of lightness as playfulness, not taking yourself or events so seriously. You can imagine that the person able to do this is more likely to be adept at acceptance. It is possible that the universe is absurd and unpredictable. The desire to feel a sense of control over it, or even over oneself, is a potential source of suffering. The master has figured this out and learned to laugh and let go.

How does this present in coaching? The leaders I work with are often rooted in the desire for the control mentioned earlier. They crave a linear, rational model that allows for planning and predictable outcomes. They may be unable to change course, even though they tout the benefits and even the necessity of change. The desire for control generates suffering and, I would argue, lost productivity. It is the leader with perspective, who holds plans lightly, who is most beloved and effective. President Dwight D. Eisenhower was quoted as saying, "[S]trategic plans are worthless. Strategic planning is invaluable."[1] This implies the truth in the notion that the product of planning and work should be held lightly and, furthermore, that the benefit in this work is the connections and the process.

Journey

> Far away in the sunshine are my highest aspirations. I may not reach them, but I can see the beauty, believe in them, and try to follow where they lead.
>
> —Louisa May Alcott

Those even tangentially aware of "Eastern thought" are likely familiar with quotes such as the one mentioned earlier. The notion that the journey matters as much or more than the destination has found its way into the popular Western lexicon. Unfortunately, popular awareness has not necessarily led to popular adoption. Organizations, with their relentless focus on achieving specific outcomes are seemingly more focused than ever on the destination over the journey. The journey is forgotten in pursuit of the next objective. One of the ways I get leaders to pay attention to this is to ask questions about learning. For example, at the end of this project what would you like to know better about yourself? As you engage in this work, what opportunities do you see along the way for you to practice new ways of being or behaving?

Tim Gallwey[2] is noted for saying that coaches need merely to help their clients pay close attention to the teacher, experience. Experience is the teacher, and as we learned in grade school, learning involves paying close attention to the teacher. It is notable that the experience is the journey. Perhaps the art of coaching is simply to help clients make meaning from their experiences, leading to new ways of being. The meaning making, or learning, requires at least some attention be paid to the experience or journey.

Simplicity

> Manifest plainness, embrace simplicity.
>
> —Lao-Tzu

Perhaps more than any other single word, Eastern thought might be known for its emphasis on keeping things simple. Simple is believed to be profound. Simple is believed to be elegant. Simple is a more accurate representation of that which is true. I see clients every day who are overwhelmed by the complexity in their lives, particularly at work. We have come to believe that we need all manner of technology and infrastructure to manage our complex lives. For some it is even a badge of honor. Yet, the most commonly taught strategy in organizations today might be—do what you are good at and focus on a few critical objectives. This is an organizational version of—keep it simple.

I have come to believe that it is our complexity that keeps us safe. Simplicity is dangerous, too close to the truth, leaving nowhere to hide. In some ways, it goes back to the "who am I" question. Without the complexity, the self-importance, who am I? If I am fearful of that question and its possible answers, I may be well served by keeping my life complex.

Mindfulness

Only that day dawns to which we are awake.

—Thoreau

Similar to the expression "be here now," mindfulness suggests an ongoing awareness of both internal processes (emotional, cognitive, and physical) as well as environmental factors. It is a form of "active noticing," without doing. It often takes the form of meditation, though the master is mindful at all times. It is "non-doing" in action. It deals with the possibility that *this* is it. Everything real is contained in this moment and if I am not present to it, I am missing not just this moment but everything.

In coaching, this is evident in many ways. The most pedestrian is that all of us live distracted lives. Living in either the future (possibilities, planning) or the past (assessments, emotions), but so rarely in the present. Put this in the category of simple and not easy. Mindfulness is to be cultivated and the more desire one has for it, the more elusive it may be.

Leaders often express the desire to have something we are currently calling "executive presence." I fear that we have substituted the expression for charisma, and consequently we have little understanding of what it actually means. In the context of mindfulness and presence, executive presence would start with sharing the same moment with others. To share in that moment I have to be present in it. However, the sources of interference to being present and mindful are too numerous to list. There is great power for coaches who are able to have this conversation with their clients.

Conclusion

The reader is reminded that this chapter was not intended to be a full discussion of "Eastern thought" and in fact that the very term "Eastern thought" borders on slighting in its simplicity. However, the similarities between coaching and Eastern thought are too obvious to be ignored. It is my hope that by shining a feeble light on the relationship, we will be better able to consider the distinctions and possibilities that exist.

> Be patient toward all that is unsolved in your heart and learn to love the questions themselves, like locked rooms and like books that are written in a very foreign tongue. Do not seek the answers, which cannot be given you because you would not be able to live them.
>
> —Rainer Maria Rilke

Notes

1. John T. Woolley and Gerhard Peters, "The American Presidency Project," President Dwight D. Eisenhower, remarks at the National Defense Executive Reserve Conference, November 14, 1957 (Santa Barbara: University of California, Gerhard Peters Database), http://www.presidency.ucsb.edu/ws/?pid=10951 (accessed November 13, 2007).
2. *Tim Gallwey,* "The Inner Game: Learning to Get Out of Your Own Way" (presentation, annual conference of International Coach Federation, Orlando, FL, 1999).

CHAPTER 4

Continued Development: Self-Authorship and Self-Mastery

Frank Ball

A t every stage in our lives as coaches, the question before us is how to engage in our continuing development as a coach. The most obvious approach, especially when new to the profession, is to focus on increasing our skillfulness. Pursuing increased skillfulness often takes the form of a search for more powerful questions, new and more effective ways to establish and maintain rapport, and learning how to craft stronger agreements, and so on. This focus on increasing skillfulness is really a commonsense approach intent on examining our proficiency at any or all of the International Coach Federation (ICF) competencies and then striving to move our performance of each of them to higher levels of skillfulness. Coach training programs reinforce this approach by asking graduating students their plans for their own development going forward. Most often the student plans include "...build this skill, become better at that, take this course or program..." Although this approach is a normal and necessary part of our continuing development as coaches, the real work, the more important work, is truly in who we "be" as a coach much more than what we "do" as a coach. In mathematical terms, we'd say that skill building is necessary, but it is not sufficient to become a great coach.

In this chapter we explore a number of distinctions between the "being" and "doing" of coaching in terms of human development theory, especially as they relate to our ongoing development as coaches. We'll also look at the capabilities and challenges coaches at various levels of development face and identify some ways to surmount them.

A very useful way to look at our continued development as coaches is to first look at what is known about adult development in general. The work of Robert Kegan is among the foundational works in this field, and his model of human development tracks with the development of coaches very well. Others, too, have contributed greatly to this field of study (see the bibliography at the end of this chapter for specific citations). Kegan has identified a number of developmental stages,[1] each of which has its own characteristics, challenges, and opportunities. For our purposes, Kegan's Stages 3 through 5 have the most relevance, and we will focus our attention on those three stages, looking at how coaches at those stages might be distinguished from one another, and how development through those stages over time occurs. Kegan named the three stages of interest to us:

- Other-dependent
- Self-authoring
- Self-aware

Let's look at the three stages to see how they compare to one another and examine what is behind the worldview and actions of a coach at each stage.

Other-dependent

When we look at a coach at Kegan's Stage 3, the term "other-dependent" means that the person looks outside himself or herself for values and standards. In a sense, the power lies outside the person. As a coach, they are like a malleable object being shaped into a "coach" as defined by an external power—the ICF—or their coach training program. In training, their focus is very extrinsic, focused on how the profession defines coaching standards, competencies, best practices, and so on. Their coaching journey at this point is a search for right answers, and once known, those right answers become internalized so that the external structure is replicated inside the Stage 3 coach as an adopted value system, or as Kegan describes it, the internalized other. A coach solidly embedded in Stage 3 would likely focus his or her developmental attention exclusively on what external bodies say a good coach does. External sources could consist of where they studied coaching, what their coach peers have to say, what the coaching books and articles prescribe, as well as standards set by the ICF. The key distinction is the total reliance on "other-than-self" for the "right" answer. The Stage 3 coach looks outside themselves to become more skillful in taking those actions and living those values set by the community of coaching and its professional body. Such a coach would have limited distinctions beyond those created by the profession and other coaches. This coach's world would include a lot of coaching "shoulds" and "oughts." And the coach may not have much trust of his or her own insights into ways to coach differently beyond those already approved. A coach at Stage 3 would have relatively few tools available to respond to the individual differences of each client, client situation, and client-coach dyad.

Self-authoring

A coach who is at Kegan's Stage 4, in contrast, is at the stage he calls "self-authoring." At this stage, the coach has developed his or her own value system that they use as a basis for their self-identify as a person (coach). They are driven to live their own values and develop their own unique way of coaching that is anchored in their beliefs rather than relying exclusively on the beliefs of others. A key distinction that sets Stage 4 coaches apart from Stage 3 coaches is their strongly felt need to adhere to their values over the values of external bodies even if doing so has a personal or professional risk. This stance is often visible when a person declares that living up to their values is more important than acceptance of others. For example, a coach moving developmentally from Stage 3 to Stage 4 might decline an opportunity to coach within an organization whose values are inconsistent with his or her own.

A phrase that captures a bit of the journey to Stage 4 as a coach is finding one's coaching voice. Most coach training programs, Georgetown among them, spend a great deal of time and effort in the course to help students find their unique voice as a coach. What this means in addition to the idea of having one's own language about coaching, is that one has developed an idiosyncratic way of "being" as a coach as distinctive as one's voice and as incapable of separation from the coach as one's voice is. A coach who has found his or her voice can be critical of and reject some of the accepted wisdom about coaching, regardless of the credibility or power of its source. The location of power is internal within them. Their values, beliefs, views, and actions take precedence, and they are willing to accept any consequences of living their values in action with clients.

Self-aware

A Stage 5 coach has shifted once again, this time moving back from a "self" centered location of power back to an "external" or "other" location of power. At this level of development, the coach now begins to become aware of the limitations of his or her values, beliefs, and so on, no matter how effective they are or how "right" they feel. Self-righteous beliefs and actions fade. Coaches moving along the journey toward Stage 5 become even more open to alternative points of view and are able to take multiple perspectives from all around them. They are open to the ideas of other coaches, other fields of endeavor, their clients, and their own experience even when things aren't going according to their beliefs. At this stage, they are willing to abandon the very idiosyncratic values they were willing to risk a great deal for when they were firmly in Stage 4. There is a realization that their views, no matter how well founded, can benefit from exposure and possible modification because of others. There is a certain letting go of certainty in the efficaciousness of their viewpoints. Much creativity is possible at this level of development since the dogma of neither the external power, such as ICF, nor the internal beliefs predominates. A Stage 5 coach is willing to surrender his or her sense of how things are to learn more and to find new ways of being and doing. This surrender to something living and outside ourselves is sometimes called flow. Stage 5 coaches are able to find that place of grounded yet free flowing creativity frequently. Their learning and self-mastery comes as much from the surrender of self as from any intentional action to learn. In sum, ego is no longer driving their actions.

Recurring Shifts in the Locus of Power

By now you've probably noticed the shifting back and forth of the locus of power from outside the coach (ICF, society, coaching colleagues, and society) at Stage 3 to inside the coach (internal values, beliefs, and standards) at Stage 4, and then back again to outside the coach (the client, other coaches, and the environment at Stage 5). To the extent that we look somewhere for insight, answers, or strength, the location of those changes throughout the developmental journey. Moreover, even when, as at Stages 3 and 5, they are outside the individual coach, they are outside the coach in a different way. At Stage 3 the external power is imposed and unquestioned, and at Stage 5 it is invited into collaboration to support the Stage 5 coach's continuing development. The Stage 5 coach does this because of his or her growing awareness of the limitations of their unique way of being a coach, and their desire to continue their own development, even at the cost of being prepared to abandon what, for them, has been the "right" way to coach. They are willing to surrender their self-ness to continue learning and growing.

At this point you may be thinking this is all very interesting, but what has this got to do with my continuing development as a coach. Here it comes. None of these levels is absolute, and most of us are moving through the levels at differing speeds. In a sense we're all on a journey; we're just at different points along the journey. The implications for our continuing development begin with determining with some accuracy where we are along the way, in developmental terms.

Coaches residing predominantly at Stage 3 should challenge and discipline themselves to look beyond the tools and techniques that external forces prescribe and which mastery of may seem so desirable. The real work moving from Stage 3 to Stage 4 is finding one's coaching voice in the fullest meaning of that concept. The work is inner work. Look for your own values. What is true for you? If you're looking elsewhere to know what the "right" answer is, then your real developmental work is to look inside. That may seem counterintuitive, and you may hear yourself saying, "...but I have to know the chords before I can trust myself to play spontaneously...and I don't know the chords well enough yet." On the other hand, you might hear yourself feeling defensive if someone challenges your viewpoint and values. An overheard conversation such as that in your head is a good sign that you're residing in Stage 3 and to progress as a coach, it may be time for you to challenge yourself to explore your own inner landscape of values and beliefs and to bring those to the surface in a way that they show up in your coaching.

One of the pieces of work that becomes obligatory when you wish to move out of Stage 3 is to examine all of the strongly held assumptions and "knowing" that you have gained through the years. Learning what works, what is yours, what you can clearly discard, and what you want to keep, are developmental actions that will launch your journey toward Stage 4 self-authoring. This can be daunting. It may take overturning some long-held beliefs about "the way things are or ought to be."

This is a lot easier to do if you have a coach yourself, one who can help you pick up the pen and truly self-author who you "be" as a coach. A specific focus of your developmental work could be to trust yourself more in your coaching. To be effective in supporting your journey toward Stage 4, your coach has to be at a level beyond where you currently are. Regardless of our development level, it is almost impossible to think ourselves out of that level toward the next by using the thinking that is characteristic of the level we're in.

For example, if a coach is solidly embedded in Stage 3, the "rightness" of responding to external "shoulds" and "oughts" is so clear that it would be very difficult and perhaps downright subversive for a coach to imagine putting his or her values ahead of conventional wisdom. Similarly, a firmly embedded Stage 4 coach would likely be so convinced of the "rightness" of his or her approach as to be very slow to admit into their thinking the idea of using someone else's approach rather than their own.

Coaches residing predominantly in Stage 4 are generally much more comfortable that they have found the optimal way to be a coach given who they are. In addition, to a large extent that is true. They can become a very finely tuned version of themselves and be great coaches. That greatness, however, has the limitation of a single perspective. At some point Stage 4 coaches begin to see the limitations of their way of being and invite others in or begin to modify their way of being in response to others. It is a voluntary relinquishing of autonomy at Stage 5 rather than an involuntary one at Stage 3. The coach approaching Stage 5 realizes that his or her continued growth is only possible by embracing other views and ways of being.

You can be sure you're strongly embedded in being a Stage 4 coach if you're very sure you've figured this coaching thing out and you resist encroachment on your autonomy by others such as ICF, clients, other coaches, or client organizations. Your developmental work would benefit from opening yourself up more to inconsistent data, differing points of view, and alternatives for action beyond those you would normally engage in. Again, it is necessary to work with a coach who is more developmentally advanced than you are to make the journey to the next stage possible.

Conclusion

Often the question comes up about what makes a great coach. The answer is a coach engaged in ongoing work on him or herself. The answer is *not* someone who asks great questions. There is no combination of skills developed to a superb level that is the mark of a great coach alone. All our "doing" is affected profoundly by the way in which we "be." Coaches at different developmental levels engage in the same activities differently, with different intention and certainly different impact. Questions asked by coaches at different levels will come from a different place and will create a different set of possibilities and outcomes for both the client and the coach.

We believe that using a model such as Kegan's provides a roadmap for coach development. It has clear definitions, sharp distinctions among levels, and suggests where the real work for any developmental level lies.

Self-development of this type is a lifelong activity and is best done with the support, encouragement, and challenge of a skilled coach who has studied human development as it applies to coaching and who has done the work on self necessary to be at your developmental level or beyond. A coach who is "behind" you developmentally will not have yet made the shift you are working on and doesn't have the "way of being" necessary to help you move forward developmentally.

As Buddha said when asked why answers to our questions are so hard to find, the answer we seek is in the place most of us are least likely to look—inside ourselves. Doing your work on self, using the levels of human development identified by

Kegan and adapted to coaching by skilled developmental coaches is the pathway to self-authorship and self-mastery. Let the journey begin.

Note

1. To learn more about your own stage of development, you can take the Leadership Circle Profile, created by Bob Anderson, or the Leadership Development Profile, created by Susanne R. Cook-Greuter, or work with a coach certified to use the Subject-Object Interview as taught by Robert Kegan and Otto Laske.

Bibliography

Kegan, Robert. *In Over Our Heads: The Mental Demands of Modern Life*. Cambridge, MA: Harvard University Press, 1994.

———. *The Evolving Self: Problem and Process in Human Development*. Cambridge, MA: Harvard University Press, 1982.

Laske, Otto. *Measuring Hidden Dimensions: The Art and Science of Fully Engaging Adults*. Medford, MA: Interdevelopmental Institute Press, 2006.

Torbert, Bill, Susanne Cook-Grueter, Delmar Fisher, Erica Foldy, Alain Gauthier, Jackie Keeley, David Rooke et al. *Action Inquiry: The Secret of Timely and Transforming Leadership*. San Francisco, CA: Berrett-Koehler, 2004.

PART II

Doing

CHAPTER 5

In the Spirit of Coaching

Sheila Haji

It started out like a typical "Meet and Greet." A group of mid-level corporate managers and external coaches mingled and chatted in hopes of finding the perfect chemistry to launch a six-month leadership development partnership. I was one of twenty prospective coaches working to ease the tension in the room. Some of the managers shook hands easily and fell naturally into conversations with the coaches while others hung back with a mixture of detachment and skepticism. One of the wallflowers was a middle-aged man with a melancholy expression and intense eyes. We made eye contact and to my surprise he approached me with an outstretched hand and a shy smile. His name was Jeffrey* and he told me in a quiet voice that he had noticed a "centered-ness" about me that intrigued him. Jeffrey then began to ply me with questions about my coaching philosophy, style, and approach. As I spoke, he listened intently, seeming to take mental note of every word. When I asked Jeffrey to tell me about himself he spoke as if he was surprised and relieved to give voice to his innermost thoughts.

Jeffrey told me about his quest for a meaningful and full personal and professional life. He spoke passionately about wanting to wake up in the morning with a sense of excitement about his work. He wondered if he was living his true purpose and if the organization would be changed for the better by his being in it. These questions were keeping him awake at night and he wanted answers. Finally Jeffrey looked at me with a direct, sincere gaze and said, "I want what you have." When I asked him to explain, he responded with one word, "Spirit." (Sheila Haji)

What Is Spirit?

In my experience as a coach, I have seen clients buckle under the weight of organizational pressures and demands. With only a few hours of downtime between

---

* Fictitious name

intense cycles of "busyness," executives and manager are often caught up in the process of *doing* and lose sight of what it means to simply *be*.

Over the years, I have met leaders and managers who yearn to *be* more authentic; to *be* more intentional about what they do and how they do it; and to *be* a part of a nurturing community. This longing is the essence of spirit at work. When I speak of spirit, I mean the manifestation of consciousness, intention, and connection.

Unfortunately, overworked executives and managers often move through their days, weeks, and months in a state of "waking unconsciousness." I have heard clients express the following:

- Leading on auto-pilot with no clear path or destination
- Living in a constant state of crisis
- Feeling unfulfilled by accomplishments such as promotions and raises
- Feeling like a professional "fraud"
- Having little or no time to nurture professional or community relationships
- Experiencing burnout, pessimism, or boredom
- Neglecting family and friends
- Losing community ties

The antidote for "waking unconsciousness" may indeed be spirit. I have had the privilege to witness amazing leadership transformations by executives and managers, on a quest for spirit.

As a coach, I have helped guide leaders on their journey with the support of three powerful practices:

- Contemplative reflection (consciousness)
- Leading with intention (intention)
- Relationship building (connection)

Consciousness

Pat Turner is distressed by the results of her recent 360-degree feedback. It seems that despite her tireless leadership efforts and significant contributions to the corporate bottom line, her direct reports and peers perceive Pat to be moody, insensitive, and hypercritical of others. Pat admits that over the past year she has had to manage the pressures of work as well as a family health crisis; however she is surprised and hurt that her colleagues and staff fail to acknowledge her gallant attempts to "leave personal emotions at the corporate door."

Three-hundred-sixty-degree feedback often prompts leaders to embark on a path of self-discovery, which for clients like Pat may ultimately invoke spirit.

To help her see new possibilities for being and doing, I introduced Pat to the practice of journaling. To inspire her thinking, I offered the following reflection topics:

- My best moment of the day was....
- I felt most relaxed when I....
- I gained a new appreciation for....
- I want to learn more about....
- I want to stay curious about....

Journaling helped Pat to realize that she had been more defensive than curious about her feedback data. As a result, Pat made a commitment to meet individually with her staff members and peers to thank them for giving her their honest assessments. Interestingly, the one-on-one conversations were often the best moments of Pat's day. In one face-to-face meeting, Pat took a risk and shared the story of her family health crisis with a colleague. To her surprise, the colleague had experienced a similar situation in her own life. Whether it was intuition, or the presence of spirit, that gave her the courage to confide in her peer, Pat was conscious of the fact that by being vulnerable she had initiated a tender, memorable moment at work.

Intention

Since joining his firm, three years ago, Jonathan Winston* has been on the corporate fast track. Labeled as a "high potential" Jonathan willingly let his bosses direct his steps up the corporate ladder. Jonathan has proven himself to be a star contributor, having performed well on all of his mission critical assignments. Now, his boss has recommended Jonathan for a coveted senior vice president position, which would make Jonathan one of the youngest executives in the firm's history. Although he is flattered by the nomination, Jonathan feels as if he is living out someone else's vision for his life.

Because he lacked a clear intention, Jonathan is facing what I describe as a crisis of spirit. Clients, like Jonathan, often express the following:

- Feeling directionless and unfocused
- Letting things happen versus making things happen
- Missing out on opportunities
- Being a victim of circumstance
- Feeling disillusioned or unfulfilled by success

I challenged Jonathan to declare a compelling intention for his future. We worked together over several weeks to identify the moments in his life when he felt most authentic. A pattern emerged, which inspired Jonathan to make a bold declaration for himself. He wanted to be in service to others. His intention was to make a career shift within his organization that would mean taking a position several levels below his current position. Although his colleagues felt Jonathan was making a huge mistake, Jonathan said that for the first time in his professional life his heart and mind were in alignment.

Jonathan's life-changing decision affirmed my belief that intention is the cornerstone of spirit. When leaders envision how they want to be, it informs what they do, and gives them the confidence and courage to act.

Connection

It is normal for Jill Myers to work in excess of eighty hours per week. Jill is the first person to arrive at the office and the last one to close up at night. Although her work schedule leaves little time for exercise, hobbies, vacation, or community service, Jill sees no way out from the pile of assignments and projects requiring her attention.

Lately, Jill is feeling stressed and overwhelmed. She worries that her boss and peers will think she is an ineffectual leader who can't handle the pressures of a dynamic work environment. Jill also fears she may suffer a physical or emotional breakdown if she continues to work at her current pace.

Leaders, who are chronically busy, often feel disconnected from co-workers, family, and friends. In addition they may experience the following:

- Never having enough time for self or others
- Feeling out of balance
- An exaggerated fear of failure
- Stress related health problems
- Feeling unappreciated and undervalued

As her coach, I challenged Jill's assessment that she had to "go it alone" to be a successful leader. I asked her to consider the following questions:

- To change this situation, how will I need to be?
- What do I need to believe about myself?
- What do I need to believe about others?
- What do I need to do?

Jill's responses highlighted several voids in her life. She was not getting the support that she needed nor was she comfortable with asking for help. We spoke about ways to build networks of support inside and outside of work. Jill came up with a four-part action plan. The first action was for Jill to have a conversation with her boss about needing to balance her work and life. Secondly, Jill was to plan a weekly activity with family or friends. The third action was to join a professional network that offered peer coaching and support. The final part of the plan was for Jill to delegate a critical project to one of her direct reports.

Although it took several months, Jill successfully completed all four parts of her plan. I asked Jill to tell me how it felt to ask for and receive help. I was struck by the emotion in her eyes as she spoke about feeling humbled and gratified by the generous support she had received from others. As I listened to her speak, I had the feeling that I was seeing her true spirit for the first time.

Implications for Coaching

The first step to supporting a client in search of spirit may be to encourage self-observation practices, such as the following:

- Keep a "Consciousness Journal": At least once or twice a day, write down the different types of emotions experienced throughout the day. For example, *sadness, anger, or joy.* Beside each word write the reasons for the emotion. For example, "I felt sad when no one asked me how I was feeling after being out of the office on sick leave for three days." At the end of the week notice patterns, themes, lessons learned, and opportunities for creating different outcomes.

- Notice Intention: At the start of each day ask yourself, "What is my intention for this day?" A sample intention may be, "to invite feedback from my colleagues and direct reports." Journal what happened as a result of setting your intention. How are you different? What did you learn? What are the implications for you as a leader?
- Connection Reflection: Look at your monthly calendar. Notice how you choose to spend your time on any given day, week, or month.
  - Do you make commitments only to cancel them because you feel overbooked or overwhelmed?
  - Would your boss, peers, and direct reports describe you as a "behind the desk" leader or an "out on the floor" leader?
  - Write down the positive outcomes of connectedness. Ask yourself the following:
    - What do I get and give from networking?
    - What are the benefits of volunteering?
    - How does my leadership position allow me to help others?
- Hold on/Let go: Notice what you choose to hold on to and why? Ask yourself the following:
  - Is this important to do now and why?
  - What difference will it make if I let this activity go?
  - Do I need help?
  - What would be the benefit of delegating or partnering with others to do this work?
  - What is keeping me from asking for help?

Learning to engage in activities that slow down the cycles of "busyness" enhances consciousness; facilitates intentional thought and action; and reinforces the positive aspects of connectedness. Coaches may recommend the following contemplative practices:

- Take a moment: Each day schedule 5–10 minutes for yourself. Set an intention to be still and quiet. Be conscious of your breathing. Connect to each physical sensation. Notice thoughts and feelings without judgment. Indulge fully in the moment as if it is a delicious and decadent treat. Notice how you feel afterward. Set an intention to repeat the process at least once a day. Gradually build up your quiet time to 30–60 minutes a day.
- Tie intentions to actions: Create a leadership development plan for yourself, which documents action, intention, and desired outcomes. Share intentions with others and monitor progress to determine when intentions are in or out of alignment. Make adjustments to actions as needed.
- Find your center: Attend a yoga, tai chi, martial arts, or pottery class. Each discipline teaches "centeredness" as an intentional thought, feeling, and action.
- Walk a mile or two in silence: Practice walking in silence without headphones or chatter. Notice the sights and sounds in nature. Journal or draw your observations. Keep a leaf, rock, or feather on your desk to remind yourself of your connection to the outside world.

- Practice "being" versus "doing": Set an intention to be fully present to an act versus multitasking. Clear your calendar and your mind to facilitate listening and attentiveness.
- Create rituals: Once or twice a year initiate a leadership retreat for yourself or for your entire staff. Build in time for reflection, intention setting, and connection.

Conclusion

As a coach, I have been enriched by my experience of helping clients pursue their aspirations to lead with spirit. The degree to which managers and leaders embrace practices that enhance consciousness, intention, and connection, the more likely they are to find spirit at work.

CHAPTER 6

G.R.A.C.E. at Work—Strong Relationships for Powerful Results

Eric de Nijs

Coaching is, by its very nature, a relationship. Many have labeled it a partnership, while others call it an alliance. However you choose to describe it, it is still a relationship, and that relationship is at the heart and soul of coaching. The coaching relationship's vitality, balance, and strength are what determine a client's success.

Webster's Dictionary defines relationship as "a state of affairs existing between those having relations or dealings." What is most important to understand, however, is not the definition, but the condition of the relationship. Webster's definition *implies a relationship* between those "having relations or dealings." However, in our warp-speed world we tend to remove the relationship from the relations. People and organizations may have dealings together, but the art, science, and practice of relationships has been abandoned. It is critical that the coach never let this happen, but rather be consciously working to establish meaningful coaching and leadership relationships.

Developing relationships is the single-most critical success element for any leadership or coaching model. Coaches who develop powerful, purposeful productive relationships with their clients are more likely to inspire greater productivity, growth, innovation, and overall performance. Without a powerful relationship, when the coach and client have only those "relations or dealings" rather than relationship, coaching is flat, unproductive, and wasted. The pure essence of successful and powerful coaching is a powerful relationship.

Since relationship-building is fast becoming a dying art, many people are unsure of themselves and their ability to develop these powerful and productive relationships. This chapter introduces a simple model, easy to remember and follow, yet powerful in its results. It is a model of human dynamics that not only enables a coach to build the best relationships for client success, but also serves as an effective leadership guide for clients to follow as well. It is not a list of competencies or skills. It is about the behavior of relationships. The profession of coaching has a great body of academic learning, including volumes on appropriate competencies, skills, and behaviors. All of that learning, each skill, competency, or behavior, can effectively be placed in one or several of the categories of this relationship model. The purpose of this model is to provide an easy and effective methodology, an "attitude alignment" model, for powerful relationships that yield productive and purposeful results for your client.

G.R.A.C.E. at Work: A New Model for
Powerful, Purposeful, Productive Relationships

Powerful relationships are based on goodwill and a mutual commitment to a shared purpose that provides affirmation, inspiration, and personal transformation. These relationships emerge only through the presence and practice of five key components whose initials form the acronym G.R.A.C.E. These are Goodwill, Results, Authenticity, Connectivity, and Empowerment (figure 6.1).

"G.R.A.C.E. at Work" was originally designed as a leadership model for application in the business environment, based on what is known to yield results, as a human interaction model. Coaches are leaders who powerfully impact the lives of their clients, often leaders themselves. This model provides a solid framework and structure around which the coaching relationship is built, maintained, and balanced. It is easy to remember, and it serves also as an excellent model for clients who lead others. The five elements of G.R.A.C.E. are blended in combination and equal balance. All five must be present in the relationship to guarantee results.

Goodwill: It All Begins Here

Goodwill involves assuming positive intent, suspending judgment, looking out for the other person's best interest, giving without condition, offering forgiveness,

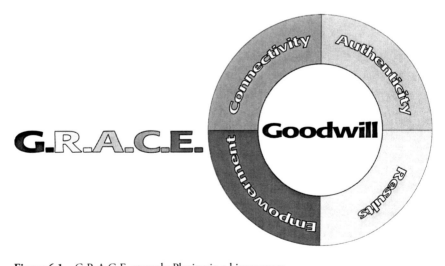

Figure 6.1 G.R.A.C.E. at work: Playing in a bigger space

being at peace with what is, and providing support and safety in times of risk and failure. It's about making things all right regardless of what is happening in the relationship. It all begins with Goodwill. The leader creates a "safe place" for working relationships to flourish, where people work together to achieve similar and collaborative goals.

Goodwill doesn't mean ignoring the effects of poor decisions. It means creating the conditions, the safe place, so both parties know the other is looking out for his or her best interests. Sometimes that might involve giving without condition or extending forgiveness. Sometimes it can mean simply being at peace with what is. Goodwill is closely linked to trust and creates the psychological safety net that encourages people to take the risks associated with breakthrough performance.

In the coaching relationship, the coach will understand, however, that instead of mutual and collaborative goals, all the goals will focus on the client, not the coach. This differs from the standard leadership relationship where both parties have goals and objectives, and the goodwill is based on making those mutually appreciated goals. This is most often not true in the coaching relationship. The nature of coaching demands that the coach holds the client's best interests as his or her own. Hopefully, both coach and client, however, approach the relationship basing their actions and words on mutual goodwill.

Here's an example that illustrates the goodwill concept. A retired vice president of a diversified international food company reflected on his rise through the organization. Young and quite ambitious when he joined the company, Karl was eager to make his mark. But, after a string of failures, the company president summoned him. Fearing the worst, Karl prepared for the meeting with dread. Instead, what he experienced was a conversation that addressed opportunities for redemption, not because he deserved it, but because of his manager's commitment to people. The conversation established the basis for what was to be a long and profitable relationship. Jim, Karl's manager, set the stage so that they could achieve shared success. He created a "safe space" for the two to collaborate. Although he didn't want to see Karl self-destruct, he also made it clear he couldn't afford any more of Karl's mistakes. Jim saw Karl's potential and established a relationship that would bring out his best.

Results: Formula for Purpose

There are actually two "R"s in this component: Reason and Results. It is the reason for being in a relationship which ultimately yields results. It focuses on the ability of both parties to mutually create meaning and value. It is a shared sense of purpose. Obviously, there must be a relationship of some sort to put goodwill to work. The working relationship between the coach and client is the REASON for being together. That reason is always to share in purpose and generate RESULTS and value for both.

Effective coaches help their clients identify their purpose and passion. G.R.A.C.E. helps answer the questions, "What's my reason for being?" and "Why are we in this relationship?" Long after leaving an organization or exiting a relationship, people realize that success isn't just about the numbers. It's about contributing by doing the things they love to do—things that are meaningful. Research conducted by the CLC Learning and Development Roundtable found that "by changing the way employees think about themselves, their jobs, and their organizations, managers have another means of obtaining dramatic improvements in the performance of their employees." Effective coaches, and leaders, recognize this desire as a powerful motivator for people, and they leverage it to create commitment to the vision and purpose of the organization, or of the client.

Authenticity: Essential Reality

Authenticity is being real with yourself and others, choosing how you wish to relate to others, declaring what your stand is, holding yourself accountable for your actions, rewarding yourself appropriately, being open and vulnerable, openly communicating needs, desires, moods, attitudes, values, and feelings—even about the other person. Being real—and being all that you can be—is essential to any relationship, but especially to one with expectations for real (authentic) results. Open and uncompromising standards, positive attitudes, and the desire to be exactly who you are, are the heart of a fruitful relationship. Authenticity keeps all relationships balanced and healthy. Each person must first identify, then "own up" to his or her own place of reality. Successful relationships thrive when both parties are exactly who they are, say exactly what they mean, and use the same standards for self and others.

Great leadership, and great coaching, begin by knowing and leveraging strengths and weaknesses. Self-awareness in coaches and leaders, and promoting it in others, represents a huge opportunity to create consistency between the walk and the talk and provides a measure of transparency to others that fosters trust in a relationship.

Connectivity: Cocreated Value

Connectivity means finding ways to identify with, affirm, and encourage the other person, understanding how the other person feels, what is important to them, sharing assumptions and beliefs, identifying and realizing differences in intention and impact on others, and the genuine desire to associate with and relate to others. When goodwill, a reason for being in relationship, and authenticity combine, they advance the relationship to the place of real connectivity. Connectivity is about empathizing with others, finding ways to engage them in the pursuit of mutual goals, and cocreating value with the people they coach. This brings to mind my client, Andrea, a successful IT executive whose expertise was greatly enhanced by a strong conceptual capacity. Andrea also had an exceptional knack for leveraging her intuition in problem solving, and she made no apologies for it. She was good at what she did, and she accomplished a lot. One of her major weaknesses, however, was not taking the time to learn from her co-workers. Andrea didn't allow that free flow of communication with others, because her agenda was focused on selling herself and her solutions. Quite simply, Andrea did not connect with others. Consequently, she lost many opportunities to engage the hearts and minds of her employees. She consistently received low scores on the associate satisfaction survey items related to manager-associate relations. Through coaching, Andrea came to realize that this behavior limited the innovation needed to succeed in the long run. Andrea needed to learn how to connect with her colleagues so they felt heard, respected, and engaged. By sharing more of what she was focused on and by asking questions and learning what was important to the other person, Andrea was able to facilitate a deeper conversation with her colleagues and generate greater ownership on the team's initiatives.

It is the coach's responsibility to create these connection points through careful and deliberate observance and understanding of the client's most effective methods of engagement. Coaches connect with clients and essentially "team up" for shared results. When coach and client connect, through shared motives, values, goals, and understanding—and through effective engagement practices—the subsequent bond can yield powerful results. The safe place of G.R.A.C.E. easily affords this vital connectivity.

Empowerment: Enabling Success

Empowerment is helping others overcome obstacles, developing new skills, establishing a safe environment to succeed (for self and others), creating catalysts for change, helping others see potential and possibilities, being open to possibilities, allowing time for testing and learning, and seeing the larger whole but being aware of smaller components. Empowerment is about enabling clients to achieve their own success, not doing it for them. It is about creating a "nutrient-rich" environment for free, unfettered growth.

It is essential that the coach maintain the critical balance of challenge and support, sufficiently motivating others to take risks, to see new things and do new things, while still holding the client accountable. A good coach must create a dynamic tension, a balance, which motivates the client to advance his or her skills, but still provide that safe place of encouragement and support. The coach creates and maintains this same balance between advocacy and inquiry, and task and relationship.

Coaches and clients need to cocreate the boundaries for empowerment, learning, and responsibility. Trust also plays a vital role in empowerment, and it begins with a common understanding of expectations and mutual commitments of goals, roles, and consequences.

Proven and Powerful Checklist

Accountability is a topic that most people avoid like the plague. However, it is essential for the coach. The great coach systematically reviews his or her performance, always seeking areas of improvement. He or she is constantly learning, constantly checking, and constantly improving. Figure 6.2 is a checklist that captures the main concepts of the G.R.A.C.E. at Work model, presented in a manner to allow coaches to monitor and realign their relationship building behaviors, while at the same time building those same skills in their clients, leaders themselves. A coach who practices G.R.A.C.E. at Work will build the kind of relationship that delivers results

Coach's Personal Checklist	Coaching (and Modeling) to Client Checklist
1. Am I approaching this coaching relationship with goodwill and positive intent for my client?	1. Is my client approaching his or her relationships with goodwill and positive intent? What does that look like?
2. Have I suspended any judgment I may tend to make regarding this client?	2. Is my client holding onto judgments and prejudices, or is he or she able to suspend/release them to move on?
3. Am I truly interested in, and looking out for, my client's best interests?	3. Is my client interested in others, developing them, mentoring them, or is he or she completely self-interested?
4. Am I giving to him or her, without condition?	4. Is my client giving without condition, or has he or she set unrealistic or unmet expectations on others?
5. Do I and will I freely extend forgiveness if needed?	5. Is my client able to freely extend forgiveness if needed, or is he or she harboring unforgiveness, a grudge, or living in past "wrongs?"
6. Am I able to be at peace with what is in this relationship?	6. Does my client know contentment in the moment, or is he or she at unrest? How do I help my client find peace with what is, yet still set appropriate goals?
7. Have I created an environment of trust and safety for my client?	7. Is my client trustful of me, and others? Is he or she able to create an environment of trust with others?
1. Am I aware of my client's dreams and goals? Can I describe what he or she thinks success looks like?	1. Does my client know what he or she is looking for? Can the client describe what success is and looks like? Will my client be able to recognize when his or her goals are achieved?
2. Do I fully understand and embrace the purpose of this coaching relationship—the intended results?	2. Does my client understand the purpose of this coaching relationship, and has he or she clearly stated the intended results? Can my client translate this ability to identify intention and shared value in other relationships?
3. Am I able to keep myself fully out of my client's story?	3. Is my client able to support the intentions, purpose, and goals of others without imposing his or her own values, goals, or intentions?
4. Will I be genuinely pleased for my client when he or she achieves the success desired?	4. Is my client able to be genuinely pleased with success in others?
5. Have I identified, and do I understand, the intended and unintended consequences of the stated results?	5. Has my client fully explored, identified, and accepted the intended or unintended consequences of his or her desired results?
6. Have I identified my own purpose and passion, and is this coaching relationship built within that passion?	6. Can my client identify his or her purpose and passion? Can they help others do the same?
7. Have I helped this client to establish a solid plan to achieve the intended and stated results?	7. Does my client have a plan to achieve results? Do they know how to measure progress? Are they able to do this for others?

Figure 6.2 Continued

1. Can I be real and authentic with this client? Can I be genuine, able to describe and articulate my values?	1. Is my client real and authentic with me? With others? Is he or she able to articulate personal values and vision?
2. Do I keep myself accountable to "walk my talk," and do I honestly engage this client and keep him or her accountable to "walk the talk?"	2. Is my client willing to engage on an authentic level, and willing to be held accountable to "walk the talk" in this relationship? Is this person able to do this with others, and self?
3. Can I openly communicate needs, desires, moods attitudes, values, and feelings, with this client and with others?	3. Can my client openly communicate needs, desires, moods, attitudes, values and feelings with me? With others?
4. Do I have open and uncompromising standards, positive attitudes, and a deep desire to be exactly who I am with this client?	4. Does my client have uncompromising standards, positive attitudes, and a deep desire to be exactly who he or she is?
5. Do I know my strengths and weaknesses, and am I able to leverage them, especially in this coaching relationship?	5. Does my client know his or her strengths and weaknesses (areas of challenge), and is he or she able to leverage them in all relationships?
6. Am I "transparent" in this relationship?	6. Is my client "transparent" in all his or her relationships?
7. Am I exactly who I say I am? Do I say exactly what I mean? Do I use the same standards for myself and others?	7. Does my client appear to be exactly who he or she says? Does this person say what he or she means? Does my client use the same standards for self and for others?

1. Am I able to identify with, affirm and encourage my client?	1. Is my client able to identify with, affirm and encourage others?
2. Do I understand how my client feels, and what is important to him or her? Do I empathize with him or her?	2. Does my client understand how others feel, and what is important to them? Does he or she empathize with others?
3. Do I have a genuine desire to connect and associate (relate) with this person?	3. Does my client have a genuine desire to connect with and associate (relate) to others?
4. Have I enabled my client to connect with me?	4. Has my client enabled others to connect with him or her?
5. Can I put my own aspirations aside to be sensitive and of service to my client's needs?	5. Can my client put his or her aspirations aside to be sensitive and of service to the needs of others?
6. Am I able to understand, empathize with my client's situation, and appreciate the impact this situation has on her or his mood, attitudes, identity, ego, and vision for success?	6. Is my client able to understand the situations of others, and to appreciate how these situations impact the moods, attitudes, identities, egos, and vision of others?
7. Can I honestly support and share my client's motives, values, goals, and desired results from this relationship? (Can I put those before my own?)	7. Does my client honestly support and share the motives, values, goals, and desired results of others in relationship with him or her? Can he or she put the needs of others first, in order to establish solid, productive connections with others?

Figure 6.2 Continued

1. Am I able to help my client overcome obstacles, develop new skills, and create catalysts for change?	1. Is my client able to overcome obstacles and develop new skills? Is this person able to create catalysts for change in others as well?
2. Am I able to help this client be open to possibilities and potential?	2. Is my client open to possibilities and potential? Is she or he able to help others in this regard?
3. Can I help my client be aware of all components, but still see the larger "whole?"	3. Is my client able to see both the details and the whole picture, keeping perspective on both? Is he or she able to help others do this?
4. Am I able to create the right balance between challenge and support for this client?	4. Does my client know and understand the difference between challenge and support in his or her current relationships?
5. Do I have all the resources needed to assist this client in developing new skills, or advancing his or her goals?	5. Does this client have adequate resources for expected growth? Is he or she able to provide that to stimulate and assist growth in others?
6. Am I able to help my client tap into his or her own passion or purpose?	6. Does my client understand working from passion, and is he or she able to discover and enable it in others?
7. Do I allow my client the time for testing, learning, and growing, and assist him or her in recognizing reality?	7. Is my client able to take the time necessary for testing and learning in both self and others? Is she or he able to recognize reality?

Figure 6.2   G.R.A.C.E.: Full coaching checklist

for clients. A client who learns and practices G.R.A.C.E. at Work will see results organizationally, and in the individuals he or she leads, which quite often is what the coaching is all about in the first place—becoming a more effective leader.

It's Not About Me

This is not a popular sentiment today, but it is essential for the GRACE-full coach. Client success sometimes demands sacrifice. Moreover, that requires doing what's best for the client as opposed to pushing toward the coach's bias, perceptions of success for the client, or personal goals. In the game of baseball, a sacrifice fly or bunt may result in a player sacrificing his personal performance statistics to advance the team. Similarly, a sacrifice in a powerful relationship may mean that a person gives up his or her agenda, his or her need to be "right," or the need to be first. This is the pure meaning of goodwill, and evidence of the capacity to coach and lead with G.R.A.C.E. It is also an attribute that, when successfully modeled, can be learned by others.

Leading and Coaching with Grace

An interaction model for coaching relationships that facilitates trust and transparency is needed to guide performance, productivity, and ultimate success for the client. Purposeful, productive, and powerful relationships can form the basis for achieving breakthrough performance and building the capacity for future growth. G.R.A.C.E. at work can provide greater opportunities to build relationships and facilitate performance. Coaches and clients are authentic, achieve a special kind of chemistry for growth, empower each other, and extend good will. It is the creation of a safe place for people to perform—within stated boundaries—without fear of failure.

One client, Ron, the vice president of a financial services company offered his experience with leading with G.R.A.C.E. In his own words, Ron said, "I had a proven track record of delivering results and felt proud of my accomplishments. However, I received some feedback on my 360 assessment that caused me to rethink my leadership methods, and I had to make a choice. It was time to be authentic, own up to the feedback, and then reframe my approach. I could have chosen to "rest on my laurels" but that would not have allowed me to grow, nor would I have been in the strongest position to help others grow. I realized that authenticity in leadership starts with me. With this perspective in mind, I have been able to encourage others to be honest about their own leadership, competencies, and challenges, thereby further enabling our connection, and ultimately, our results."

The concepts behind the word "grace" lend themselves to this model well. *Grace* generally brings to mind two ideas. One, simply put, is unmerited favor. In other words, we are treated much better than we deserve. The other is a certain poise or elegance in movement. Both of these ideas contribute to leading and coaching with grace. G.R.A.C.E.-full coaching assumes goodwill, which will many times translate into unmerited favor. In a state of G.R.A.C.E., energy is abundant and performance effortless. Obstacles are anticipated, but with the expectation that they will be overcome. Failure is seen as an opportunity to learn. This does not imply that this kind of relationship is pain free or even easy. It requires effort, commitment, and yes, *grace*. However, the anticipation and realization of success supersedes pain and difficulty.

Coaching and leading with G.R.A.C.E. encourages people to learn new things and express themselves authentically in a safe environment. G.R.A.C.E. encourages commitment, not compliance, because G.R.A.C.E. assumes that development and high performance occur most effectively in the context of a purposeful relationship. This relationship is based on goodwill and a mutual commitment to a shared purpose that provides affirmation, inspiration, and personal transformation. Without G.R.A.C.E., what remains is a series of transactional interactions that neither satisfy nor inspire, and do not advance your clients to the success they seek. Are you insuring the success of your clients by building G.R.A.C.E.-full relationships?

CHAPTER 7

Using Story in Coaching

Margaret Echols, Karen Gravenstine,
and Sandy Mobley

Stories of Our Becoming

Since ancient times, we humans have told stories to make meaning and sense of our lives. The Hindu *Mahabharata*, Homer's epics, the Greek tragedies, the Bible, Shakespeare, Aesop's Fables, the Grimm Brothers' Fairy tales, the "sacred bundle stories" of Native American Indians, and the country and western ballads of Nashville are all powerful and amazing stories that inspire wonder and awe. In these stories, facts are mostly irrelevant. What matters is the underlying message they mean to convey—the values, passions, concerns, hopes, and dreams of the ones who tell them.

In her book, *Corporate Legends & Lore*, Peg Neuhauser writes, "the stories of our own life are a personal treasure. They are your personal sacred bundle. Those sacred bundle stories represent the best of who you are, as well as the wisdom that you have accumulated over the years of your life."[1] Listen to another's sacred bundle stories and you listen to his heart. Hear another's legend and you witness the hero within. Attend to the ballads one sings about her life and you learn the recurring refrains by which she defines herself. Stand as witness to his fables and fairy tales and you enter into the core values, principles, and morals that guide his life.

"We all tell stories about who we are, where we come from, and where we are going. These personal myths in turn shape who we become and what we believe."[2] Stories told time and time again give us a glimpse into the spirit and soul of a tribe, a nation, a people, an organization, and an individual being. The myths, legends, ballads, parables, and fables we tell about ourselves reveal our essence. In the Native American Indian culture, the role of the "story teller" is to share the most important stories of the tribe so they continue from generation to generation. We are the keeper of our own stories, telling over and over again those that define who we are—those that reveal our spirit—our soul, both as individuals and as communities.

Sometimes we keep telling our stories as though they are irrefutable facts, unquestionable and unchangeable. We often live our lives as if the stories we hold about ourselves are real. When that happens we can get stuck in our past, seeing no possibility for the future. Scientists studying brain activity found that people remembering a situation have identical brain activity as those imagining a situation. Their hypothesis is that people mentally cannot distinguish between a real and imagined situation. If people are remembering, imagining, or anticipating a negative experience, it shapes how they view the world. And so is their world shaped when they hold a positive experience.[3] This is powerful for coaching. Coaching provides an editor's role in our story. It helps others to "detect the story line in their own lives…opening up a hidden world of self-discovery and meaning."[4] Coaching invites the insertion of new chapters. It creates the opportunity to write new, unimaginable endings. It allows the possibility to change the moral of the story and the outcome of the fairy tale.

"Storytelling is fundamental to the human search for meaning whether we tell tales of the creation of the earth or of our early choices."[5] These are the stories of our becoming.

Stories for Personal Transformation

I asked Jean, my client, to tell me the story of her life, the momentous moments, and the people who have influenced/shaped her into the person she is today. She shared the highlights, both painful and joyful then said, I had never thought about how my life sounds when I talk about it as a complete picture. I heard my perceptions, my beliefs, the undercurrent of pain and dissatisfaction…and fear. Is this the story of my life? It's bleak—all black and gray. I want a better, happier story—I want bright colors, I want a hopeful mood, I want courage. How do I get there? How do I change how I view myself and my world—how do I change my story?

Who are we? Who do we think we are? How have our life experiences shaped our bodies, our emotions, our beliefs—our way of seeing, and being in, the world? What is our story, our narratives, regarding the sum total of our experiences? It is how those experiences are felt, defined, reflected upon, and talked about that become our set of beliefs. These beliefs can severely cripple our ability to take action, or strengthen and embolden us to extraordinary feats. Our stories, and what we focus on, become our reality.

The Coach's Role

Stories are essential to our capacity to truly understand each other, our world, and ourselves. Physicians who fail to listen to their patients' stories may fail to provide the correct treatment, despite knowing all the relevant medical facts. *Narrative medicine programs* are emerging—evidence of the increased focus on training doctors to listen to the stories and learn to better "read" their patients. Coaches, also, must listen deeply to their clients' narratives. We must listen beneath the words, beneath the facts, to understand the lens through which the client is viewing the world, and the effects of that view.

In the earlier example, Jean told her story to her coach. With other clients, the coach may have them write their *up until now* story to capture a picture of their life up to the present. During the first month of coaching, the coach also gave Jean some self-observation exercises to help gain even further clarity on how she is seeing her world. One exercise, for example, was the following:

- Notice things you are doing well, your successes.
- Notice the challenges you are facing and what you are doing about them.
- Write what you are noticing in a journal. Keep a daily record.

During the first few weeks, Jean observed many problems/challenges and very few successes. It was clear to both coach and client that Jean's attention and energy were centered on her missteps and daily challenges.

The coach gave Jean the assignment of writing her *best self* (her most powerful, authentic self) story. She asked Jean to write about how she wanted to show up as her best self in her work, in her relationships, and in her whole life. When they discussed this afterward, Jean was excited. She saw that she was already exhibiting some elements of her best self, yet never noticing. She saw that some of the challenges that loomed as mountains in her mind were not so large at all—she had been investing them with the power to paralyze her. Over time, she began to gain insight and see possibilities for herself not seen before. Through subsequent coaching sessions, Jean's energy and increasing belief in herself propelled her forward. She grappled with her "gremlins" and continued to shift her mental habit from focusing on problems to receiving solutions. She set her sights high and took bold action on goals she had identified. And little by little, day by day, Jean's life shifted from shades of gray, black and white to a full spectrum of vibrant color.

In the previous abbreviated story, we fleshed out Jean's "story" of her way of seeing the world up until now. We then explored Jean's real *commitment* to change. What does she want? What will that get her? How will she know?

Through coaching Jean gained increasing awareness of her *authentic* and *best self.* We uncovered layers of beliefs and experiences that had given rise to her gremlins of doubts, fears, and judgments. She began to advance to higher levels of learning, self-awareness, and emotional intelligence. Jean identified her *new story* as her best self and, through continued practice and feedback, started to live the story she had created.

SCAN

toward an understanding of who we are
and, ultimately, transformation to the person we can become.

Story > Commitment > Authentic self > New story and action

Figure 7.1 A model for using story in coaching: SCAN

Stories for Organizational Change

How does an organization build, teach, and reinforce its culture? Most organizations have mission and values statements—does anyone read them? If they do read them, do they remember them or behave according to the values? What people remember are the organizational stories, and these stories describe what has meaning to the people.

For example, when two EDS employees were held hostage in a heavily guarded prison in Iran in 1979 and political negotiations broke down, EDS chairman, Ross Perot, took matters into his own hands. He handpicked a team of volunteers from his organization to go in and rescue the employees.[6] What a powerful message that conveyed about EDS taking care of its people.

Consider the leaders of Enron or WorldCom who put the organization in jeopardy and risked employees' retirement plans for their own gain. They sent a very different message to their workforce.

When people tell newcomers to an organization about the company, they tell the stories of risks taken, mistakes made, successes, and what happened to the people who won and lost. This tells the new employees what behavior is rewarded and punished far better than value statements or employee manuals.

Just as people can use story telling for transformation, so can organizations. How many organizations have come back from difficulties because people had confidence in their leadership and the leaders were able to create a vision that the workforce believed in? Think about the rebuilding of Chrysler and the new vision or story Lee Iacocca told the workforce and their debtors to make them believe and help Chrysler come back. Moreover, Iacocca didn't tell that story only once. He made hundreds of presentations reinforcing the pride of the workforce, the preeminence of Chrysler engineering, and the strong possibility of a successful outcome.[7] Could he have succeeded without a compelling story? We don't think so.

An organizational mini-story may be its tag line or vision statement. Some examples are: GE—"We bring good things to life" or Nike—"Just do it." These visions tell employees much more about the company than employee manuals.

To be a person is to have a story to tell.[8]

"Start with Story" Coaching Exercises for Your Client

Hero's Journey

- One way to use storytelling for transformation is in helping people tell their story of what they want to create. Using Joseph Campbell's model of the hero's journey,[9] begin by asking people what they are called to do or what vision they want to bring about. Then ask them to reflect on both their fears (monsters) and their resources for support. As they tell the story from startup to struggles to success they embolden themselves and engage others in the possibilities.

Use of Metaphors

- A metaphor is a mini-story. Symbolic representations bring power and deeper meaning to transformation. The coach might ask, "If you were a flower, how would you describe yourself?" The client might see herself as a shade plant, a toad lily. Yet, she is a tall, fun-loving person who is working in a serious, harsh organization characterized by overwork and lack of personal connection. The coach might tell the client that she sees her as a sunflower—growing taller and bolder as she got more sunshine. Holding this image would allow her to look for organizational possibilities for more fun and connection (sun) and supportive leadership.
- In a career development workshop, one coach asked people to give her metaphors for their careers.
    - One person said he steps into an elevator and pushes the button for the penthouse but never gets there because other people push his buttons and derail his assent.
    - Another person said his career was like being a racecar driver. He goes around and around at high speed, but there is never a finish line.
    - With metaphors, you can help people see possibilities for change. In the first example, the coach asked, "How can you enlist others in helping you reach your destination?" In the second example she asked, "What are your own milestones for success that will tell you that you have completed the race?"

Recall and Reshape the Story

- We have clients make a list of significant turning points in their lives, and then list these events as chapters in a book, adding some narrative description.
    - Then they choose one of these turning points and describe what changed for them after this event (i.e., outlook, emotions, actions, and values).
    - Finally they identify any patterns in these events as they scan the whole story.
- We may ask a client to tell or write about a peak experience in his or her life, and to write about a painful experience. In these narratives people often realize the growth or shifts that came from these episodes.
- We ask clients to write their obituaries—"How you would like to be remembered?"
- Another story starter: "You are on the cover of Fortune magazine in five years—write the story." This exercise and the one preceding open clients to more possibilities for their lives. Clients begin to realize they still have things they want to accomplish. And so they begin to create their new stories.
- This is a good targeted exercise: "Describe a conflict you had recently with a colleague. Write the story from your point of view. Now write the story from your colleague's point of view."

A Closing Exercise for Coaches, Their Clients, Their Friends, and Their Families

Telling Your Sacred Bundle Stories

A "sacred bundle" is a symbolic collection of items—mementoes that capture the essence of who you are—your heart and soul.[10] Spend some time over the next two weeks reflecting on your life—what you value, key characteristics that describe you, your watershed experiences, the heroes and mentors who helped to form you, significant events, major disappointments, failures, or crisis—the most important things that contribute to your identity.

For each of these things find a small, symbolic, physical object that will help you remember and tell your story. Put these together in a "sacred bundle"—a basket, a precious box—someplace where you can keep them all together. Share your stories with a committed listener—someone who can help you see not only how these items describe your past history, but also support you in generating the future you want to create for yourself.

This same exercise can be done with groups—families, businesses, places of worship—with each person in the group bringing an item and telling the story that contributes to the creation of the group's "sacred bundle."

One of us, Karen Gravenstine, tells this story to illustrate, "My family created a sacred bundle as a gift for my parents for their fiftieth wedding anniversary. Each of us kids, ten in all, brought several items that reflected for us the essence of our family. We carried them to my parents' home as part of the celebration. As we each presented the object for the sacred bundle—a lovely basket my parents kept in a special place from that day on—we told the story related to it. Stories of church; reading; learning; service; vacation; singing; special foods; siblings who had died; neighbors and relatives. Some things we hadn't discussed for years! The grandchildren and the sons and daughters-in-law were in awe as they heard some family stories for the first time. They were initiated into, and we were reminded of, the essence of who we are as a family. My parents were touched by the power of the stories we told, the best of who we are as a family—the legacy they helped to create."

Conclusion

We are surrounded by our stories and the stories of others. These stories, as we have described in this chapter, have power and life. We can use them to achieve greater connection. We can revise them to achieve greater success. We invite you to use stories as a tool in your coaching practice. Recalling, telling, and revising stories can stimulate dramatic transformations for individuals and organizations. So ... what's your story?

Notes

1. Peg C. Neuhauser, *Corporate Legends & Lore: The Power of Storytelling as a Management Tool* (New York: McGraw-Hill, 1993), 68.

2. Sam Keen and Anne Valley-Fox, *Your Mythic Journey: Finding Meaning in Your Life through Writing and Storytelling* (Los Angeles: Tarcher/Putnam, 1989), David L. Miller, back cover comment.

3. B. Gonsalves, P.J. Reber, D.R. Gitelman, T.B. Parrish, M. Mesulam, and K.A. Paller, "Neural Evidence That Vivid Imagining Can Lead to False Remembering," *Psychological Science 15* (2004): 655–660.

4. See note 2 above.

5. Mary Catherine Bateson, *Composing a Life* (New York: Penguin Books, 1990), 34.

6. *Famous Texans,* "H. Ross Perot," http://www.famoustexans.com/rossperot.htm (accessed November 12, 2007).

7. Ari Weinberg, "The Dollar-A-Year Man," *Forbes*, May 8, 2002, http://www.forbes.com/2002/05/08/0508iacocca.html (accessed November 12, 2007).

8. See note 2 above, 1.

9. Joseph Campbell, *The Power of Myth* (New York: Doubleday, 1998), 14.

10. See note 1 above, 41–48.

CHAPTER 8

Whose Story Is This, Anyway? Identification with Clients in Leadership Coaching

Dave Snapp

My client Robert is a middle manager who is having trouble stepping up to the next level of leadership. After six weeks of coaching, it feels like we are closing in on his key issues: his ambition and his flight from ambition, his abundance of choices and his fear of committing to a single game plan, his sense of an inherent conflict between his career and his family life.

Then it hits me—this is just what is showing up in my life. This guy is *me!*

I'm excited because I know these issues, and I can be of help. But from somewhere inside comes a warning, "You haven't been paying enough attention to these issues for yourself. How can you expect to coach Robert? And whose story is this, anyway?"

It is almost inevitable that, as leadership coaches, we will encounter clients with situations and issues apparently similar to our own. These similarities may intrigue and stimulate us, or they may feel disquieting and uncomfortable.

Whether these initial reactions are positive or negative, they are signals we should pay attention to. Identification with a client's situation or issue may produce empathy and insight that can be helpful to the client, but it can cause significant problems.

Why can identification become problematic? When a client's situation provokes a response in us, it suggests that an active issue of our own is being stimulated. Using the analogy of electrical current, we can say that the issue is "charged" or "carries a charge." We can imagine a whole spectrum of reaction, ranging from "neutral" to "highly charged." The stronger the reaction, the greater the charge. And, often, the greater the charge, the more active, deep, or fundamental the issue is for us, and the more difficult it may be for us to see clearly and be helpful to our client. Alternatively, the more likely it is that we are responding to our own story instead of our client's.[1]

This is why the way in which coaches manage issues of identification can make the difference between masterful work with our clients and mediocre—even harmful—work.

This chapter explores the dynamics of identification in leadership coaching:

- Why does identification occur?
- How can we tell when identification is charged for us?
- How does identification affect our ability to coach leaders effectively?
- What can we do to coach effectively and ethically in such situations?

Why Does Identification Occur?

Judy learns that her client received a critical evaluation at work. Having had a similar experience, she identifies with the client situation and assumes she knows "how it is." In Judy's own case, the critical evaluation was devastating. She is anxious to support her client and probes for evidence of disappointment and sadness.

It's a common occurrence. A client describes a situation. The coach identifies with that situation, in one way or another assuming similarity where it may not exist.

Why does this happen? To some extent, it's unavoidable. One way humans try to make sense of the world is to classify incoming data about people and situations as "like me/mine" or "different than me/mine." Finding similarity provides reassurance that we can recognize and understand what is happening around us. For a coach, this may satisfy a need to understand or "know what to do."

How Can We Tell When Identification Is Charged for Us?

When identification occurs, we as coaches will often be aware of it. What may be harder is to assess whether this identification is charged for us in some way and may as a result present a challenge to our coaching. Fortunately, there are often warning signs that some degree of charged identification may be occurring. Some of these warning signs are

- An emotional response disproportionate to the situation, either positive or negative
- Pain, trauma, or discomfort in the body
- A strong desire to solve the client's problem or give advice
- A sense of being stuck, blocked, or at a total loss as to what to do
- A feeling of being in the client's story
- A persistent feeling that the coaching isn't working, whether the client agrees or not [2]

These clues may or may not indicate that the coach is "identifying" with the client's story. But they are often good signs that the coach is being "hooked" in some way and needs to take steps to figure out what is going on.

How Does Identification Affect Our Ability to Coach Leaders Effectively?

Identifying with a client's story is not necessarily a problem, and it may at times prove helpful. Similar experiences can create some familiarity with the client's territory and provide a foundation for empathetic and caring coaching.

So where might such identification present problems? In general, identification becomes a problem when the focus of the coach's attention moves from client to coach. When we over-identify with a client, we are more likely to assume similarity. Our vision suffers, and we may actually distort reality.

> Jose is currently launching his own independent coaching practice. The experience is proving exciting, but also very stressful. As his family's primary breadwinner, he is particularly anxious about money. One of Jose's first coaching clients has recently retired from a successful and lucrative business career and is planning to launch a strategy consulting business.
>
> Jose finds himself unable to stop worrying about the viability of his client's new business, though the client repeatedly assures him that he is at no financial risk. Jose also pushes "solutions" that have worked for him but don't work for the client. His client's real desire, to explore the broader meaning and value of his new career, is not met.

The dangers of identification increase when the "similar" situation or issue is a charged one for the coach. Jose is caught up with launching his own practice. He projects his anxiety, particularly about finances, onto the client situation. As a result, it is hard for him to hear his financially comfortable client's quite different needs and wants.

A coach's work is to help clients resolve patterns of breakdown or reactivity. The client is stuck, and the coach helps the client discover how to get unstuck. To be helpful in this situation, it is critical that the coach is not himself in a state of breakdown or reactivity. A coach's perception of similarity in the client situation or story may cause coaches to assume greater similarity than actually exists. A special challenge is presented when the perception of similarity triggers—or is triggered by—a coach's own active or unresolved issues. When we as coaches are in breakdown ourselves, we may "see" our clients differently.

A number of things can happen when a client's similar situation triggers a coach's active story, as it did in the case of Jose. The coach may

- miss signals;
- become focused on her own story, and lose sight of her client's story;
- buy into the client's story and get stuck with him;
- begin to work "harder" on the problem than the client is;

- push solutions or reject certain solutions;
- be unable to see alternative ways of being or acting; and
- have difficulty challenging the client or discussing a need for change.

All of these possible responses can hamper the coach's ability to help the client.

Coaching leaders in organizations involves additional considerations. We are in effect entering into the organizational "field" with our clients. Leaders function amid a network of complicated relationships and pressures. They must deal with multiple challenges, involving vision and values, competition and conflict, and ultimately success and failure. As a result, there are countless opportunities for us to be drawn into those same pressures and to lose our necessary independence and objectivity. This is especially true when our own issues, reactivity, and blind spots are apparently similar to those of the leader we are coaching, as in the following case.

> Maria made a career switch to coaching after a fairly unpleasant and unfulfilling stint as an organizational leader. She disliked the competition and conflict she experienced in her work, as well as the focus on the bottom line. She became a coach to be able to focus on building positive and supportive relationships with others.
>
> One of Maria's clients is a leader who is struggling to manage a great deal of conflict in his organization. Maria begins to harbor negative feelings about the client organization and is finding it hard to help or support her client. She begins to think that her client would be better off leaving this organization.

In this example, Maria has clear difficulty differentiating her story from her client's situation. Her own unresolved discomfort about the bottom-line focus and conflict in business organizations is aroused by her client's experience of them. As a result, her inability to separate her own reactions from her client's adversely affects her ability to be of help to her client.

Coaches working in organizational contexts need to take particular care to avoid being unduly influenced by their own experiences and stories about leaders, leadership, and organizations. It is interesting to consider that leadership coaches have generally chosen not to take full time jobs as leaders in organizations. What might this suggest about our view of what it is like to be a leader in an organization?

We need to understand these filters through which we see leaders and organizations. These include not only our general values and assumptions, but also the experiences and stories that live deep within us. We might ask ourselves: What do we like most or least about being a leader? What have been our most or least successful and fulfilling experiences? What kind of leader am I? What excites or scares me about it? What does all of this tell me about my own story about leadership and how this might affect how I coach? A similar set of questions could be asked about our experiences in organizations.

Here are just a few of the stories we may hold about leaders and organizations:

- Organizations eat people up
- Entrepreneurial organizations are better than bureaucratic organizations

- Organizational leadership is heroic
- Most leaders are dishonest
- Successful leaders need sharp elbows
- The problem with most leaders is: [fill in your own story]

How a coach's own story interacts with a client's particular leadership context can be further complicated when a coach has multiple relations in and with the organization. For example, the coach may

a) have a contract with the organization to coach this client,
b) coach others in the organization,
c) consult in the organization,
d) be on staff in the organization,
e) have a history in the organization,
f) have a relationship with key members, and
g) experience any combination of a) through f).

Besides creating boundary issues, the existence of such relationships can multiply the sources of potential triggers for the coach.

What Can We Do to Coach Effectively and Ethically in Such Situations?

In one of the vignettes earlier, Judy initially assumes that her client will react as she herself would have and begins probing "for evidence of disappointment and sadness." What Judy eventually learns, however, is that her client is, in fact, relieved. She had been fearful that her boss's assessment would be far worse, and she is also beginning to realize how little she likes or cares about her current job.

By maintaining curiosity and an awareness that the client is different from the coach, good coaches correct for any tendency to assume similarity. Further exploration often reveals client situations and responses to be distinguishable from the coach's experience in important ways. By staying open and curious, Judy learned that her client's reactions were actually quite different from her own.

In another of the vignettes, Jose was launching a new coaching business while coaching a client also in the midst of career change and thinking about next career steps. Here is more of the story, told from Jose's perspective:

This client's situation triggered me in a number of ways. Along with feeling very immediate financial worries, I was also very committed to the process of self-authoring the next stage of my life. I found myself becoming anxious for and about my client. Since I found structure helpful in my own situation, I advocated structures for him. I also wanted him to pay close attention to generating income quickly. As a coach, I became very result-focused with a client who was much more interested in a philosophical exploration of the possibilities of this next stage of his life. But it was hard for me to see the distinctions between our situations.

A number of steps helped me become more grounded. By spending some time understanding his past, I was able to see how he was different from me. Using the DISC instrument and other "neutral" assessment tools also helped me differentiate my story from his. I consulted with a mentor coach who helped me tune into the problem more clearly. Finally, concerned that my coaching was not proving helpful to the client, I initiated a discussion about my concerns with him. Sorting out what he was and wasn't getting out of the engagement gave us an opportunity to talk through these issues.

Jose got into difficulty because his related story was active and charged. But he also took a number of steps to self-correct and, in doing so, he became much more helpful to his client. The steps Jose undertook included:

1. Staying open to his client's story (as Judy also eventually did)
2. Using neutral assessment tools (examples of such instruments include the MBTI®, DISC®, BarOn EQ-I®, and FIRO-B®)
3. Consulting another coach (conversations with other coaches can help you see what you are not seeing in your coaching)
4. Sharing concerns with the client

    It is often helpful to share with the client what is happening for you as it occurs. The conversation might go something like this: "I am noticing similarities between your situation and one that I faced recently, and I am concerned that my own reactions might get in my way. I would like to hear more about how you are reacting so that I can understand ways that the situations are similar and distinct." This kind of statement invites a very real communication with the client and helps the coach to keep his or her own experience separate.

    Additional steps that are useful are

5. Paying attention to the warning signs (cited earlier, p. 84)
6. Using discretion in sharing stories

Once aware of possible similarities between the client's story and our own, we should take extra care to keep the two experiences distinct. If we decide it will be helpful to share our stories, we should frame this sharing very carefully (i.e., "I am going to share an experience that I had related to this. I am not suggesting that my experience or approach applies to your situation directly. But I offer it in case you find something useful in it"). These kinds of steps help to keep the focus on the client's experience where it belongs.

Effective uses of these action steps depend, first of all, on being aware of the personal issues that may surface in our interactions with leaders. Only through ongoing personal development work are we likely to be able to know which issues belong to us and which belong to our client. In particular, it may be useful to explore our experiences and stories about leadership and organizations. Once we have identified and dealt with those issues, we are less likely to experience the "charge" when one of our issues shows up with a client, and we will be more able to use our own experience without projecting it onto the client. As part of this ongoing inner work, coaches should engage in regular practices of reflection and centering (i.e., journaling, meditation, and bodywork) that support their self-awareness and their presence for coaching.

Self-awareness can also help us know when we are just not the right coach for a client. Most coaches have decided at some point that a particular client is not a good match. This is a hard call, but learning to differentiate a similarity that the coach can manage from one that may interfere is a critical skill to learn.

In the end, our ability to manage identification issues is an ethical concern. The Code of Ethics of the International Coach Federation states:

> I will at all times strive to recognize personal issues that may impair, conflict or interfere with my coaching performance or my professional relationships. Whenever the facts and circumstances necessitate, I will promptly seek professional assistance and determine the action to be taken, including whether it is appropriate to suspend or terminate my coaching relationship(s).[3]

Conclusion

A final way in which identification operates in leadership coaching occurs at a deeper, more fundamental level than we have discussed thus far. Our contemporary understanding of leadership effectiveness increasingly extends beyond the idea of what leaders do to who they are as people. "Leadership from within" suggests the notion that leadership has everything to do with the personal attitudes, beliefs, strengths, and character of the leader. It is these qualities that allow a leader to navigate the challenges of modern organizations in a rapidly changing environment. In addition, it is particularly to this dimension of leadership that coaches must ultimately attend. Coaches who are attending to their own personal attitudes, beliefs, strengths, and character can be more adept at guiding their clients through that exploration.

Parker J. Palmer writes with particular insight about those fundamental inner qualities that most contribute to a leader's effectiveness.

> We share responsibility for creating the external world by projecting either a spirit of light or a spirit of shadow on that which is other than us. Either a spirit of hope or a spirit of despair. Either an inner confidence in wholeness and integration, or an inner terror about life being diseased and ultimately terminal. We have a choice about what we are going to project, and in that choice we help create the world that is... What does all of this have to do with leadership?... I'll give you a quick definition of a leader: a leader is a person who has an unusual degree of power to project on other people his or her shadow, or his or her light.[4]

In the "shadow side" of leadership, as Palmer describes it, are a number of common stories that undermine a leader's ability to project light. Those include deep insecurity about one's own worth, the belief that the universe is essentially hostile and life a battleground, the belief that ultimate responsibility for everything rests with oneself, fear of the natural chaos of life, and the denial of death and the related fear of failure.

It is ultimately the power of these "shadows" or deep stories that determines the effectiveness of leaders. For coaches to help clients identify and work with these core stories and beliefs, coaches must also understand how these stories are present in their own lives. Work at this fundamental level is most critical when the leader's shadow story is also alive for the coach.

Coach and leader are in a sense on a similar journey. Both are challenged to identify their core stories, to understand how they may affect their work, and, in some cases, to choose new and different stories to live by. For coaches, this ability to recognize and manage these deep stories determines whether we shed light or darkness in our coaching.

Notes

1. Psychological theorists have explored this terrain in considerable depth. Since Freud, for example, the concept of projection—the psychic mechanism by which one attributes to others one's own unacceptable thoughts and/or emotions—has become central in psychological theorizing. Readers interested in exploring the evolution of this concept should consult Freud, Anna, *The Ego and the Mechanisms of Defense* (London: Hogarth Press and Institute of Psychoanalysis, 1937), as well as a good textbook on psychoanalytic theory, for example, Laplanche, J. and J.B. Pontalis, translated by D.N. Smith, *The Language of Psychoanalysis* (London: Karnac Books, 1966).
2. Adapted from Cashman, *Leadership from the Inside Out: Becoming a Leader for Life*, 39–42.
3. International Coach Federation, *ICF Code of Ethics, Part Three, Number 5* (approved 1/22/2005).
4. Parker J. Palmer, *Leading from Within: Reflections on Spirituality and Leadership* (Washington, DC: Servant Leadership School, 1990), 7.

Bibliography

Cashman, Kevin. *Leadership from the Inside Out: Becoming a Leader for Life.* Minneapolis, MN: TCLG, 1998.

Coleman, David. "A Coach's Lessons Learned: Principles and Guidelines for Practitioners," in Catherine Fitzgerald and Jennifer Garvey Burger, *Executive Coaching: Practices and Perspective.* Palo Alto, CA: Davies-Black, 2002.

Flaherty, James. *Coaching: Evoking Excellence in Others.* Boston: Butterworth-Heinemann, 1999.

Granberg-Michaelson, Wesley. *Leadership from Inside Out: Spirituality and Organizational Change.* New York: Crossroad, 2004.

O'Neill, Mary Beth. *Executive Coaching with Backbone and Heart.* San Francisco: Jossey-Bass, 2000.

Palmer, Parker J. *Leading from Within: Reflections on Spirituality and Leadership.* Washington, DC: Servant Leadership School, 1990.

CHAPTER 9

Congratulations—You're in Breakdown!

Jennifer Sinek

I uttered these words to a client, and received a look of shocked surprise. How could I congratulate her for being in a situation that was intolerable and causing her great pain? As we continued to talk about it, however, her expression turned to understanding, and then finally, to joy. What could lead to that?

Every effective coaching interaction either has a point of entry, a doorway to spur the client to take action, or one must be created. This is the concept of breakdown—and breakdown is essential to breaking through. Although the word sounds destructive, at its core, breakdown is generative. Breakdown provides the client with both the possibility of a new way of seeing things and a desire for this by "breaking down" the barriers to seeing our lives from a new perspective, making us question our spoken or unspoken assumptions about what's possible or impossible, what's "true" for us and for others, how the world works.

What Do We Mean by Breakdown?

Breakdown is what happens when the outcomes we experience don't match our expectations. We're not talking about a "nervous breakdown," or clinical levels of anxiety or depression—merely what most of us experience to varying degrees at different times as we move through life.

It's about seeing things that weren't visible to us before—sometimes an entirely different world. Think of the chick that begins to crack the shell, to break through, and emerge into the world. The shell was protective, but then becomes a barrier—the breakdown needs to happen for the chick to continue to grow.

However, we don't always notice the breakdown, or its upside, right off.

As human beings, just as in the rest of the universe, inertia is a natural law. We tend to keep doing what we're doing. In addition, if we're not getting or creating what we want, we often do more of it, faster or more intensely. We miss Ben Franklin's insight—that the definition of insanity is doing the same thing repeatedly and expecting different results. One must overcome this inertia to effect change.

Some of you may be familiar with what is known as the boiled frog syndrome. According to research done in the late 1800s, frogs' nervous systems are unable to distinguish incremental changes in temperature or pressure.[1] Therefore, if you were to put a frog in a pan of water and raise the temperature very gradually, eventually the frog would boil to death without noticing that the water was getting hot. However, if you put a frog in a pot of already hot water, or increase the heat quickly, it will jump right out.

We humans tend to experience this in a number of domains. Many of us don't pay close attention to slight changes in our emotional state, our health, or our performance in our jobs. Raising (or cooling) the water temperature slowly is the slow breakdown. It's the job that isn't great, but isn't awful. It's the team that's showing signs of increasing difficulty, but it hasn't really impacted the work—a lot—yet. It's the subtle signs that the organization isn't overjoyed with our work, or our management style, or our choices. Sometimes it's the coach's job to step in and point out the breakdown, directly or indirectly, either by naming the story that we see being played out or by providing the opportunity for the client to see the "hot water" in a different light, if they see it at all.

Often we live with a low level of pain in one or more areas of our lives, to the point that the pain becomes invisible to us. It is so familiar that we no longer see it. On the surface, we may realize that things aren't quite what we want them to be or that we're not as happy as we expected to be, but we tell ourselves that that's just the way life is—our expectations were too high, just live with it.

Alternatively, we think we can't change it—it will take too much energy or risk, or change who we fundamentally are. And all the while, it's sapping our energy, keeping us from the future we desire and deserve.

Sometimes, when the coach turns the client's attention to the heat, it helps the client both see the current state with all its warts and more clearly envision the life or situation that they truly desire, it shifts the perspective and allows them to see new possibilities—and to have the energy to bring them to reality.

The client whom I mentioned at the start shifted from shock at my congratulating her for being in breakdown to joy in just a couple of conversations. She realized that she *had* to make a major shift, that she could no longer just get by, trying to manage the pieces or change them incrementally. Once she achieved this clarity, the energy that had been being sapped by her situation (and her angst about it) was freed up. She was able to envision and focus on a future she truly desired, which continued to fuel her energy and her joy.

Energy for Change

Energy for change comes from what pulls us forward—the vision—and what drives us from behind—the desire to get rid of what we don't want. And when we're creating the future, it is valuable to know what we don't want to include in it, as well as what we do.

The push (discomfort, dissonance, and pain) times the pull (the vision) yields the energy available for change to occur (figure 9.1).

Discomfort X Vision = Energy for Change

Figure 9.1 A formula for change

Our rising awareness of discomfort or dissonance helps us stop and reflect—and really think about what we *do* want. This vision of the present allows us then to have a point of comparison to our future vision and shows us where we need to take action to create the situation we desire.

A few years ago, I was involved in a project that turned out to be a much larger commitment than I had agreed to take on. It was also much different work than I had anticipated, much of which I didn't enjoy or experience as bringing my value to the world. The longer-than-expected hours on top of an already busy schedule came out of my nights (sleep), weekends (recreation), and most importantly, my time with my husband and young children. However, I had committed to the project, and my story was that I had to continue, even though it was sapping my energy. I told myself repeatedly that it would change once we had gotten past the "start-up phase," an ever-receding milestone. I was so busy trying to get everything done so that I could spend some time with my family, and perhaps get a bit of sleep, that I didn't look at what was happening, how out of whack with my values my life was becoming.

Fortunately, something happened to trigger an additional level of pain. I received a call inviting me to be part of a significant project, one that truly spoke to who I am, to my values, and to my continuing development. The pain came from my initial reaction, which was that I had to turn it down—that there was no way I could add one more thing, even something I dearly desired, to my already crazily overbooked life.

I experienced even greater pain as a colleague coached me, helping me to explore and paint the picture of this future I desired in even more vivid color. What a fit with my values, my vision! How nourishing being part of this would be, in addition to being an avenue for me to help others on their path! As I thought about it more and more, the vividness of that image and the contrasting pain of turning it down brought my life into sharp relief. I started thinking more about the impact on my family, about the percentage of my toddler's life that had already been affected by my being consumed with this project—and I knew I had to make a change. It was no longer a question of finding a way to add this new project to my life—it became a question of how to remove the other project from my life to create open space for what I did want. Once I made that shift in focus, two things began to happen immediately. First, the pain became more real, much less tolerable. How had I been downplaying or ignoring it all this time?! Second, my energy became focused both on creating the change—removing myself from this contract—and also beyond that into exploring changes that would help me continue to move closer to living my life according to my values and dreams. *This* energy was positive—and generative. The process took energy, but like a good workout, the movement itself was regenerative.

Had I not experienced that trigger, that quick rise in the level of discomfort I was experiencing, who knows how much longer I would have continued on the same, negative path. As it was, the increase in the level of discomfort, combined with the increasingly clear vision and draw of the future I desired, supplied the energy I needed to make the change.

Types of Breakdown

Breakdowns come in all shapes and sizes. Some are externally induced or triggered (i.e., situational or crisis-related breakdowns). This could be the loss of a job, being passed over for a promotion, a team the client just can't get to work together, and a bad performance evaluation. It could be the death or illness of a loved one that causes the client to question how he is spending his own life. On the positive side, an unexpected promotion or new job opportunity can also trigger breakdowns, raising fears of failure or success.

Some breakdowns are internally triggered. These can be put into a few categories (table 9.1). On the negative side:

- The client is experiencing pain or dissatisfaction, but doesn't see a clear way out. Sometimes it's because they just aren't happy—they are tired, frustrated, or something is just "not right." Or, they just don't feel they are being as effective as they could be. Some may even have just made a seemingly positive transition, perhaps a new promotion, but it didn't bring the happiness, success, power, self-confidence, or relief they believed it would.
- The client is feeling numb, feels like something is wrong—just not connected to something they care about. This is becoming an increasingly prevalent issue and is having increasingly significant impacts on both our work effectiveness and our lives and relationships outside work.[2]

Moreover, on the positive side:

- It's about what's next. The client is fairly content with the present, but knows there's more…a next step. The vision of the future isn't clear, but the client knows that pretty soon, the present will no longer satisfy. The itch for growth, for continued transformation, has reached awareness and is calling to be scratched.

OK, So Now We Know There's a Breakdown.
What Is the Coach's Role?

The coach helps the client to see or experience more fully the breakdown they're in or headed for. How? By keeping the mirror up that reflects the breakdown as a breakdown. This may increase the client's perceived level of pain, though the intent

Table 9.1 Types of breakdown

	External catalyst	*Internal catalyst*
Positive	Unexpected Promotion, New Job/ Opportunity → Anticipation or Fear of Failure or Success	Looking for the next step in development or transformation
Negative	Crisis-related, for example, job loss, bad performance evaluation, illness, death of someone close	Experiencing pain or dissatisfaction, but doesn't see a way out or feeling numb, disconnected

is merely to see it more accurately and free up energy to create the future the client desires.

With any type of breakdown, it's critical that it's the internal link that's driving the change. If the catalyst is external, then it's important that we help the client translate it into something that matters to them, that has connection to something they truly value and believe in. That's what allows them to move beyond the pain of the breakdown into generating the vision of the future that will focus the energy and pull them forward.

So, as coaches we

- Invite our client's to see the breakdown more fully and experience its impacts on different areas of their life. We do this through structured self-observation exercises and self-reflection. For example, to what extent are you creating the results you want, and what's the story you're telling yourself about where you are and are not? Where is the friction, the nagging, annoying, or empty places? To go back to the chick analogy, where is their shell becoming too small? We gently intensify the clients' experience of pain by encouraging them to engage in, and reflect on, a particular area that seems to be a root of an issue in their life. We focus them intellectually, in terms of the emotions they are experiencing with it, the physical sensations, and how they show up. What is the physical "shape" of their breakdown? How do they hold their bodies in that space?
- Help our clients find spots of joy. Often the comparison or contrast to the rest of the client's life or presenting situation brings the pain in those areas into sharp relief—that creates both an opening and energy for change. The joy provides an oasis, a place to rest and recharge during the process of change. When they think of these elements of joy and life, how do their emotions shift? What do they notice in their body—sensations, form? We help them to own these and build from them.
- Help our clients to author or flesh out an alternative vision of a truly compelling future, one that speaks to who they are and what they value. Have them envision this fully—intellectually, and in terms of their mood, emotions, and bearing. How does it feel in their body as they put themselves in that new future? What brings more life to it? This all provides the pull to the future as well as a point of comparison to the life they are currently leading, which helps them to discern where there are opportunities for change and growth.
- Help the client generate and live into an alternative story—one that serves this vision for the future that he has created. Who must he be to be successful in this vision? What stories about himself or the world does he need to write or rewrite to be successful? Ground it in skills, but also in mood, presence, and structures of support. It can involve developing new moves and presence physically so he can step into the new vision powerfully and effectively.

So, What If We Can See the Breakdown, But the Client Can't?

This happens frequently in situations where we may be gathering information from the client's co-workers in addition to what we hear directly from the client. What we can best do is reflect the behavior, condition, sharing, and experience of the client as we are observing it and invite them to consider a different perspective on it. Or together come up with yet another way to look at the issue. Often the client has inklings about the issue that he or she may not be fully conscious of that become much clearer with additional perspectives and information. We can also suggest self-observation exercises that invite the client to notice things from a different perspective. We must also realize that the client may not be ready to address the issue at that point in time—or that we may be off base!

What If the Client Is Already Experiencing the Breakdown?

Great—the key is to keep the client in dynamic tension—to get sufficient clarity around what's contributing to the pain, while focusing them on the future they would like to create.

Conclusion

Coaches often fall into the trap of helping their clients feel better and decreasing their level of pain. We care about our clients, and we don't like to see people in pain. Although this is a positive long-term goal, sometimes in the meantime it actually does the client a disservice, keeping them stuck in their current situation, robbing them of the energy they need to make the move, to take the risk that will help them create the life they truly want.

Sometimes we need to turn up their sensation of the heat by asking questions that focus their attention on the thermometer, by providing invitation and support for the client to experience their breakdown, so the client's life doesn't get boiled away, evaporate, or simply leave them cold. The client doesn't want to wake up five, ten, or twenty years from now and say, "What happened? How did I get here?" We help them wake up *now*, if they're ready, to the gradually changing temperatures in different areas of their lives and see new possibilities for what they want to create.

We point out the breaking down of the coherence in their lives—mind, body, emotions, and spirit—and help them see new choices to make their lives whole. Therefore, as coaches, we must welcome breakdown and focus on how we can create the space and the opportunities for our clients to step into their breakdowns, experience them, and use them as openings—as invitations to growing into and creating the futures they desire.

Notes

1. Scripture, Edward Wheeler, *The New Psychology.* (New York: Charles Scribner and Sons, 1897), 300.
2. Joyce, Amy, "Boredom Numbs the Work World," *Washington Post*, August 10, 2005, D01; Gallup, Inc., "Gallup Study Finds That Misery at Work Is Likely to Cause Unhappiness at Home," *Gallup Management Journal*, June 23, 2003.

CHAPTER 10

The Role of Emotions in Coaching

Randy Chittum

It is accepted practice for leadership coaches to coach in the domains of mind (language), body (somatic), and emotion. Conventional wisdom suggests that mind, body, and emotions are all connected and the coach can "enter" the conversation in any of the three domains and all three may shift. This chapter focuses explicitly on the role of emotions in coaching.

Emotions are often misunderstood in Western culture and I would argue, especially in business organizations. Executive leaders in particular may see themselves as tough-minded and imagine that leading from feelings or emotions may make them somehow less serious about the business. What many fail to understand is the already significant role that emotions play in the serious side of business. I enjoy telling executives about what happens when the amygdala (the site of emotional memory) is severed from the rest of the brain. What happens is that the person who suffers from this cannot make even the simplest decisions. When faced with something as mundane as where to have lunch, this person can list in detail the pros and cons of all available options and cannot make an actual choice. This would seem to suggest that emotions play an unconscious role in all decision making. Pretending this is not so makes us less masterful of our life, not more.

What Is an Emotion?

The cognitive understanding of emotion seems to be the most useful approach for coaches. Philosophers have suggested that all emotion is propositional. In other words emotions are a mental construct connected to a proposition, or belief. Without the accompanying belief, there is no cause for emotion. For example, when someone at work raises their voice to me, my emotional experience of defensiveness is rooted in the belief I have that I deserve to be treated with respect. The person who responds to the same situation with fear might have an underlying belief that raised voices signify danger. We all have a unique set of beliefs that have been formed over all the years of our existence.

If one accepts that beliefs and thoughts create the possibility of a particular range of emotion, it is not a far leap to suggest that emotions similarly create the possibility of a range of behaviors. This BELIEF—EMOTION—BEHAVIOR model is used widely by coaches. I believe it is much harder to coach without understanding how these are linked together for the leader I am coaching.

I often ask—do you have emotions or do your emotions have you? By asking this I intend to have leaders think about to what extent they are in control of their emotional experience. Understanding underlying beliefs and the emotions to which they predispose us creates leverage for sustainable change.

Coaching is largely about helping clients see new possibilities for action. What could be more powerful and sustainable than helping clients achieve some insight into their own emotion generating process? If my client is working toward being more approachable, we have numerous ways to get at that issue. I would argue that the least powerful is to work at the behavior level. Discussing how one would look (behavior) if one were to be more approachable is likely to leave the client feeling incongruous, and that type of change often proves unsustainable. However, if we can look deeper to the emotions that are present when she shows up as unapproachable and then uncover the beliefs or thoughts that lead to that emotion, we have the possibility of interrupting the process at a level that truly impacts. In this real life example, this client was experiencing an emotion of irritation that was built on a belief that others were not as smart as she. Although it took time and practice to challenge that belief and to discover a more useful emotion, when the change came it was a sea change.

To this point we have adequately distinguished between how one deals with emotions and how one deals with the underlying beliefs or thoughts. Coaches refer to these as "stories" and they are treated elsewhere in this book. For the remainder of this chapter we focus in on the role of emotions as a unique way to transform.

What Is Emotional Intelligence?

You may find yourself working in an organization that is attempting to practice "emotional intelligence" in their leadership. The essence of emotional intelligence is awareness of your own emotions, awareness of the emotions of others, and the ability to consciously choose an emotion. Each is dealt with in detail.

I find that many leaders are limited when it comes to accurately sensing their own emotions and even more limited when it comes to naming that emotion. They seem to often get stuck at "good" or "frustrated." I believe one task of developing emotional intelligence is to develop greater distinction in our language about emotions. What distinguishes joy from happiness? Anger from rage? Love from admiration? I have had leaders express to me that they do not have an experience of emotion in normal settings, and I respond by saying that being numb to emotions is not the same as not having them. I do not buy the notion of emotional neutrality. We are always experiencing some emotion, in admittedly greater and lesser degrees.

I am fond of asking leaders I coach to keep a log or journal of emotions they have noticed during the day. I want to develop their internal radar to notice more quickly and accurately what they are experiencing in their internal landscape. I imagine some of my clients eventually tire of me asking the question—and what emotion were you experiencing when that occurred? How do you think that emotion made possible certain behaviors and limited you from others? Over time and with enough data points, leaders will often start to notice patterns that can lead to especially powerful conversations.

Having an awareness of the emotions of others is often more daunting for leaders. Both empathy and care are required to do this. Although coaches might have a natural affinity for attending to the emotions of others, many leaders do not. There seem to be two primary schools of thought as to how we become aware of the emotions of others. I think it does not matter to which theory you ascribe, but it does matter that this muscle is developed.

One school of thought is that emotional energy is an open system and emotional energy is a field that others who are attuned can experience. Another prominent view is that emotions are displayed in our body language in ways that we cannot always consciously identify but are nonetheless aware of. The bottom line is that without the capacity to notice and identify the emotions of others, one cannot be fully emotionally intelligent.

This is of course easy to practice. I encourage leaders who are challenged in this area to practice all the time making their best assessment as to another's emotional state. Further, I suggest that in those places where it feels safe, that they check out their "guess" as a way to calibrate over time.

Finally, the most powerful skill of all is the ability to choose your emotion. If you accept that emotions lead to behavior, then you can readily see the power in the ability to choose an emotion. For example, I worked with a leader who got easily flustered and off message whenever she had to tell truth to power, in her words. The nature of her job meant that she had to do this often. We agreed that the first step was to pay more attention to the emotion she was experiencing in the moment. After several experiences she noted, not surprisingly, that she felt anxious, and more surprisingly, that she felt hopeless—that nothing good would come from the risk she was taking. After a coaching conversation she decided that she would try to get centered on an emotion of optimism before the next such experience. Though it took several iterations, she reported that staying centered on that emotion did a lot to change her behavior. For example, from an optimistic stance she reported that she was more assertive, that her body shifted to a more powerful stance, and that she kept her conversation more in the future (hopeful) and less in the past (defensive). Although we could have identified those useful behaviors, I believe the emotional work created a more sustainable change for her.

The current working definition of emotional intelligence has shifted from the original. On hearing the words "emotional intelligence," many leaders imagine emotional intelligence to be a competency model that has been created to enable more emotionally intelligent leadership. That model is probably similar to the one put forth by Goleman in his book *Primal Leadership*. At their best, competency models provide a model that allows a leader to imagine his or her leadership differently

Table 10.1 Emotional intelligence

Self-awareness	Self-management	Leading others	Organization leadership
Emotional self-awareness	Optimism	Coaching others	Enrolling others
Accurate self-assessment	Personal control Personal energy	Purposeful conversations	Principle driven
Appropriate self-regard	Adaptability Lightness		Change advocate
	EMPATHY		
	AUTHENTICITY		

and bigger. At its worst, a competency model becomes a set of rigid rules for how one must behave. It is the responsibility of the coach to use a model in a way that is expansive, not limiting. Table 10.1 is an example of an "Emotional Intelligence" competency model that I created and use in my leadership development work. If you were to compare several competency models, you will notice that they are far more similar than different.

How Are Emotion and Body Connected?

Leaders are often fascinated with this topic, and I have found that keeping the conversation at a higher level seems to work best. In particular they are fascinated with the idea of "awfulizing" and "hijacking." Awfulizing is a concept put forth by Albert Ellis in his Rational Emotive Behavior Theory (REBT). The essence of REBT is that we all have irrational beliefs that cause us to amplify the significance of particular events. For example, if my boss does not respond to my very important voice mail I might start to awfulize that he is upset with me or he doesn't care about the project or perhaps thinks I am incompetent. Although there is nothing rational about it, most people report doing it often. We seem to awfulize more often when there is missing information. For example, I worked with a leader who often found himself presenting information to new groups. He consistently awfulized about how that might go even though he had ample evidence that the fear was unfounded.

Leaders will often report that when they are awfulizing they have some very distinct experiences in their body. They might report sweating, increased heart rate, sinking feeling in the gut, flushed face, and so on. Although one might enter this conversation by learning somatic responses, one might equally enter through emotion and language in an attempt to uncover the underlying thinking and as discussed earlier, a more productive emotional stance.

I have yet to encounter a leader who is not fascinated with the notion of hijacking. Hijacking is the term used to express the experience of being totally out of control, often in a state of anger or rage. The amygdala serves as the site of our emotional memories and as such is a filter for those experiences that might be a threat. When the amygdala experiences something it perceives as a threat, it metaphorically hijacks the rest of the brain and the body. In a full-blown hijack, the amygdala might send signals that flood the brain with chemicals and the body with hormones and adrenaline that prepare it to deal with a threat. The amygdala has been a part of us for a long time and serves a useful role. However, in the world in which most of us live, the threats we experience are primarily to our ego, our self-esteem, and our pride and not necessarily our physical well-being. Although the threats may have changed, the amygdala and its purpose have not. What that means is that we might get hijacked from the way someone speaks to us, ignores us, or mistreats us. We might get hijacked because the traffic is heavy or our flight is delayed. We might get hijacked because an important meeting got cancelled or our presentation did not go well. Since what is perceived as a threat is unique to each individual what might hijack you might not hijack me.

The danger is in our response to being hijacked. Most of us have developed conditioned tendencies that serve as default patterns when we are hijacked and therefore unable to think clearly. One person's conditioned tendency might be to lash out and fight while another person might want to fade into the woodwork. The point is that you are no longer in control and that your conditioned tendency might not serve you, or others, in that moment. Yet, in that moment, the power of the tendency will convince you that you are right. It is a primal experience, and one that we can be drawn to.

The leaders with whom I work can all report instances of being hijacked that led to a negative outcome in a relationship. Many can report multiple instances in any given day. Living this out of control life is the opposite of the intentional way I prefer to see leaders lead. It is hard work to help leaders learn how to mitigate this. It starts, like all emotional intelligence, with increased self-awareness. When, and with whom am I more likely to become hijacked? What early indicators can I identify that let me know I am on the path to a hijack? Once I learn to identify it, how can I employ breathing and meditation strategies to help mitigate the event? I believe that most leaders experience two kinds of hijacking. The first is a full-blown immediate hijack when nothing is going to keep you from being hijacked. The second is a more gradual hijack when you might see it coming. In the second, I have seen the strategies listed earlier help leaders make a significant improvement in how they manage themselves. In the first I make sure that leaders know that it takes approximately twenty minutes to feel clear of a hijack. One organization I know bought hourglasses for many of their leaders as a way to reinforce the message that, once hijacked, the strategy might be to keep from doing harm to others.

Conclusion

In my experience, the work of emotional intelligence and using emotions in coaching is not difficult to understand but can be challenging to implement. In emotions we are venturing into that space for leaders that bridges the external and internal worlds. As such it is very powerful and it can also feel risky to those who have not engaged in such conversations before. I find that a few well-worn examples with leaders can make it easy to help them see the value. I will often ask them if they can imagine they would behave differently if they showed up to a meeting in an emotion of curiosity and hope versus an emotion of skepticism. It is not hard for most leaders to call upon their own experiences at this point to help them see the power of an underlying emotion.

Another activity that I use in teaching leadership workshops ends with the leaders in the room distinguishing what makes the most respected leaders in their lives successful. What we learn is that in their own experiences, the vast majority of what seems to matter is in the world of emotional intelligence and far less in the world of intelligence or technical ability. This always proves very powerful since the data belongs to them.

In summary, I have found that engaging leaders in the world of emotions and emotional intelligence has generated a substantial return. Although it is arguably a stepping-stone to even greater leverage in the world of thoughts and beliefs, it is also a wonderful play to stay over and do real work with real sustainable results.

Bibliography

Ellis, Albert and Robert Harper. *A Guide to Rational Living.* North Hollywood, CA: Melvin Powers Wilshire Book, 1997.

Goleman, Daniel. *Primal Leadership: Realizing the Power of Emotional Intelligence.* Boston: Harvard Business School Publishing, 2002.

CHAPTER 11

Using Somatics to Coach Leaders

Margaret Echols and Sandy Mobley

Our leadership coaching approach includes basic distinctions related to language, emotions, and body; we increase our power as observers by obtaining more distinctions in language, deeper and wider access to our range of emotions (and moods), and greater *awareness of our body*. As our own leadership coaching experience has grown, we have developed an increasing recognition and appreciation of the rich possibilities in exploring more deeply the critical role the body plays in the clients' learning and in helping our clients transform. It is routine for coaches to ask their clients, "What are you feeling?" but rarely is the emotion or mood linked to the client's body sensations or body posture.

In working with somatics—that is, the domain of the body—coaches learn to make deep connections between language, body, and emotions, and they learn to become more powerful observers of others and ourselves. We discern what the body can tell us about who we are and how we are living. Before they can assist clients somatically, coaches need to experience for themselves how they are in their own bodies, where they are open and where they are contracted, and where there is possibility and where there is limitation.

To work with leaders *through the body*, coaches learn to observe, in themselves and then in others, when language, emotions, and body are congruent or aligned and when they are not. They learn to observe, in themselves and others, reflexive ways in which people respond to certain triggers or life events. Through awareness and somatic practices, we expand our capacity for action. As coaches practice and cultivate the power of being centered (i.e., connected, present, open, and focused) in more situations, more frequently, they also learn to recover more quickly when off center. They shift from simply being coaches to becoming *embodied* leadership coaches.

Understanding the Gap

An amazingly hard human lesson to grasp is how often we fail at something we've set out to do. Think about the commitments that you've made to keep your desk neat, to return phone calls or respond to e-mails in one day, or to get to meetings on time. Since most of our education had been biased toward cognitive learning (i.e., facts, theory, etc.), we were shocked to learn in an initial Strozzi Institute leadership course how often *knowing* doesn't translate into *doing*.

In a physical (somatic) exercise designed to model making a request, we were told to walk toward the person we were making a request of with our hand out and touch the person just below the throat with an open palm. One coach remembers: "With the best of intentions my hand always ended up on the other person's shoulder. I don't have vision problems, and I could walk up to someone and touch them under the throat, but in the context of making a request, I missed every time. That's when I saw my own gap. My body knew something my mind did not."

For example, many people *know* the importance of making an effective request and can even recite the criteria perfectly. However, under pressure or in certain situations, they often fall into old ineffective patterns. Alternatively, they might say the right words, but their tone of voice or body language conveys an undermining message. Seeing this dilemma made us more aware that, in working with executives, we needed to look for and bridge this gap.

After the somatic exercise, the coach continues, "my awareness was raised further as I listened to how I made requests. To staff I said, 'Please make sure you include me in that client meeting.' But with the boss, the same 'request' sounded like, 'It would be useful to me to attend client meetings.' I clearly *knew* how to make an effective request, yet wasn't able to *do* so in some situations. This made me curious about what happens in that knowing-doing gap."

Human beings are conditioned through upbringing and culture to behave in ways that might have served at one time, but are no longer effective. These behaviors are so ingrained that we don't realize we have a choice. For example, a leader we know was taught as a child to *not* make direct requests of others. This behavior became so automatic that it occurred whenever she wanted something; she had buried the ability to make direct requests. "I can remember being at my aunt's house when I was eight years old, desperately wanting an Eskimo Pie ice cream from her freezer and knowing that I dared not ask for it. I could only make a series of hints. 'My throat is burning up,' I said, prompting my aunt to offer water. 'No,' I responded, water won't do it; it needs to be *colder* than water. Perhaps some milk, she suggested. 'No, milk won't work; I don't like the taste of it, but that is closer to what I'm looking for.' Finally, my aunt asked if I'd like an ice cream." Imagine the inefficiency and waste of time if someone used that process at work!

Instead, the leader in our story above learned to make powerful requests of the staff that left no room for interpretation. By bringing this skill into her conversations with her superiors, she realized she would save herself a lot of aggravation and disappointment when they couldn't decode her veiled requests. "Until I became aware of this conditioned response, I could only hint and hope that others would know what I desired and respond positively," she says. To undo the conditioning, awareness of the behavior had to come first. To be effective, coaches must help leaders recognize the ingrained, habituated responses that they can't see and assist them in adopting more productive behaviors.

Clients aren't disembodied heads, required only to *think* leadership. Without the ability to *act*, leaders can't motivate others, align behavior, or influence change. Action occurs through the body. Action follows awareness, so it is important to notice what we are paying attention to. For example, if a leader is focusing on keeping others happy, he may not make requests that he feels are unpopular. On the flip side, if the leader is only concerned with getting the work done and not how others feel about doing the work, he runs the risk of alienating the workforce.

A key factor for effective leadership is authenticity—alignment between saying and doing. People evaluate their leaders more by what they *do* than what they *say*. Albert Mehrabian from UCLA studied this behavioral difference. He found that when people communicated feelings if there was dissonance between what was said and how that person behaved, the audience judged the person's actual words to have only a 7 percent impact, while the person's voice and body language had much higher impact, at 38 percent and 55 percent respectively.[1] Clearly a person's actions and voice, with a 93 percent impact, carry far more weight than the words a person uses.

In his book *The Anatomy of Change*, Richard Strozzi Heckler writes, "Somatics... defines the body as a functional, living whole rather than as a mechanical structure. Somatics does not see a split between the mind and body but views the soma as a unified expression of all that we think, feel, perceive, and express."[2] Somatic coaches show clients how their body language correlates with often hidden and limiting inner feelings, narratives, and mindsets. Specifically designed, somatically based practices allow these internal states to shift, enabling clients to take new actions to achieve their goals. For example, if a man grew up being told that "nice boys" don't brag, he may drop his voice and look away from his peers when asked to talk about his projects in a team meeting. He may have no awareness that hiding his talent is limiting his career progression. Once these behaviors are brought to his attention, he will still need time and somatic practices to keep his voice strong and maintain eye contact when talking about his work.

Getting Centered and Using Somatics for Coaching

To understand somatics and apply it to coaching, you must be attuned to your own body and your feeling. Many people have become anesthetized to feelings and tell themselves—that is, tell their bodies—what they can and can't feel. A person may feel sad at the death of a relative or the loss of a meaningful job, but feels compelled to put on a happy face and dismiss the feelings. Another person whose boss yells at her several times a week may say, "Oh, he is under pressure and doesn't really mean it." For both people, their bodies ache nonetheless. Denying feelings doesn't ease pain. In addition, numbing painful feelings decreases the capacity to experience other feelings—joy, fear, surprise, and so on.

On the other hand, some people can be overloaded by the intensity of their feelings to the point that it becomes intolerable and they boil over in rage or panic.

Daniel Goleman refers to this in his book *Working with Emotional Intelligence* as an amygdala hijack.[3] In these situations, the primal part of the brain senses an old and uncomfortable emotion, and the person is thrown into one of three basic responses—fight, flight, or freeze. The higher-functioning part of the brain is cut off, and the behavior that results is seldom pretty.

To avoid having to swallow feelings or to be ruled by them, it helps to have a place of safety inside oneself that allows time for choice and greater ranges of possibilities. The first step to finding that internal oasis in the body is to learn what it feels like to be centered. Being centered in your body is like shifting to neutral in a car with a manual transmission. It is the place of flexibility that allows for easy movement in any direction. It is a place where you can access your power, focus on what you care about, and tap into the inner wisdom of your body, feelings, and emotions.

There are times when being centered can mean the difference between life and death. Consider the police officer who has a split second to decide whether the person in the heavy overcoat coming his way is carrying a bomb, a weapon, or something harmless such as a cell phone. Being centered can affect whether you win a negotiation, get a job, or hear what is really bothering your teenager.

Somatics begins with you as a coach. It is important to be centered before beginning a coaching session. This allows you to be open and connected to your client. You become a more powerful observer because your focus is on your client and his needs, not your worries about what to say next or whether you sound intelligent. Centering keeps your internal chatter at bay and opens you to hear what the client has to say. Your ability to center helps your client center as well. Think about how one scared horse spooks the others in a corral, or the impact on others of a hysterical person at the scene of an accident. Being open, centered, and confident helps the client become open and calm, too.

To center, pay attention to your breath. Is it low in your belly and moving fully through your body? Bringing your attention to your breath helps you center. Notice your posture. Are you slouched or rigid? If so, sit or stand tall with your weight evenly distributed on each side and from front to back. What about your forehead—is it wrinkled or relaxed? Notice your eyes. Are they staring fixedly or wide open like a deer in the headlights? Relax your eyes—let them soften and increase your peripheral vision. How about your jaw? Is it held tightly? Are you grinding your teeth? Open your mouth as wide as you can and then relax your jaw. How about your shoulders? Are they pulled up tightly near your ears as you carry the weight of the world? Tighten them more and then relax them, feeling the tension slide away. These are some of the key areas where we hold tension. Tension dilutes center. If we are feeling tightness or pain, our attention goes to these areas and away from feeling centered.

It may be useful to do a centering practice with your client at the start of your session. Coaching sessions often take place in the middle of a busy day. Helping your client get centered allows her to let go of other concerns and be fully present for the session. The more you can bring your client's awareness to her stance and sensations, the better. Pay attention to your client's body. Are her shoulders high? It could mean she is taking on too much responsibility. Notice tightness in the jaw area. This may indicate the need to control things or that she is *chewing* on a difficult problem.

How is her eye contact? Do you see a "deer in the headlights" look, an intense stare, a sleepy gaze? What do these things mean to you? You are helping your client see what has been invisible to her. For example, you may point out that she smiles broadly when she is saying no. Then she wonders why people don't accept it when she turns down a request.

Rather than keep a checklist that says if you see this, it means that, it is more useful to be curious. You might sometimes mirror what you see to the client and ask what that posture or look provokes in her. That tends to give you more insight about what the client is experiencing, and she in turn sees herself from new perspectives.

How It Works: Somatics in Action

To illustrate how you, as a leadership coach, can incorporate an understanding of somatics into how you would coach a leader, here's how one coach we know recounts her own experience:

Carol is a senior government official in an important position with the Department of Defense. I assumed she'd be somewhat rigid in her posture, buttoned down and stern. When a slight woman dressed in a flowered blouse and light blue skirt, with wispy blonde hair and a shy demeanor, met me on our first appointment, I presumed she was Carol's administrative assistant coming to escort me through security. Imagine my surprise when she introduced herself as Carol.

Carol possesses a brilliant mind and is one of only three women to rise above the director level. I learned that she is an excellent project leader, able to see the big picture while still keeping track of all the details needed to make a project succeed. Possessing strong influencing skills, she would thrive in a more collaborative work environment, but her difficulty making direct requests allows others to take advantage of her in this competitive workplace. Carol was referred to me because to meet her goals, it is essential that she get other parts of the organization to work together. To do this she must learn to make requests effectively.

When I asked Carol to show me how she makes requests, her body and words betrayed her intent. She blinked her eyes nervously, her mouth twitched, and her posture became slumped. She appeared to be begging. Her language became indirect, prefacing her requests with words like, "I would like it *if...*" or "We need..." or even "I wish..." She told me people would respond to her with nods, but rarely would anyone take action. She was burning out from lack of support.

I asked her to give me examples of assertive people in her organization. She described only men. I asked her to tell me about some assertive females. She said there were two, both of whom she described as aggressive, attacking terrors who frequently raised their voices, barked out orders, and never listened. She could not identify a single woman who was assertive in a positive way. In her world, women were either vicious sharks or meek little mice. She felt revulsion at the thought of being a shark.

I began by demonstrating a continuum of behaviors between Mouse and Shark. First I made a request at the Mouse end. I rounded my shoulders, crouched down, looked up through my eyelashes, avoided eye contact, and said in a soft voice, "It would be nice, uh, uh, do you think maybe we could finish the project today?"

Carol observed that the Mouse-me was so hesitant that she was unclear what my request actually was and felt no urgency to comply. I asked her to match my Mouse posture. She did it easily and said that this stance felt all too familiar.

I then demonstrated the Shark-me. I puffed up my chest and demanded, "I want the completed project on my desk by the end of the day, or you can look for work elsewhere." She took a step back, her face froze into a mask, and the light went out in her eyes. I asked her what she experienced and she said she felt afraid. "But," she added in a feisty voice, "if you didn't have the authority, you could hold your breath before I'd respond to a demand phrased like that." I noted that she sounded angry. She agreed and said, "People who abuse their power really infuriate me." I asked her to notice her posture. She was standing tall and making direct eye contact. "This is you stepping into your power," I said. "Notice how it feels." I suggested there might be some benefit to harnessing her inner Shark. "For example, you notice this feeling when someone has stepped over a boundary. Instead of shrinking, you can use the feeling to get in touch with your power and prevent someone from pushing you where you don't want to go."

I then demonstrated a centered, confident, and direct request for her. I stood with my feet shoulder-width apart, my back straight and aligned with head over shoulders over hips over feet, all in one continuous line. I made direct eye contact. Breathing in a relaxed manner, I spoke in a strong, even voice, "Please have the project on my desk by the end of the day." As I made the request, I noticed that Carol also seemed relaxed. She met my eye contact and her posture shifted from slouched to more erect. She was surprised that I could be so strong without being offensive, and she said she felt "invited" to hear my request.

For the rest of the session, I modeled and she practiced moving in small increments along the Mouse-Shark continuum. Sometimes when people make a change, they go too far in the opposite direction. My goal was for Carol to know what degree of directness was appropriate for her. Awareness is the first step toward making a change. At the end of the session, Carol was aware not only of her inability to lead her organization from the Mouse end of the spectrum but also of a range of responses and their impact on her. As we walked toward the elevator, a colleague walked by and called her Cheryl. I asked if her name was Carol or Cheryl. She admitted it was Cheryl. She had let me call her Carol throughout the entire first session because she was embarrassed to correct me.

Cheryl's homework for the next week was to practice making requests in a direct, not indirect, way—such as asking her change-resistant secretary to redo the filing system or asking her coach to call her by her correct name. When we met again, Cheryl had made requests, and for her, that was a positive step forward. I began by calling her Carol. She quickly asked me to call her Cheryl. As she described successes, it became clear that she had made most requests of people she thought would be amenable. For the following week, I challenged her to make more difficult requests and to notice her body language and what she was feeling and make notes for us to discuss at our next session. My goal was to help Cheryl *feel* how to make requests from a centered place and to notice her own and others' responses when she did so. I wanted her to embody making strong requests and not lapse into her Mouse body, which made requests that were easy to ignore.

At our next meeting, she reported that she had been able to make more challenging requests of her staff, such as asking them to take on more project responsibilities. Most of her difficulty had occurred when asking peers in other departments for help. She recounted many instances when she had helped others with resources, provided support for their proposals, and even times when she shared money from her budget to help fund others' projects. However, when she needed assistance, her peers consistently failed to reciprocate. Two things became evident: (1) she never let others know that helping them was a cost to her, so they thought she had excess budget and resources, and (2) she never stated her expectation that they reciprocate. She had set up an expectation of a one-way relationship (she gave, they didn't) and they were happy to keep it that way.

Underlying Cheryl's difficulty was her quaint notion that if she did nice things, people would naturally reciprocate. She wouldn't *have to* make requests. I asked her how she would feel making a request of her peers. She said she actually had several requests in mind. Her posture was strong and I could see that she was harnessing her Sharkness. She said that she was tired of their ignoring her and never offering help with her projects. I asked her to remember the sensation in her body when someone called her by the wrong name and instead of ignoring the feeling, to use it to get in touch with how irritating it feels to be dismissed and ignored.

Her homework for the next session was to continue making challenging requests and to pay attention to her feelings when she made them.

When we met again we discussed requests she made to her peers. She reported several successes and one devastating failure. She had asked Tom, notoriously rude and the most alpha dog on the team, to loan two people from his department to assist with a project that had a tight deadline. He ignored her and simply walked away. She felt angry and hurt, but rather than bury the feeling, she followed him to his office and made the request again. He didn't look away from his computer as he said, "Look, my people are overworked. I can't help you." She didn't know what to say then. She felt so low she could have slipped under the door.

I suggested we practice. I role-played Tom and asked her to make a request of me. As direct as Cheryl had been in a previous session when she asked me to call her by her correct name, her posture reverted to Mouse with resigned body, slumped shoulders, and downcast eyes. I asked her what she noticed. She said that as much as she wanted to be strong, she felt all her emotions pulling her to be indirect. "What feelings?" I asked. "Be specific." "I think...just the pain of being rejected," she said. As a peer, she had no power to reverse his rejection. Tom's "no" represented disrespect and powerlessness and she feared that when he rejected her request she looked even weaker for asking. This was another layer that kept Cheryl from making direct requests. It brought back all the shame she felt as a teen asking her father for money when he said no, most painfully when she asked him for money to go on a class trip and he said no. Moreover, it brought back as well the sadness of having to tell her friends that she couldn't go with them and her loneliness the week they were gone.

I wondered if Cheryl realized that making a request means the other person has the power to say no as well as yes. I asked her if she was making a request or if she were *demanding* that he do something. "I hoped he would agree, but realized he could say no." She took a deep breath and sighed. I asked what the sigh was about. "Maybe I never feel that *I* can say no," Cheryl admitted, "so I resent it from others." Now, another layer had surfaced. Cheryl didn't allow herself to say no, so she didn't think others had the right to do so. Furthermore, she felt someone saying no to her request was a sign of disrespect. Working through the body is interesting because at each step, the body reveals more of what is being held back.

The next step for Cheryl was to learn to accept a "no" without relapsing into her internal story of disrespect and powerless. As in learning to make direct requests, gaining the ability to accept a rejected request took three sessions before Cheryl could maintain her poise without crumbling into Mouse. One key to change for Cheryl was to recognize that when her shoulders curled and her chest tightened, she could practice dropping her breath into her belly and get centered. From here, she recognized that she felt less afraid. It brought back the memory of how she anchored before a track meet in college—the crouch in the blocks before the starting gun. Accessing her center deactivated her Mouse-body, where her breath was high and her chest felt tight. As in making requests, Cheryl found being centered made all the difference in calibrating how forceful to be. Later that day, she asked her boss for an additional person. Although he said no, she said the rejection wasn't hard to take at all. Moreover, she felt proud of herself for having the courage to make the request.

A few weeks later, I got a surprise telephone call from Cheryl. "This amazing thing happened," she said. "Tom said no to me again." "Then why do you sound so happy?" I asked.

She related that while making the request she had been able to drop her breath, stand tall, and stay centered the whole time. She felt the strength of her stance made him pay attention to her. And even though he said no, he looked up at her and said courteously, "Sorry, I can't help you this week."

"He was so polite I thought maybe an alien had invaded his body," Cheryl joked.

I asked how she felt. She said she felt courageous and inspired to ask for what she wanted and to say no when she needed to. "What does that feel like in your body?" I asked. "I feel tall and powerful like when I crossed the finish line in a race," she said, "like I can take care of myself."

Conclusion

To achieve our goals or be who we long to be, we must be able to take new actions. New ways of engaging can feel uncomfortable, sometimes even unsafe. Being centered allows us to try new moves and to make the moves in ways that work. Having a coach as an ally to weather the discomfort of learning new actions and calibrating how far to go makes it easier to take risks. Consider the pain Cheryl, in the story earlier, felt at being taken advantage of and feeling unsupported by her peers. To learn that she could get support by behaving differently was a life-changing experience for her. Imagine how many possibilities opened when she became able to make direct requests and decline others' requests.

When we consider that we all have behaviors that limit our effectiveness, we gain an even greater appreciation of the power of somatics to increase our awareness and capacity to change—both in our clients and in ourselves. Thinking about a change is a necessity, not an end. Change must be embodied. Over time new behavior becomes deeply rooted and can be relied on to produce the results we want.

Notes

1. Albert Mehrabian, *Silent Messages* (Belmont, CA: Wadsworth, 1971), 77.
2. Richard Strozzi Heckler, *The Anatomy of Change: A Way to Move through Life's Transitions* (Berkeley, CA: North Atlantic Books, 1984, 1993), 9.
3. Daniel Goleman, *Working with Emotional Intelligence* (New York: Bantam Books, 1998), 74–76.

CHAPTER 12

Distinctions for Coaching Leaders

Beth Bloomfield

Coaching leaders is, in many ways, different from coaching everyone else; and yet, in many ways, it is much the same. Leaders are, after all, human beings first and foremost. What's different is the special pressure of being "in charge," ultimately responsible for people and results, which means they are "on" all the time, under constant scrutiny, subject to endless second-guessing and their own impossibly high standards. In my work with leaders in a variety of organizations, I find that most of them struggle with the same issues of managing themselves, characterized by the set of distinctions examined here. Readers beware: There are no easy answers, only thoughts and ideas, and of course, more questions.

Management Versus Leadership

Why do executives all want to be known as great "leaders" but worry that the words "good manager" in their performance review are the kiss of death to higher aspirations? The notion that management is bad and leadership is somehow good has grown out of a decades-old idea that there is a dichotomy between the two.[1]

Management skills are denigrated or completely overlooked in the popular literature of business these days, while books on leadership are perennial bestsellers. Management is frequently characterized as old school and fear-driven, while leadership is seen as enlightened and trust-based. Management is seen as the province of number-crunching mid-level drones, while leadership is the creative work of extraordinary or even heroic figures.

My own premise is that although there is a distinction, the dichotomy here is a false one. Management skills and leadership "jazz"[2] are both essential elements in building and sustaining a healthy and productive organization in today's world, and good management is complementary to, rather than opposed to, strong leadership. It's curious that American businesses spend vast sums annually on leadership development without any real evidence to show that it actually works, while training in the fundamentals of management is neglected in many organizations.

Management practices are what bring order and focus to an otherwise chaotic environment, and good management is a distinct professional set of knowledge and activities that is necessary to achieving consistent and reproducible results. Successful leaders must be adept at strategy and execution, vision and organization, creativity and structure, motivation and measurement.

Leaders can better align the organization by including a set of core management practices along with core business processes and core values. They should focus on developing a common set of management practices that can be explained and taught to managers at all levels. Here are a few questions to ask the leader you are coaching:

- What are the current management practices in your organization? Where are the areas of commonality? Where are there differences, and why?
- Is there a good understanding of management fundamentals by all levels of managers? Are the fundamentals being practiced? If not, why not?
- Are your management practices tied to your organization's strategy, goals, and expectations for its managers?
- What management practices need to be developed to address key gaps in your organization's performance and business results?
- Is there a system in your organization for mentoring and coaching managers in the fundamentals of good management, and how to apply them to your particular organizational context?

Looking at management as a part of the whole system of the organization will help the leader develop a more appreciative understanding of its value to the bottom line. Good management should fit hand-in-glove with a leader's approach to leadership. Without one, the other isn't very likely to succeed.

Power Versus Influence

One of the hardest lessons of leadership for those new to the role is that practically everything they have to get done must be done by others. For those accustomed to excelling as individual contributors, the transition to leadership can be a bumpy ride, especially in today's workplace. They can no longer rely solely on the power of their position in the hierarchy to command and control their employees because today's leaner organizations depend on more fluid structures and collaborative processes. Effective leadership requires the ability to influence people in a variety of ways, across a range of organizational structures.

We all influence others in some way, it's just that we seldom realize that we do or how we do it. By becoming more intentional in the use of influence, and by practicing it more consciously, it's possible for a leader to build some extra "muscle" and get noticeably better results. The foundation of influencing skill is "personal power," as distinct from the power of the leader's position. The leader is the one in control of his personal power. It's up to him to build the necessary trust, respect, and commitment of others.

To influence others to do something we want them to do, the first place most of us go is logic. We marshal the most logical and rational arguments in favor of our proposal, in an effort to appeal to the intellectual and analytical capacities of the stakeholders. To sweeten the pot, we cite lots and lots of good data in our appeal to their minds. If we're especially shrewd, we make sure we make the pitch in terms of the best choice for their interests or the most benefit to them. Most of us are good at making rational arguments.

That would be fine if people decided what to do only on the basis of logic. But of course, people are more complicated—they have emotions, and they are frequently not aware of how much they rely on emotion to make decisions. Therefore, if a leader wants to be a more powerful influencer, he'll also appeal to a person's values, their self-image, and their sense of belonging. He'll couch his request in terms of a larger purpose or vision and express confidence in the person's ability to accomplish the job. To be most effective, he'll need to listen well for clues about what really motivates them. Finally, he'd be wise to appeal to the need for connection and relationship that we all share. By building connection, he invites a more solid and continuing commitment by others to his proposal and his broader goals.

Begin coaching on influencing skills by asking the leader you are coaching to notice the many ways in which he seeks to influence others and to note which avenue he typically uses—logic, emotion, or relationship. If he relies too heavily on one, he's missing opportunities to bring people along. Ask him to practice extending his range in different situations, and notice how people respond. The objective is to develop his own style of influence, and build his own personal power to get things done.

Intelligence Versus Curiosity

What distinguishes the truly strategic thinkers from the larger group of general managers in most organizations? Certainly well-honed analytic skills and intellectual sophistication are the price of admission. We can also point to a recognized set of carefully cultivated habits of thought and action and maybe to some innate qualities of being as well. One thing I've noticed in my work, though, is that the biggest thinkers are the habitually curious people.

In this day and age of specialization, niche marketing, and technical expertise, it can be tough to make the leap from "go-to" person in one particular area to "big picture" player on a larger stage. It's hard to let go of the very thing that has made you so successful—up until now. But strategic leadership lives in the very broad context of history, culture, politics, economics, demographics, science—the rich broth in which we all swim. To get strategy right, you have to be conversant in all these domains.

Given the perpetual busyness of life today, that might seem impossible, not to mention downright unappealing. That's where curiosity comes in. If a leader can reframe the question of how to manage the torrent of information coming at him, to one of how to manage himself in the midst of the flow, the entire picture changes. If he can remember what it was like, at other times in his life, to have what some Eastern cultures call "beginner's mind," he's well-positioned to think big. Stay curious about the world and all things in it, and the world will open itself to you.

Here are six practices you can use in coaching a leader to build healthy strategic thinking "muscle" by getting curious and getting smart about his particular strategic context:

1. Become a "first-class noticer," as novelist Saul Bellow put it. Survey the people and places in which you find yourself during the course of your day. What's different, unusual, or interesting about them?
2. Develop your peripheral vision. Broaden your focus beyond what's in front of you. Cast your glance from side to side. What do you notice that's out there on the fringes?
3. Acquire a voracious appetite for knowledge and understanding. There's nothing too small or too subtle for you to notice and learn from. What would it be like to see the world from these various vantage points?
4. Cultivate a discerning eye, ear, and mind. Learn to tell the difference between quality and quantity in news, information, and opinion. Which sources are trustworthy, which providers are reliable? Be mindful of what your purpose is, and where you want to go. What criteria will you use to sort out the meaningful from the merely interesting along the way?
5. Learn how to speed-read, both figuratively and literally. Build your skills for scanning both the information environment as a whole, and the mountain of reading material that's available to you. What's the "take-away," the one priceless nugget you want to remember from any given book, article, program, speaker, Web site?
6. Exercise ruthless editing. Cast your net widely, but be prepared to cast off most of what you catch. Once you've read, seen, or heard enough to form a strong impression, you can pare away the nonessentials. What's the simplest and most direct way to describe something you have observed or learned?

Balance Versus Integration

I often hear requests for help in achieving better "work-life balance" from senior executives who are stressed out by incredibly busy lives and impossibly competing commitments. That sense of being constantly out of balance between the demands of the job and the requirements of the home and family seems to afflict women executives more than men, but it certainly isn't exclusive to them. Sometimes it seems as though equality of the sexes in the workplace has just spread the pain of being torn in different directions.

Usually, these busy leaders are looking for the magic bullet, for some powerful methodology or practice that will neatly resolve the dilemma for them. "I need a better time management system" is one I hear a lot. Alternatively, "I need to figure out how to do more of my work at home." I usually point out that none of us can "manage" time, time happens with or without us at the same rate of speed. It's what we choose to do with it that creates the problem, so what we have to manage is ourselves.

There is another way to appreciate the balance question, found in the distinction between living a "balanced" life and living an "integrated" life. Webster's defines the verb *integrate* as "to form, coordinate, or blend into a functioning or unified whole."

Applied to how we live our lives, that's a powerful paradigm for change. For leaders who can't realistically set rigid boundaries in time and space between work and home life, integration offers a model that intuitively feels right.

Here are seven strategies you can introduce to the leaders you coach, choices they can make for an integrated life:

1. Give up the idea that there's "work" and there's "life." Isn't it *all* life?
2. Design your work to fit the life you want, and your life to complement your work (versus to support it). Think about when, where, and how you want to work so that it blends more seamlessly into when, where, and how you do your life.
3. Be "out there," in both work and life. Live as though you are your work, versus your work defines who you are. Get curious about your world and everything in it, and get comfortable with not knowing all the answers all the time.
4. Decide what your life is about, and live *all* of it that way. What is your purpose? Seek authenticity in all domains of life, be who you really are, all the time.
5. Work with people you want to be with. Why not be friends with your clients, colleagues, and customers? It's less about setting boundaries than it is about being respectful and compassionate towards others, and being "clean" (honest and appropriate) in your relationships.
6. Give up the idea that you can "achieve" balance (or integration!). You will always be a work in progress, and you will never get there. So? Forgive yourself for not being perfect.
7. Not everything in work and in life is that serious. It's not *all* about life and death. And, it's not all about you, either. Try thinking about "my life as a comedy" once in a while to bring yourself back to earth.

Stamina Versus Resilience

Leaders at all levels these days are expected to have the stamina of an Energizer Bunny, to "go the distance" and "stay the course" no matter what. The physical and psychological demands of "extreme jobs" are unquestioned in many organizations today, with little heed to what that really means for the individual or the people he must lead. However, as an older and much wiser colleague always used to say, "Nobody goes through life unscathed." If you live long enough, sooner or later "stuff happens." Why do some people snap back, while others snap under the stress of unanticipated occurrences? The quality of resilience is very often the determinant of success in work, as well as in life. Studies show that resilience matters more to sustained high performance than do education, experience, or training. Resilience, more than stamina, is crucial to effective leadership.

Here's the dictionary definition of "resilience": (1) The ability to recover quickly from illness, change, or misfortune; buoyancy. (2) The property of a material that enables it to resume its original shape or position after being bent, stretched, or compressed; elasticity.

The important thing to note here is that we are *not* talking about being unaffected by events and forces in our world but rather about the capacity to move with them and then reestablish a working balance.

According to experts, the main building blocks of resilience are the capacity to accept reality and stand up to it; the ability to find meaning in life; and the ability to improvise. Other important factors are a strong sense of self; the belief that you are the author of your own life; and the ability to be flexible. It's an interesting mix of mental, emotional, physical, and spiritual qualities, all of which can be cultivated. My own experience in coaching leaders in a variety of organizational settings confirms the observation.

Authors Jim Loehr and Tony Schwartz have researched how winning athletes train for high performance, and they translate their findings into practical strategies for corporate leaders in their book, *The Power of Full Engagement: Managing Energy, Not Time, Is the Key to High Performance and Personal Renewal*.[3] Fundamental to their approach is the idea that you can't manage time—you only have a fixed quantity—but you can manage the energy available to you, and the quantity and quality of that is not fixed.

We build mental, emotional, and spiritual capacity in the same way we build physical capacity—by expending energy beyond our usual limits and then recovering. So, effective energy management in all domains requires cycles of expenditure (stress) and renewal (recovery) of energy. Building resilience means mastering the practice of these rhythmic cycles. Resilient leaders have developed rituals that help promote cycling—going to the gym at the same time every day, for example, or sitting down to dinner with the family every night.

Loehr and Schwartz note that the demands on today's executives dwarf the challenges faced by professional athletes.[4] Executives must sustain peak performance while athletes play in relatively short bursts of energy. Athletes spend most of their time training and very little performing—executives just the opposite. Athletes have off-seasons, while most executives are lucky to get three or four weeks of vacation. An athlete's career averages five to seven years, while most executives will work for 40–50 years. As a coach of leaders and those aspiring to leadership, it's very important that you work with your clients to help them develop lifelong habits that will support resilience in the face of the inevitable personal and professional setbacks they will experience in the course of that long career.

Focus Versus Reflection

Survey after survey, bolstered by anecdotal evidence from virtually all my executive clients, indicates that work is expanding almost exponentially. There's no end to this trend in sight, and the stakes are increasingly high for executives who must deliver solid business results from whatever project or assignment they have taken on. Leaders need an edge to keep up, and it had better be a sharp one if they want to sustain peak performance.

The top three challenges faced by executives today are time pressure, financial pressure, and the imbalance they feel between work and life. They often feel out of control, as though they are perpetually reacting to events. To help my leader/clients regain a sense of control, of "authorship" of their own lives, I frequently begin with the development of a critical skill: focus. The ability to focus on what's important, when it's important, is one of the things that distinguish successful from unsuccessful leaders.

Focus is a learned skill, and it also can be practiced until it becomes habit. In addition, as with any other habit, it lives in the body, our biological being. That's important, because most people tend to think that focus is strictly a mental process and a matter of emotional self-discipline. When we talk about someone being "unfocused," we often conjure an image of dishevelment and incompetence, almost a morally deficiency.

Focus, when practiced well, is not about homing in on one thing to the exclusion of all others. It is an essential element in what is often called "flow," and it involves agility and grace, the ability to move almost seamlessly from one thing to the next with a minimum of settle time. The key to developing this kind of focus is what I call "attention training"—the physical practice of mastering a mental shift. Here's a set of practices you can adapt for the leader you are coaching to help him achieve better focus:

- To focus, you have to set aside all the things you are *not* going to focus on—you have to define the universe of what's important by eliminating the unimportant. Begin by tracking all the things you do in a day, a week, a month, and choosing *not* to pay attention to the distractions.
- Choose one important matter to attend to for an hour or more each day, working with a clearly articulated goal in mind, one that includes both a time element and a quantitative measurable outcome. While you are working, if something else comes up, turn it away until your focused work session is complete.
- As you increase your ability to concentrate on this one matter for a prescribed period, add another important matter, treating it in the same way. Use physical actions—turning off your phone or computer, closing your door, asking your assistant to screen calls and visitors—to reinforce your focused attention.
- Limit the number of important matters you will attend to to three, and as you reach your goal for one, move another new matter to your set of three. As other matters come to your attention, pass them on to others, or turn them away.

At the beginning, it may seem impossible to control this much of the time in a day. If the leader treats this practice as a conscious choice, though, and puts physical structures of support in place, he'll begin to build the muscle for focus. After a while, this way of attending to what matters will become habitual, and the habit will be reinforced when he enjoys the fruits of success. By training his attention, he'll develop a felt sense of greater autonomy and control in work and life, and discover the secret to sustained peak performance.

The requisite partner to focus is reflection, the complement to the reactive or "process" thinking that tends to govern our waking hours. Reflection is necessary to cement the things you are continually learning in your memory, because it enables you to assign meaning to the myriad of experiences you have every day. Reflection is the "time out" your brain needs to process the mix of sensory perceptions, emotions, and communications you are being bombarded with all the time. Reflection is how you figure out what you think, and therefore who you really are.

Frequently my leadership coaching clients tell me they can't find the time for reflection, or they don't think they know how to do it. Very often, when we probe what's behind those assessments, we discover that there's another really huge or "master" assessment, namely that if you're not constantly in action you aren't really accomplishing anything. This is such a powerful assumption in these times that it is often literally impossible for people to see how driven by it they are. It's as though we were all afflicted with some profound variety of attention deficit disorder.

Why are we so reluctant to sit quietly with our own thoughts? Is it because of our modern existential phobia of inactivity as akin to death? Alternatively, perhaps our physical addiction to the adrenalin rush of constant busyness? Suffice it to say that if you aren't reflecting in a conscious way, your brain is doing it for you automatically, running the program in the background—and you might not like the logic it is using while unsupervised by you. Dedicated reflection practice will raise the whole thought process to the conscious level, and it is a necessary precursor to planful action. If you skip this step, you're far less likely to get to where you really want to go in business and in life.

The good news is that the leader you coach doesn't have to retreat to a mountaintop to bring more reflective thought into his life. Ask him to start wherever he is and build some reflection time into his daily routine. If he already exercises most days, suggest that he turn off the iPod for five or ten minutes and turn his thoughts inward as he walks or jogs on the treadmill. If he already keeps a journal or a "learning log," throw in a good question for deep reflection once a week or so. If he does the dishes every evening, ask him to turn off the TV and enjoy his time at the sink by spending it with his own thoughts.

Your coachee will soon see that reflection happens regardless of the surroundings or the length of time he may devote to it. He may find it adds to the experience to set up a regular reflection ritual, perhaps settling into a favorite armchair with some soft music and a cup of hot tea. However, the brain doesn't require any of that. A good "quieting" practice, such as taking a few deep breaths or centering himself, will quickly put him into the posture for good reflective thought. Anywhere, anytime.

Notes

1. An influential thinker on this point was Abraham Zaleznik, a professor at the Harvard Business School, who published an oft-cited article on the social psychology of managers,

"Managers and Leaders: Are They Different?," *Harvard Business Review,* May–June 1977, 67.

2. Depree, Max, *Leadership Jazz* (New York: Currency Doubleday, 1992).

3. Loehr, Jim, and Tony Schwartz, *The Power of Full Engagement: Managing Energy, Not Time, Is the Key to High Performance and Personal Renewal* (New York: Free Press, 2003).

4. Ibid., 8–9.

PART III

Using

CHAPTER 13

ALIFE™: A Listening Model for Coaching

Christine M. Wahl and Neil Stroul

A group of coaches, sitting around a conference table, sharing their best practices. Batting ideas around. Getting juice from the life in the discussion. One of them, Neil Stroul, offered up a framework that he had developed to organize the stories he was hearing from leaders, and he said that this framework helped him calibrate how he listened. We talked about what a leader has to do, what and how a leader thinks, and how a leader ought to learn. One of the other coaches, Karen Gravenstine, mused aloud that these organizing principles could be reordered to create an acronym "ALIFE." We've used it that way ever since.

ALIFE™ stands for Authenticity, Leadership, Intentionality, Fear/Courage, and Execution. Each of these concepts has distinctions that coaches can use to work with leaders. We have found that just by listening through the lens of ALIFE™, when we listen to leaders' "stories" we can zero in on areas that the leader may be blind to.

Over time we have refined our thinking about these concepts and offer it to our students as a grounding model for beginning coaching. We have also presented it to a number of audiences—coaches, leaders, HR managers, and OD consultants—that have given consistent feedback on its usefulness. This chapter outlines key attributes of the ALIFE™ model.

Authenticity—What Does It Mean to Be an Authentic Leader?

Authenticity is contagious.[1]

—Paul Wieand

Authenticity is one of those terms that people hear and understand on some level—but don't really "get." Many people think of it as just being yourself—but we don't see it that way. It's deeper and bigger than that.

As coaches, we are supremely interested in helping our clients bring their authentic selves forward; at the deeper levels our clients need to learn who they are when they are showing up as their "best self," and our task as coaches is to help them identify what that authentic, best self is capable of, and how to assist them in summoning forth that best version of themselves. In our view, it is essential to being a great leader. For most of us—coaches and leaders alike—it is a lifelong process.

How can you tell an authentic leader? Most of us can *feel* it when someone is authentic, and so we can say that it has something to do with one's *presence*. Moreover, we feel connected to them in some way. An authentic leader creates trust. An authentic leader is generative. An authentic leader draws from deep internal source material, understands that people aren't perfect, and works with them anyway.

An authentic leader tells his/her "truth" in such a way as to invite dialogue that embraces the "truths" of others.

At a deeper level, being authentic means that we express our fundamental sense of purpose and that we are working, with awareness, to be the person we aspire to be, the person we *must be* if we are truly to feel that our deeper sense of purpose is being fulfilled.

Most people in organizations learn to "play the game" at some level, and they may push their own deeper needs to the background. However, this is a story that does not serve the leader and inevitably generates an inauthentic way of being. The human operating system can support a certain amount of this, but over time, too much of it leads to being out of synch with ourselves, and our authentic self becomes buried. Another version of "playing the game" looks like this: completely ignoring your own quiet voice in favor of those louder ones, inside of you and outside of you, that encourage you to do what everyone else does to get ahead—multitask, be accessible nearly 24/7, work longer, harder, faster, get more done, stay later, and come in earlier. You get the picture. These belief systems that keep you in the more-harder-faster-better loop are debilitating over time, and they override your authentic voice. When we hit a crisis of burnout, illness, or some other sort of suffering, it may be our authentic self demanding our attention. The coach's job is to help the client notice their flagging energy and see opportunities to more fully express themselves, so their authenticity begins to come forward.

A leader striving to be more authentic has the pull to stay in touch with the vision of the person s/he aspires to be, and to challenge him/herself more and more to *be that person* by noticing daily exactly what life is calling for. The coach's job is to encourage and support the leader to live in the question, "am I bringing my best self forward?"

Our belief is that every day, each of us has the chance to greet life from a more authentic stance. That's the beauty of it—we get opportunity after opportunity to show up as the person we aspire to be.

As coaches, we listen to our leader clients tell us about the obstacles they face at work, what they want to get done, and what makes it so hard. In many cases, what they are describing is their desire to bring their fuller self forward. We listen for those places where their authenticity is thwarted, where their presence diminishes, and where they feel no power. This is always an opening for coaching.

The poet David Whyte[2] offered the concept that the soul would rather fail doing what it must do, than succeed doing what someone else thinks it ought to do. This is the mission deep within our operating system, the one that helps us bring our authentic voice forward. Awareness is the first step on this path.

Leadership

> Go to the people. Learn from them. Live with them. Start with what they know. Build with what they have. The best of leaders, when the job is done, when the task is accomplished, the people will say, "we have done it ourselves."
>
> —Lao Tzu

In listening to stories that leaders tell us, we are discerning how this person sees him/herself as a leader. We are wondering what distinctions related to leadership exist in the client's mind. Are they a leader in title? Are they a leader in spirit? Do they embody leadership? Do they walk their talk? Do they communicate their leadership, both in speech and action? Do others perceive them as a leader? What do they know about the demands of being a leader? To what extent, do they operate with a "leader's mindset?"

Let's look at leadership as a series of public acts. In our minds, being able to *be* a leader is based on reflection and self-knowledge, and executives "show up" as leaders when they move into action. It does no good to just think grand leadership thoughts. Every leader has chances, both big and small, to embody leadership through their actions daily. Another distinction important to consider is that leadership moves more toward the future than management, which stays more in the present. Leading often requires a strategic focus, while managing requires an operational focus. The question we are wondering as we listen is how is this client showing up daily? Is this client "out there" acting as a leader? Is this client focusing on the future, on what is possible? Is this client thinking strategically?

Now, let's view leadership as a mindset. Actions that a leader takes will be fueled by the context she is in and the story she tells herself about that context. If a leader lives in a story of possibility, her actions will reflect that. If a leader lives in a story of resignation, her actions will reflect that. In each case, the possible outcomes can have a dramatic impact on the leader's organization. A leader's actions are informed and supported by the amount and quality of self-reflection she engages in, how well she knows her "self," and how well she takes lessons from feedback.

Powerful leaders today are those who can read a situation and know how to act within it. They do not assume that their "style" is applicable to every challenging situation. There are times to be autocratic, authoritarian, supportive, inspirational, and logical. Coaches need to listen to the leader's distinctions about being a leader and help the leader shore them up wherever necessary.

Intentionality

> Power is…the capacity to translate intention into reality and sustain it.
> Leadership is the wise use of this power.[3]
>
> —Warren Bennis

Leadership without intentionality will lead you to move in a direction that may well be contrary to where you actually want to go. Notwithstanding the occasional magic of serendipity, we believe intentionality is key to great leadership and is based on integrity and authenticity. Intentionality is also integral to achieving a vision. Intentional means purposeful, focused clearly on an outcome. Most of us have worked for leaders who lacked intentionality—and the result was chaos. It reflects the classic metaphor of a ship adrift, with no one at the helm.

One client we worked with needed to discover the power of intention. He did not have a big goal; instead, he blew with the wind. Whatever the organization needed, he would try to mold himself into that. In the process, he lost a sense of energy and gained a sense of resignation. His authentic self was buried somewhere under the external expectations he was trying to meet. He clearly needed a sense of intention. When his team was faltering, he tried something new. He *declared the intention* of pulling them together and inspiring them to do better. He became willing to step up to the plate and envision a new kind of success: intention in action.

We have frequently encountered executives who have inherited an agenda from a predecessor or senior executive and have not worked out a way to integrate the previous mission with their own aspirations. As a result, their intentions become vague and lack potency. The coach's task is to help the leader attain the requisite clarity so that they can then become intentional.

Think of intention as the point around which a leader can rally energy and ignite the energy of followers. A leader can have intentions around just about anything, such as:

- personal development as a leader
- commitment to develop others
- commitment to wholeness, for yourself, and others
- commitment to clear communication
- commitment to partner with colleagues
- commitment to increase market share
- desire to bring the organization to a new way of thinking
- desire to create an image of your organization that is admired and valued by others
- desire to create an organization that is respectful, innovative, and welcoming for everyone who works there

The list can be endless. Coaches listen for a leader's intention or lack of it and help the leader choose those areas to focus on that will create energy and leverage for self and for the organization. Coaches help leaders create a crystal-clear intention, make a commitment to it, and live it! As a result, the leader will be quicker to make decisions (intention is a compass pointing north), will generate creativity, and will stretch beyond what was thought possible.

Fear/Courage

Never let the fear of striking out get in your way.

—Babe Ruth

Fear—it is often difficult to admit that we feel afraid. We try to suppress its insidious hijack of our purpose, and regardless, fear will hold us in its thrall. Humans (even leaders) are hardwired to be fearful. It rightfully protects us from threats that we feel. Yet, sometimes the threats are not real. The famous quote, "there is nothing to fear but fear itself" may ring truer than most of us imagine, partly because when we imagine the worst, it's easy for us to see how possible "the worst" could be, and we begin to believe the imagined scenario.

Fear keeps us small. Courage helps us live larger. Courage is not the opposite of fear, but it helps us past our fears. Imagine a great leader acting out of fear. What if, for example, Churchill had acted out of fear? Or Roosevelt? Acting courageously is something every leader must do. Powerful people are able to *transform their fear into courage.* Leaders must find courage to lead, make the hard decisions, and move past their fears, all in service of preserving an organization's integrity and supporting its future.

Coaches who listen for the leader's fear, however hidden or nuanced it may be, can help the leader step to the other side of the fear to lead more courageously. In many instances, leaders are simply unable to recognize that they are fearful. It is the coach's task not only to help the leader "put her hand in the flame," but also to give the fear a name. Naming a fear allows a leader to *claim* (own) the fear that is the first step in regaining their personal power and moving into courage.

Personal courage is necessary for leaders. There are times when the demands of work life unabashedly trounce on boundaries of balance—little or no time for personal pursuits outside of work, for family, for reflection. In many systems, it takes courage to model balance and effectively nourish an ability to be present. "Systems" will take as much as a leader is willing to give them. Who sets the limits?

From a coaching perspective, fear takes many forms. Fear shows up when a person has to speak publicly, have a difficult conversation, defend an argument, stand up to authority, or go against the norm. Leaders can have a fearful response to e-mail! It matters not if it's a big thing or a little thing that causes fear; the point is to recognize ways past it whenever possible. Getting to the other side of fear is empowering and energizing.

We had a client who needed to hire a second-in-command. The client procrastinated, made excuses, laid blame for not hiring at the feet of the HR recruiters she was working with. Months went by, and the position was still vacant. Although she lamented her workload and verbally wished for a strong leader under her, the truth was that she was afraid that if she hired someone strong, they would take over her position and she would be out of a job. Once this fear was identified, and the client could come to terms with the dragons that were managing her mind around this issue, she was able to comfortably hire someone remarkable and reap the benefits of strong leadership supporting her vision and mission.

Execution

> People think of execution as the tactical side of business, something leaders delegate while they focus on the perceived "bigger" issue. This idea is completely wrong. Execution is not just tactics—it is a discipline and a system. It has to be built into a company's strategy, its goals, and its culture.[4]
>
> —Ram Charon

Execution is key to the cycle of action and key to leading others. Anyone who is a leader undoubtedly has a mandate to create a future and make things happen. Leaders who are unable themselves to move into action and get others to move into action fail to deliver on their mandates. Recognizing *what is* and *what needs to be* is the first step. Filling the gap to get to what needs to be is where execution or action is necessary.

Execution, therefore, is necessary to leadership.

Leaders do not have the luxury to just sit and think big thoughts. Though thinking big thoughts is necessary (we encourage every leader to find time—and hold it sacred—to kick back and think big), thoughts and ideas need to be translated into action. Declaring a big thought—a new future, for instance, is not enough. Though the declaration is the first step, it is not the only step. Leaders need to execute on their ideas and engage others in moving forward. The job of a coach is to listen for the ways that the leader moves into action, such as balanced versus rushed, thoughtful versus spontaneous, in partnership versus lone-ranger-like, and networked or system-oriented versus tunnel-visioned. Then, a coach helps the leader notice the timing of the action and its effects on the leader's organization.

We have found over time that this model offers a very deep and rich way to listen to a leader's story. We share ALIFE™ with the leaders that we coach. As the coaching progresses, our coachees often start our conversations by saying, "today, we will talk about fear" or "today, I need help refocusing on intention." And off we go. The richness that comes from listening through this lens never fails to show an opening where the leader can respond to a development opportunity.

Below are some questions for reflection in each area of the ALIFE™ model. They can be used for conversation, journaling, or daily reflection, and we encourage our readers to share them with leaders to deepen their understanding and commitment to leading authentically, courageously, intentionally, and producing amazing results.

Personal Reflections

Authenticity

- When I'm experiencing "life is at its best" what am I able to notice about how I'm feeling, what I'm doing, what's happening around me?
- If I could hear others eulogize me at my funeral, for what would I want to be remembered, and how would I want to be described?
- What talents or abilities do I possess, that, when I'm applying them, I feel a sense of rightness or wholeness?

Leadership

- Who lives in my memory or imagination as examples of great leadership? What qualities do those leaders embody?
- What am I able to notice about my own experiences as a follower? Are there universal principles of leading that inspire others to follow?
- What do I stand for? Do I hold key values that could form the basis for a leadership agenda?

Intentionality

- When I reflect on possibilities, is there a particular future that I could be committed to creating?
- What do I know about my key stakeholders? What do they want/need from me?
- If I'm feeling thwarted or bogged down, what do I know about the obstacles to success?
- What would it take for me to declare an intention, find support for fulfilling it, and stay committed to it?

Fear/Courage

- Am I able to recognize where fear lives in my body? Am I able to recognize when I'm afraid?
- What do I know about my own defensive habits? Are there patterns I follow when I'm afraid?
- Am I able to recollect episodes from my own history when I successfully converted fear into courage? What allowed me to shift?

Execution

- Is it possible that I am my own source of interference? In what way? Are there actions in which I need to stop engaging in order to be more effective?
- What do I know about my own sources of resistance and avoidance? Might there be actions that I need to initiate that I have been procrastinating?
- Are there actions I have not taken because I am insufficiently competent? What might I need to learn?

Notes

1. Pamela Kruger, "A Leader's Journey," *Fast Company 25* (June 1999): 116.
2. David Whyte, "The Three Marriages: Work, Self and Other" (presentation, Georgetown University Coaching Reunion, Sterling, VA, 2005).
3. Warren Bennis and Burt Nanus, *Leaders: Strategies for Taking Charge* (New York: HarperCollins, 2003), 16–17.
4. Ram Charon, "The Discipline of Execution," *Corporate EVENT Magazine* 1, no. 3 (2005): 17.

CHAPTER 14

Coaching in Organizations

Randy Chittum

In the same ways that coaches and clients come in all shapes and sizes, the environments in which coaching occurs are all different. For the sake of discussion, there is a distinction that needs to be drawn. The first type of coaching is "life" coaching. This type of coaching is more likely to focus on the client's life ambitions, which may or may not be related to work, career, and leadership success. The second type of coaching is "organizational," or "leadership" coaching, and it is the focus of this chapter.

It is a misnomer to suggest that life coaches and their clients do not deal with living and working in systems and organizations. It is similarly misleading to suggest that leadership coaches do not deal with "life" and issues greater than the role of leadership. That said, for the coach whose expressed interest is in coaching in organizations, there are implications beyond mastering the art and skill of coaching. This coach must also give due diligence to understanding organizational systems in general, and the client's system in particular.

This chapter attempts first to outline and discuss some of the considerations of coaching leaders in organizations, and second to address some of the issues related to entry or contracting.

Issues Related to Working in Organizations

Organizations as Systems

Coaches, like the leaders being coached, are subject to the powerful influences of organizational systems. By their nature, systems are complex and nuanced and often serve primarily the continued survival of the system. Social psychologists led by Lewin, argue that we consistently and significantly underestimate the impact of the environment on our behavior. This is called fundamental attribution error. I would suggest that coaches, with our focus and even fascination with the person, could be especially ignorant of our tendency to err in this way. In organizational development parlance, there is the notion of being "co-opted" by the system. When someone becomes co-opted, she begins to unknowingly act in ways that are consistent with system influences and expectations. She is likely unaware of this co-opting process because of its very power. It speaks to our desire to fit in and to be accepted, among other things. Coaches that work in organizations can be co-opted and may be likely to underestimate the power of the system and environment on her clients.

Organizational Dynamics

Bolman and Deal (1984) suggest that to understand an organization, four perspectives must be considered. The first is structural. Most organizations have an organizational structure that details reporting relationships, roles and responsibilities, authority and so forth. For the novice, there can be a temptation to stop at the structural understanding. It all seems so clear and easy to understand when you print the strategic plan, business plan, and organization chart! The coach with deeper distinctions about organizations will understand that this lens, although useful, is far from a complete picture.

The second perspective is the political. Simply defined as competition for scarce resources, politics are an important part of how organizations work. Who has budget authority? Who makes decisions about resource allocation? How are alliances formed and utilized? Where is there missing transparency in the organization and who benefits and who is harmed? What topics are off limits, and with whom? These types of questions will help you understand the political landscape of an organization.

The third perspective is human resources. This perspective addresses how people are tended to. How are employees recruited and hired? How are they oriented and trained? Evaluated? Rewarded? What is the philosophy of succession and development? What is the stated goal related to diversity and what is the reality? How are employees treated formally (benefits, policies, and procedures)? How are employees treated by managers?

Finally, understanding an organization requires attention to the culture or spirit of the organization. What stories are told that create a sense of organizational identity? What rituals and celebrations exist and what do they teach us about what the organization truly values? For example, what would it tell you if a "performance-based" culture celebrated only longevity? Reading organizational culture takes a great deal of mindfulness and time in the organization.

The leadership coach in an organization may not have to fully diagnose the organization in the ways described earlier. However, the basic distinctions are important because this is the world in which you work. Given our tendency for fundamental attribution error, it seems even more important that we acknowledge the sway of the systems in which our clients work.

Teams

Teams are ubiquitous in today's organizations. You can almost certainly expect that any leader you coach will both be a part of a team, and probably lead a team, if not more than one. The extensive use of teams has aided organizations to be more effective through better use of human capital and more clear opportunities to strategically align efforts. However, being a leader or member of a team increases the level of complexity. There are several important distinctions to notice when working with leaders in the context of a team-based environment.

The first issue is that leading a team is different than leading a group of individuals, more commonly thought of as a functional department, or perhaps a working group. A team implies shared purpose and interdependence. The strength of teamwork is found when synergy is created, thereby making the team greater than the sum of its parts. Therefore, leading a team is dramatically different from leading a collection of people. The team leader has to have the capability to balance declarations with consensus, manage relationships among others, enroll others in a shared vision, and manage planning processes. Also, since the work of teams happens through meetings, the leader of teams should be a skilled facilitator, with a strong understanding of group dynamics and processes.

The second issue to consider is that teams are sometimes compensated differently. Team members may be rewarded for individual performance and for team performance and success. Managing compensation and rewards is a unique and perhaps necessary skill for the leader of teams.

Organization Initiatives

When you enter an organization, you may find yourself in the middle of any number of organizational initiatives. In fact, you may be there to help a leader engage in one or more of those initiatives. Some of the more common possibilities are listed here.

Strategic planning is a common organizational effort that consumes much energy from leaders. You may encounter leaders who are immersed in that process. Having broader strategic vision is one of the most cited developmental needs for leaders, particularly those who are being developed for more senior leadership positions. Strategic planning processes are often a wonderful time to be coaching because it is all about creating a new future, which coincides nicely with most coaching philosophies. It is also an interesting time to be coaching because it is often stressful for the leader, giving you a glimpse into how the leader handles stress.

Succession planning is becoming ever more popular as organizations realize that the demographics of retiring leaders do not support the need for long-term leadership at the very top levels of the organization. Many organizations are preparing for the expected competition for leaders as current leaders retire. The most likely intersection for the coach is that you may be coaching a leader who is in a succession management program. This coaching may not vary significantly from coaching a leader who is not in a succession management program. The possible sources of interference include the awareness of greater evaluation by senior leaders, the potential feeling of competition between leaders, and the desire to impress decision makers.

It seems that organizations are in constant change, some planned and some not. Leaders today must excel at leading change efforts. It is likely that the leader you are coaching is either responsible for, or influenced by, or both, a significant change effort. The midst of this uncertainty presents great opportunities for coaching. Some would argue that leading in change is the best test of leadership. As the coach, you get to see the client in all sorts of challenging situations. It will be in your best interests to have some distinctions about managing organizational change.

Assessments

One of the great benefits of coaching in organizations is that you have ready access to feedback about the client. It may take the form of past performance reviews, or leadership assessments that you might do or others might have already done. It is increasingly popular to do a verbal 360 review in which the coach interviews direct reports and other people in key relationships with the client. All this data is available to the coach and client. There is a danger in thinking that what you hear from a client while sitting in his/her office is the whole picture. The leadership coach often needs additional information to be effective. For example, I have had many clients who had stories or mental models that limited what they could notice. What clients notice is often significantly impacted by his/her beliefs. In one case a client was completely convinced that he listened well and made others feel included. As he described his view I found it very compelling, in part because of the conviction of his beliefs. Had I not looked other places for contrary data I might have headed down a less fruitful path. This client was shocked to hear that others did not share his view of his listening skill and quickly became committed to improving.

Many organizations have leadership competency models that have been developed to paint a picture of the effective leader in that organization. Competency models are often the framework used for promotion and hiring, performance reviews, and compensation. Competency models are behavior-based, researched models that typically explain the difference between very high performers and average performers. The behavioral evaluation is often multirater, or 360 in nature. It is an excellent opportunity for leaders to learn how others perceive their leadership on a variety of dimensions. The organizational implication is to get more people to behave more like the high performers. For those reasons, they can be of great importance to the person being coached.

Although the idea of such a model has an appeal, there is a potential downside. To the extent that the model becomes that which the client must become, possibilities are limited. There is much evidence that truly effective leadership is an "inside-out" process. Coaching or teaching to the model is the opposite, an "outside-in" process. Each coach must find for him/herself the balance between using organizational tools such as competency models and a more generative approach.

An organization may request that a leadership assessment be performed using a standardized assessment tool. The advantage to this method is that these assessments often provide a benchmark against other leaders. Leaders often like to know how they "measure up." It is important when using a tool such as this that the client know exactly what questions will be asked and of whom. It is beyond the scope of this chapter to recommend specific assessment tools. Reliability and validity studies should be readily available for the more reputable tools. Perhaps most important, be sure to choose an instrument that will be consistent with the organizational culture and will speak to the client.

The reports are usually very formal, with lots of graphs and data to be absorbed. It may take both coach and client some time to ascertain the implications of such a report. There is one word of caution when using these tools. Clients can sometime assign great importance to these reports, in part because they look so official. Be mindful that they are one view into one aspect of a very complex person!

There is ample, and growing, evidence to suggest that there is greater leverage in focusing on developing a few clear strengths as opposed to trying to develop every possible dimension of leadership. For example, Zenger and Folkman (2002) in *The Extraordinary Leader* write, "Our research has led us to conclude that great leaders are not defined by the absence of weakness, but rather by the presence of clear strengths."[1] They go on to say that 84 percent of the leaders they studied have no clear weaknesses but are not perceived to be strong leaders. This is a very important concept to discuss when debriefing a leadership feedback report. I find that leaders are generally first interested in improving in areas of weakness and find the "strengths" movement counter-intuitive.

Issues Related to Entry and Contracting

Accountability

The coach in an organization quickly learns the importance of transparency around accountability. Consider the possible complexity of a coach hired by the human resources officer, to work with the leader of a division, who reports to a vice president. For whom do you work? Who is your real client? It is naïve to assume that you work only for the person you are coaching. Organizations invest in coaching with the expectation of seeing a positive result. You and your client are bound by those expectations.

I have recently heard organizations defined as "collections of agreements." This is one place where the coach can be a good role model for establishing clear agreements. What constitutes that agreement will differ for each of us, based on our need for certainty and our coaching offer.

One school of thought is total transparency. Meet with everyone at once and clarify the relationships and expectations. Clarify your role with each person so that all are clear. Be especially careful to reach an agreement about confidentiality. You can make any agreement you want, but make sure it is clear, transparent, and that you honor it. I generally try to make the agreement that the only way I will discuss the coaching is if the person being coached is in the room at the time. This provides some assurance to the person being coached that he/she will always be aware of any discussions of his/her performance.

Finally, here are two specific words of caution. First, be very careful of being used by the boss to deliver news that he/she was unwilling to deliver. In addition to leaving the person being coached more effective, I would like to leave the relationship with her boss more effective. That is best accomplished by helping the client and supervisor learn how to have a meaningful and truthful dialogue. Second, beware of being asked to fix "broken" clients. My experience, and that of most coaches I know, is that this is a risky proposition. The temptation to help is strong. The danger is rooted in the possibility that this person has essentially already failed and you are the last effort to prove that the person cannot be "fixed." The timelines for change may be unreasonable. The possibilities are severely limited. The emotions are often so overwhelming that purposeful, future-based coaching can hardly occur at all.

The story of one of my very first coaching clients comes to mind. I was hired by the board to coach the executive director of a nonprofit organization. Her performance had suffered for years and a frustrated board had reached the point of bringing in outside help. Convinced I could help, I agreed to the six-month window for her to show "significant improvement." Unclear as to what that meant, she and I moved heroically down the path of self-discovery. Six months later the board deemed her cured and all was well. Three months after the coaching engagement ended she was fired. What I failed to understand was the extent to which the "coaching" had deteriorated into "managing perceptions." Although this felt and looked good at the time, six months was not long enough for her to recover emotionally and make significant transformative change.

Outcomes

Today's organizations want to measure everything. The mantra seems to be, "that which is measured, gets done." This organizational edict may wend its way to your coaching relationships. You may be asked to demonstrate ROI, or speak to how the organization will benefit from your coaching presence. In fairness, remember that the organization does not exist to provide you with opportunities to coach! They are rightly interested in how you can help them to achieve their organizational mission, through enhanced leadership capacity. This is another area in which there is no right answer. You will have to determine what your coaching offer means in light of expressed goals on the part of the organization.

Here are a few things to consider. How will you respond if the desired goals do not match up with the client's interests? What if the client is seriously considering leaving the organization? Knowing that transformative work involves the client exploring new possibilities and reaching his/her own conclusions, how will you proceed if those possibilities will take the client further from the organization's stated objectives? How will you respond to the internal pull to "teach to the test?" Your responses to these, and other questions like these, should be part of your offer and discussed up front. The ultimate question at stake here is, "Who is my client?" If my client is the person I am coaching, I will likely respond one way. If my client is the organization, I may respond differently. The most harmful wrong answer is to not have an answer in advance.

The organization into which you enter will have an assessment of the value of coaching long before you arrive. That assessment might include how open one should be about having a coach; in other words, whether it is a bad thing to have a coach or a good thing to have a coach. Either assessment will open certain possibilities for the coaching and close down others. I have found it useful to explore this issue early in the relationship, often in contracting. Some of that exploration is factual—how many leaders in this organization have coaches? For what reasons are coaches typically hired? What have been the outcomes of the last three or four coaching engagements? Some of that exploration is emotional—how does it feel to have a coach? How do you imagine feeling if others know you have a coach?

Conclusion

This chapter has likely raised more questions than it has answered. One key issue is being clear about who you are as a coach and about your coaching offer. Another is to stay mindful of the organization and its influence on you and your client. Chris Argyris is noted for, among other things, his writings about "espoused theory" and "theory in action." He suggests that we have two theories, the one we state to the public and likely believe, and the one that actually guides our actions. I believe that these differences are explained in large part by the power of the environment. Beyond your own mindfulness, I find it useful to have coaching partners with whom I confidentially share coaching experiences. Sometimes the brilliant insight to which I seem blind is right there in front of me.

Coaching leaders in organizations is a rich and rewarding experience. This coaching allows for the opportunity to use context and backdrop to enhance the coaching relationship. The opportunities for significant learning are endless.

Note

1. Zenger and Folkman, *The Extraordinary Leader: Turning Good Managers into Great Leaders,* 20.

Bibliography

Argyris, Chris and Donald A. Schon. *Theory in Practice.* San Francisco, CA: Jossey-Bass, 1974.

Bolman, Lee and Terrence Deal. *Modern Approaches to Understanding and Managing Organizations.* San Francisco, CA: Jossey-Bass, 1984.

Lewin, Kurt. *A Dynamic Theory of Personality.* New York: McGraw-Hill, 1935.

Zenger, John and Joseph Folkman. *The Extraordinary Leader: Turning Good Managers into Great Leaders.* New York: McGraw-Hill, 2002, 20.

CHAPTER 15

Moving the Client Forward: Designing Effective Actions

Frank Ball and Beth Bloomfield

As coaches of leaders, we are quite skilled and practiced in building rapport with our leader/clients, asking penetrating questions, listening deeply, and understanding our clients and the worlds in which they live. When we're with them, great things often happen. A new distinction is seen, a helpful insight is grasped, and the leader can often begin to write a new story for himself during the meeting. Powerful though those interactions may be, the question remains, "how do we keep the momentum moving forward between sessions?"

One of the most critical skills of a coach is the ability to design effective, purposeful activities for clients to engage in between coaching sessions. This is how the coach helps the client continue to move the action forward when the coach isn't there. If our work with our leader/clients is to be more than the sum of the individual meetings, we need to think beyond those conversations.

In this chapter we introduce a process to link the coach's assessment of the client's current state and coaching goals to specific activities to help close the gap between them. We also explore five specific types of activities coaches can ask their clients to engage in between coaching sessions, during the middle part of the coaching "Life Cycle." We define and describe each activity in turn, provide examples, and show how they produce the desired results. These activities are unique to coaching and distinguish the skillful coach from those whose impact is more limited.

In the "Life Cycle" of coaching every coaching engagement has a beginning, a middle, and an end (figure 15.1). If you think of the beginning only as contracting, intake, investigating, and rapport building, you'll miss an important opportunity to be purposeful and intentional in your coaching through design of an individual

Beginning		Middle	End
Up-front work	**Program design**	**The coaching itself**	**Closing**
Contracting • Duration • Frequency • Payment • Agreements • Other terms ***Rapport & Trust Building*** • "Intake" • The Story ***Investigating*** • Presenting issues • Assessment instruments • Interviews • Workplace observations	• Current state • Goals/Objectives • Grounded assessments • Format • Timeline • Conditioning • Methodologies	***During the Session:*** • Purposeful conversations • Immediate concerns • Exploring the story • Staying in the question • Models, tools, role-plays, etc. • Congruence of mind, body, emotions • Reviewing commitments • Results of insights; learnings • Feedback for coach and client • Recontracting/new agreements • Noticing & offering distinctions ***Between Sessions:*** • Inquiry • Self-observations • Practices • Exercises • Resources (books, poems, videos, etc.) • Structures of Support (day planners, exercise buddies, etc.)	• Pre/Postcoaching comparisons • Action plan • Next steps • Evaluation of program • Feedback for coach • Ritual/gifts

Figure 15.1 The flow of coaching

Source: ©Frank Ball & Beth Bloomfield

coaching program using coaching-specific activities. Why should you as a leadership coach be thinking in terms of a "program" for your leader/client? Working programmatically provides structure to the engagement, ties the coaching to measurable outcomes, and places coaching in a systems context—all important aspects of coaching leaders in organizations.

The Elements of Program Design

We can identify five key characteristics of a well-designed coaching program for a leader/client:

- *Purposefulness*: "Begin with the end in mind."
- *Rigor*: This makes possible purposeful conversations (versus merely interesting).
- *Impact*: Purposeful conversations are what give coaching its impact and distinguish it from other approaches to personal and professional development for leaders.

- *Consistency*: Through the rigor of good design, you achieve consistent results for the leader.
- *Breakthrough results*: Good design is the only way you can be sure of getting *breakthrough* out of "breakdown."

Program design is done together by coach and leader/client, in a process of "co-creation." Both work together to describe the leader's current state, using the information and insight derived from the up-front work of investigation and assessment (whether through means of formal assessment instruments or a more organic process of inquiry). As a coach, you help the leader see "the way things are," focusing especially on what's missing and what's getting in the way of the leader reaching his goals. The leader has the prerogative of describing his own desired end state, although the coach can help ensure that the goals are realistic and attainable, while at the same time big enough to stretch the leader and build his capacity for continuing growth and development.

Out of this work, the coach must formulate theories or working hypotheses for why the leader is who he is, why he behaves as he does, and how change might happen for him. These are actually "grounded assessments" of where the gaps are between current state and desired outcome. As the coach, you may choose to make these assessments together with the leader or keep them to yourself until later on in the coaching process, if you assess that the leader's tolerance for hearing potentially unwelcome news is low. In that case, part of your work will be to increase his capacity for receiving feedback, however unflattering to his ego. We should add that our preference is for direct communication with the leader/client from the beginning of the engagement; a key coaching competency is delivering feedback and well-grounded assessments in a way that is respectful, useful, and kind.

Up until this point, we have been working with the "what" of the individual coaching program design. Now we will move to the "how"—how are you, the coach, going to help the leader/client bridge the gaps? This is where the design of effective actions is integrated into the structure of the overall coaching program. Key elements of this part of the design include those that mainly involve your effort as the coach and those that mainly involve the leader's effort. The coach is responsible for determining the sequencing of coaching-specific activities—what's the order, what are the milestones—and for conditioning the client—is he "in shape" for coaching? If not, what actions will you request he take to get himself ready for the hard work ahead?

The leader, on the other hand, is in charge of his own learning style—what does he know about what works best for him, and how does he communicate that to the coach? He is in the best position to assess his own learning gradient—how quickly can he integrate change? How steep is the slope? In addition, both coach and leader/client should seek some early wins, to give them both a strong foundation to build on as the coaching progresses.

With all these elements in mind, it's up to the coach to plot a pathway, using coach-specific methodologies, including learning activities specific to coaching. It's good practice to share the roadmap with your client, and to invite his comment and reactions to it. That way, the coaching process becomes more transparent and the coaching program you have designed together becomes a touchstone that you can both return to periodically to gauge your progress along the path, and if necessary, to change your route. Remember the ultimate purpose of coaching is to build capacity for learning and self-generation in the client.

Designing Actions

At last! You're coaching! You have entered the middle phase of the coaching engagement, and it's time to put your program design to the test. And now, also, you are called upon to supplement your powerful coaching conversations with some powerful activities for the leader to use to continue and perhaps to accelerate his learning between sessions. During the program design process, you should have thought through the types of activities that you want to use, but the commitments you ask the leader to make—whether you call them "homework" or "fieldwork"—should be specific to the issues and concerns raised in the coaching itself, and so may be difficult to anticipate ahead of time.

For that reason, most leadership coaches maintain a "toolkit" of activities they can turn to and adapt to the particular needs of the individual leader/client at that point in his coaching. We categorize these activities, specific to the middle of coaching programs, into five basic types:

- Self-observations
- Practices
- Inquiries
- Exercises
- Structures of support

Self-observations

To the extent that leadership coaching is about helping the leader see differently so that he can then act differently, becoming able to observe oneself more skillfully is the first step leading to change (table 15.1). This enhanced ability to observe oneself is also the source of the leader's ability to self-correct and is the ultimate source

Table 15.1 Steps to create self-observations

1. Identify an opening or situation you want to know more about.
2. List questions on how you think, show up, and act in that situation.
3. Split yourself in halves: an observer and an actor.
4. In real life, have the observer watch the actor using one or more of the questions in step 2.
5. Record what you observe and learn. Look for patterns and trends.

of sustained excellent performance. Well-designed self-observations are a key tool coaches use to take the first step of creating insights. We define them as:

A precisely defined set of observations that a client performs over a period of time, whose purpose is to create self-awareness, provide grounded assessments for decision making, and build capacity for self-correction.

Self-observations can be focused on either the leader's interior landscape of thoughts and emotions or his exterior landscape of actions and results. For example, the leader might be asked to notice his thoughts and feelings when in certain situations. On the other hand, the leader could be asked to notice the volume of his voice, his rate of speech, posture, and gestures in certain situations. The intention is to focus the leader's attention on a place where he is not now focusing to bring new things into his awareness.

Shifting and increasing awareness is the first step leading to change. For example, if a client declares that he intends to lose weight this year and doesn't start to pay attention to what and how much he puts into his mouth differently than before, it's unlikely that he will lose weight. The new practice of dieting is reinforced through observation of himself in action (what and how much he eats). Through observing himself in action he develops the means to self-correct and self-manage in a way that supports the change he has declared he wants to call into being.

Details that contribute to the effectiveness of self-observations include specifying times or occasions when the observations are to be made. The leader/client will be asked to collect data over time. This is where the practice of journaling comes in; the two support each other. By keeping a record of his observations the leader will be able to discern patterns and trends in his own behavior and what prompts it. Over time the leader will be able to notice what works and what doesn't, and when he is effective and when he is not. Many of our leader/clients may have difficulty slowing down enough to self-observe.

Often the coach will ask the leader to engage in a practice of "not doing," such as meditation, to slow the leader down and support the self-observation.

Practices

To the extent that self-observation leads to insight and new understanding, the next coaching-specific activities that build on this learning are practices (table 15.2). They are focused on building the leader's ability to take effective actions through

Table 15.2 Steps to create practices

1. Gather data (observe).
2. Set a goal: What do you want to change, learn about, or deepen?
3. Create a practice to do often (at least daily).
4. Reflect periodically on what you're learning.
5. Self-correct—fine-tune the practice or create a new one.

embodying the learning self-observations and other activities described in this chapter produce. A practice is:

> A behavior that is performed iteratively with the intention of improving a quality or competence, and building automaticity and transparency in the client.

Practice doesn't make perfect. Practice makes permanent that which is practiced.

In addition to building new capacities for effective actions within our leader/ clients, practice can also be used to interrupt the action or cause a break in the leader's automaticity. For example, a leader who is working to include others more into his decision making may adopt a practice of asking "what do *you* think?" whenever a colleague presents a problem needing resolution. By stopping his automatic response to answer the question right away, the leader creates the possibility of a different outcome. When accompanied with a self-observation to notice when it is easy or difficult to engage in the practice, the leader can learn more about those factors that affect his ability to act with purposefulness and skillfulness. Practices and self-observations, then, support each other.

Often in the beginning of the coaching relationship the coach may ask the leader to begin one or more practices of self-care regardless of any other practices agreed upon. These contribute to the process of getting the leader into condition to be coached.

In contrast to self-observations that can focus on thoughts and emotions as well as actions and results, practices usually involve the domain of the body and have the leader doing something in the physical world. In a sense they can be thought of as the means through which learning is made permanent through embodiment of the learning. This is what happens when you learn any new skill—playing the piano, or tennis, or riding a bike—you can read or hear about it, you can watch it being done, but not until you practice it repeatedly do you build the muscle for it.

Inquiries

The capacity for reflective thought is a hallmark of an effective leader, yet in today's blur of events and activity, few of us have the opportunity to engage in it. We hear repeatedly from our executive clients that allowing themselves to pause for reflection is one of the great benefits of coaching. Part of our role as coaches is to help them make the space for reflection in their lives well past the conclusion of the coaching engagement.

Inquiries are the tools we use to open up the leader for reflective thought (table 15.3). We define an inquiry as:

> An investigation of values and beliefs; moods and emotions; behaviors and actions; connections and relationships; and social, cultural, and historical contexts, in order to build awareness and understanding of a client's situation and ultimately to build the client's capacity for self-correction and self-generation.

Table 15.3 Steps to create an inquiry

1. Identify an opening or situation you want to know more about.
2. List questions on how you and others show up, behave, and interact in that situation.
3. Observe and ask, "What's behind that?" (at least 3 times).
4. Record what you observe and learn. Look for patterns and trends.
5. Ask new questions.

Inquiries are questions coaches ask leaders to "sit with" between coaching sessions and often over an extended period. One of the key elements of an inquiry is that its purpose is not so much for the leader to find an answer to the question asked as it is to inhabit the question in a way that heightens understanding. In some ways asking a leader to "sit with the question" is like a coach using silence during a coaching session rather than speaking or asking. Much richness can arise when the space is afforded for that possibility.

It has been our experience that people lose all their curiosity about a thing (i.e., stop learning) when they think they have the answer. One key, we've found, to the effectiveness and impact of an inquiry is to ask the leader to avoid answering the question to permit new thoughts and alternative explanations to surface.

Exercises

We have noticed a fair amount of confusion among both our leadership coaching students and sometimes our executive clients about the use of the term "exercise" as distinct from self-observation or practice. To be clear, in the coaching context we view an exercise as having a specific meaning stemming from its function; an exercise is:

A focused activity, finite in scope, that a client performs with the purpose of gaining clarity or understanding, in preparation for (or in support of) a shift in the client's consciousness or behavior.

As distinct from practices, which are repeated over time, exercises generally tend to be one-off activities used to provide the client with new information or new understanding—clarity. Examples include written exercises such as the "Future Self" exercise described in *Co-Active Coaching: New Skills for Coaching People toward Success in Work and Life*[1] or a "Day in the Life" written exercise.

Structures of Support

Finally, we recognize one other category of activity, the creation or adoption of what we call a structure of support (table 15.4), defined as:

A mechanism, object, social construct, or person(s) that supports a client in putting new practices or behaviors in place.

Table 15.4   Creating a structure of support

- Who
- What
- When/how often
- Where
- How

Frequently, a structure of support builds in accountability for the leader in staying with new practices and behaviors. Examples might include calendars and planners, an exercise buddy or trainer, an assistant, or a traditional support group. Some would say that hiring a coach is a structure of support in itself!

Structures of support can be as simple as a post-it note on the computer screen to remind the leader to self-observe or a sign on the desk with "WAIT" written on it to remind him to ask "*Why Am I Talking?*" In our dieting example earlier in this chapter, attending weight watchers meetings could be a structure of support for the client.

A Few Other Considerations

It's always best when the leadership coach and client can cocreate the various activities the leader will commit to engage in between sessions. There will be occasions, though, when the leader will be so stuck in his story that he will not be able to imagine an exercise that will yield a new insight or build the capacity to act in new, more effective ways. The coach must be prepared to step in and design an activity, using one of the five methods presented here, to get the leader unstuck and moving forward with new eyes and new actions. Moreover, even if you aren't feeling particularly brilliant in the moment, you can always promise to research and send one along soon after the coaching session.

It's important to be clear here that we are not advocating the use of "tips and tools" in some sort of cookbook recipe for good and effective coaching for leaders. Absent a fundamental grasp of the distinctions of leadership coaching and some meaningful experience in their application to real leaders with real coachable issues, the kinds of coaching activities we describe here are little better than interesting diversions. Coaching is both science and art, and the skillful practitioner brings both to the design of coaching programs and actions that are unique for each individual being coached.

What's required is a thorough understanding of the mechanisms at work in each type of coaching activity, and a dash of inspiration that can come from virtually anywhere. Some of our favorite sources of inspiration, beyond the ubiquitous self-help and business books, include interview questions asked by thoughtful journalists, stories told in novels or films, metaphors suggested by poetry, and even games played by children. Lightness and wonder help set the stage for learning, and both should inform your design of coaching activities for your executive clients.

The five coaching-specific activities described earlier are often combined to great effect. For example, a new leader/client might be asked to complete the "Future Self" exercise described in *Co-Active Coaching: New Skills for Coaching People Toward Success in Work and Life*.[2] Based on the results of that exercise, the coach might assign a specific inquiry for the leader to sit with over time, collecting thoughts and insights using a journal (a structure of support.) Based on the insights gained through inquiry and journaling, the leader and coach might codesign a series of practices and self-observations through which the leader can build the capacity to take new, more effective actions and observe himself in action in a way that permits self-correction and thereby sustained excellent performance. Finally, structures of support can assist the leader in the journey from where and who they are now to where and who they aspire to become.

Something to consider is the gradient of the learning curve you are asking your client to climb. Your leader/client is already living a life full of other commitments, and anything you request he take on in support of his learning and growth will be competing for space in an already very full schedule. So one aspect of gradient is the quantity of the additional work we ask our executive clients to do between coaching sessions.

The second aspect of gradient is the degree of difficulty of the activities we're asking them to complete. For example, journaling or starting a practice of seated meditation may be very easy for some clients and very difficult for others. We must gauge our clients' receptivity and readiness to take on and be successful at those activities we assign them.

Likewise, it's important to pause periodically, perhaps at mutually agreed milestones in the coaching engagement, to recalibrate the program with the leader, to check your assessments about him, and if necessary, to revise your design or change your planned activities and methodologies.

Another consideration for the coach is to make sure that the activities you ask the leader to engage in address all domains of learning—the cognitive, the emotional, and the body. This is especially important if the client is dramatically underdeveloped in one or more of the domains. Big breakthroughs are possible if the coach has the courage to take the leader where he hasn't spent much time before. Sometimes it's also easier to work in the less familiar domains because the person is less well-defended there—his story that is keeping him stuck isn't as strongly entrenched there.

When asking leaders to engage in specified activities between coaching conversations, the coach is wise to have them complete the activities over an extended period before either adding more practices or changing them. In the case of self-observations, for example, their impact is much greater if the leader self-observes over an extended period to allow for trends and inconsistencies to emerge. Using a journal to capture those observations as they occur then provides a sound basis for insight, learning, and growth. Although insight can occur in a flash in "coaching time," deep change of the sort coaching seeks to bring about takes a long time and a lot of hard work to become permanent.

In a coaching relationship, growth and learning occur over time in a way that is cumulative. One of the roles of the leadership coach, in addition to designing and assigning great activities for the leader/client to engage in between sessions, is to insure progress and accountability.

Coaches often dedicate a specific portion of their coaching sessions to a check-in around the assignments since the last time they met with their client. Key aspects of the discussion include whether the assignment was done, what difficulty (ease) the leader experienced in completing the assignment, what outcomes the leader achieved, and what he learned about the topic, himself, or coaching. This conversation is where key learnings are identified, where the efficacy of assignments can be measured, where course corrections can be made, and where progress can be noticed and celebrated.

The coach and leader then have a sound basis to either drop, modify, or continue the assigned between-session work to continue the learning and growth experienced in the direction of the coaching goals agreed upon at the beginning of the relationship. This process is yet another way in which rigor is insured, and the leadership coaching relationship is purposeful and not merely interesting.

Notes

1. Whitworth, Laura, Henry Kimsey-House, and Phil Sandahl, *Co-Active Coaching: New Skills for Coaching People toward Success in Work and Life.* (Palo Alto, CA: Davies-Black, 1998), 216–221.
2. Ibid.

CHAPTER 16

Assessments for Insight, Learning, And Choice in Coaching

Sue E. McLeod

You've probably had the experience of coaching a leader when you were sure that how they saw themselves wasn't consistent with their behavior or what you believed was authentic for them. These people seem to be playing a role, or focus on their intentions—what they meant to do, what they were thinking at the time, or the story that they tell about themselves—rather than what actually happened. Assessments can play an important role in generating self-awareness in the leaders we coach, and provide information, beyond the leader's self-perceptions, that can be directly applied to their most challenging situations.

As coaches, we create opportunities for new insights that open the doors for improved performance and authentic leadership. Assessment data can open new ways of thinking or behaving, by bringing to light new information that the leader couldn't see before. It can also affirm what the leader already knows, but thought was hidden or invisible to others. It often provides a powerful mirror to allow the leader to say, "Yes, that's me" and to take more responsibility for their own behavior and how it impacts the people and results of their organizations.

We seem to expect that leaders will be unaware of their weaknesses and the negative impacts they have on others. I have seen this quite a bit in my experience. However, I'm always struck by the leaders who do not fully know their strengths and their natural gifts, or appreciate how their gifts help to make them successful. By giving an objective and neutral perspective, assessments can be powerful tools for "accentuating the positive" as well as "eliminating the negative."

What Are Assessments?

Assessments are, in general, information that assesses selected aspects of the leader's behavior, skills, performance, styles, or preferences. In this chapter, I'll refer to using the following types of assessments in coaching[1]:

- Self-assessments of personality and style assessments that indicate preferences for behaviors, thought patterns, attitudes, or approaches under normal or stress situations. I'll refer to the results of these assessments as preferences. I like that language because it implies choice and flexibility, which is what we're trying to engender in the leaders we coach.
- External assessments of behavior or results that use data from sources other than the leader, such as 360-degree assessments with data.

It's important to note that these assessments are just that—assessments. They are one view of the leader, from their own eyes or from the eyes of selected others, created at a particular point in time using a particular frame of reference. They are not "the truth," they are not the definition of the whole person, nor do they completely describe the past or predict the future. Given that perspective, I take the results seriously—they have meaning and are valuable—and hold them lightly, especially when using them to create new actions in the future.

From "Automatic" to Choice

In my coaching, I first want to understand the leader's "automatic" approach. "Automatic" is the way the leader reacts without advance planning or thinking. For example, as an intuitive type, my automatic response to new information is to ask, "Why is this important? What's new and different about this approach?" Someone with an automatic approach that is more analytical might ask, "Where's the proof that this will work? What's missing?" These are two very different responses to hearing new information.

Once we understand the "automatic," we start noticing whether it works or not, or, more specifically, *when* it works and *when* it doesn't. For example, my automatic response doesn't work well when the situation requires a critical eye for the details. The analytical approach may not work well when it's time to brainstorm creative, new approaches.

In situations where the automatic isn't working, the leader and I can turn our attention to new choices that might change the results.

Assessments are tools that can be used for each step of this process. They tell us about the leader's past and current behavior. They provide data about what the leader is doing well—what's working—and where they may have difficulties or challenges. They present this information in an objective and neutral way, taking out the judgments and negative (or positive) connotations that we associate with certain traits. Assessments also give leaders new insights into how they are seen by others. This can uncover the gap between their intentions and the impact they are really having. Finally, many assessments provide a well-researched conceptual model of human behavior that can be used to generate new options for action.

Self-assessment

There is a wide variety of self-assessments on the market today, many with strong research behind them. They measure many things—personality types, thinking style preference, values, leadership traits, critical thinking skills, emotional intelligence, body and energy patterns, behavior patterns, and so on. The most effective assessments will be the ones that you, as coach, can use effectively. This means you should be trained or well studied in the conceptual model, have practice interpreting the results and applying it in the coaching context of creating new awareness and new future behaviors.

The training and study in the assessments you use should prepare you to introduce the assessment and interpret the results with the leader. Here we focus on the coaching aspects—creating distinctions and insights and finding openings for new actions.

Insights for the Leaders

What insights can you create for your leaders with these self-assessments? First you can develop an understanding of their "automatic" responses or behaviors. Some assessments even include measures of responses to stress. In your coaching, explore the stories of how they see their preferences day to day. Can they distinguish their preferences from the set of possible preferences in the assessment? Can they describe and recognize the preferences of others? With your guidance, they can understand the distinctions of styles, types, or preferences in the conceptual model behind the assessment.

Another insight to create for the leader is how their automatic preferences translate to behavior. You want them to "see" their preferences in action, so they can recognize their behavior when it happens. For example, understanding how I process information gave me more insight into how I conducted meetings. My agenda follows my preference for information to be presented in a particular order. When others present information to me using their own preferences, different from mine, I find myself bored, disengaged, or frustrated because they didn't give me the "foundation" information that I wanted.

Finally, the ability to step out of their "automatic" to choose another response requires your leader to be able to think about a situation objectively before behaving. Use the assessment model to discuss some of the challenging situations they find themselves in. Ask what style is *appropriate* that might be very different from what they *want to* do. I have one leader who has a strong preference for creating new ideas, seeing the big picture, and being innovative. This doesn't work in some of the things he needs to do well to be successful, such as managing budgets or executing a structured decision-making process that is working well. Make the connection between his preference and the less-than-stellar results, and you have an opening for new action. By having your leader think about what's needed is a situation, then mapping their own preferences and behaviors against what's needed, you can help them see how their preferences impact their success.

Path to Understanding Others

The assessment that you use for the leader to understand herself can also help her understand others. Sometimes just the awareness that other styles exist and that people think and behave differently is an important thing for a leader to understand. Without that understanding, they can carry unstated expectations that others think, feel, and behave the same as the leader, with the resulting frustration when those expectations are not met.

I hear so many complaints about people who "should have" done something or used a different approach. I've found this reflects the leader's assumption that others would approach the situation the same way they would. Yet, most of us use our most comfortable styles when we approach our work. Our intention is to do our best, not to frustrate others by doing it a different way. For example, the person who seems to be sabotaging the new policy by repeatedly bringing up how people who are affected might feel during the change may just be asking that their preference for considering people and feelings be included in the decision making.

The assessment puts a neutral and objective picture of humanness on the table. Once you can see that someone is operating out of a preference for a different approach, the emotion can subside. Then it's easier to consider the other point of view, ask what the situation needs, and make a choice. In the earlier example, considering how people will feel is an important component of developing and communicating a policy change. Changing the perception of "sabotage" to "adding a valuable perspective" can make a tremendous difference in the success of the policy change, as well as smooth the relationship between the "saboteur" and the leader.

Here are the basic questions to ask your leader when coaching using a self-assessment:

1. How do you *want* to act, given your preferences?
2. What can you *expect* from others, given their preferences?
3. What's *needed* in this situation for the project, initiative, or task to be successful?
4. How *will* you act and what will you ask of others, to be successful?

External Assessments

External assessments provide a different view of the leader's behavior, impact, and results within the organization. This view is a valuable addition to the leader's self-perception. The external view gives both leader and coach more information about the impact of the leader's behavior on the people with whom they work most closely. These assessments can also give an organizational or leadership context for the coaching.

Three-hundred-sixty-degree assessments collect information from all sides of the leader—self, supervisor, direct reports, and peers. Some are even designed to get the perspectives of other key people with experience and insight into the leader including friends, family members, customers, and suppliers.

The Value of an Outside Perspective

It's important to remember that the inside perspective (from inside the leader) is just one perspective and is often clouded by the leader's knowledge of their intentions and their internal standards of behavior or performance. Their ability to gauge their impact on others depends on the level of awareness and the amount of time they spend reflecting on how others reacted. By gathering information from other people in the organization, the coach and leader discover how other people see the leader, what expectations they have, and how the leader is measuring up to those expectations. Hearing about performance and impact from outside also makes it more difficult for the leader to "hide" from the impact and implications. We all have the illusion that our mistakes and faults are overlooked—it's often an awakening for the leader to realize that everyone sees their weak points, in action! Alternatively, some leaders' performance doesn't measure up to their own incredibly high standards. It can be a relief to find that others are satisfied with their performance.

Getting multiple perspectives is also valuable. Each person's view of the leader is colored by their own filters and experiences of the world. By gathering data from multiple sources, the coach and leader will begin to see patterns in the feedback—what's consistent, what's different among the people asked. The areas where there are consistent messages are more difficult to ignore. As one of my leaders used to say—if one person calls you a horse, you can think about it; if three people call you a horse, you might consider buying a saddle.

Another advantage to multiple perspectives is insight into how the leader is perceived in different layers in the organization. Is this someone who "manages up," spending time and energy impressing the boss while ignoring direct reports? Or is the leader protective of direct reports to the detriment of building relationships with key peer organizations?

Types of Assessments

Three-hundred-sixty-degree assessments can be formal instruments developed and scored by companies who specialize in studying and assessing leadership behavior. These can be "off-the-shelf," that is, commercially available for use in any organization, or they can be custom designed for an organization, often based on a model of competencies that the organization deems are necessary for success. Like the self-assessments, I recommend that you be well-versed in these formal assessments before using them in your coaching.

If a formal assessment isn't available, or doesn't seem appropriate with the leader you are coaching, you can offer to collect 360-degree feedback using a set of structured interviews. This method allows you to tailor the information you collect to the specifics of the leader's situation. You're also likely to get some interesting insights through these conversations that don't usually come out of the more formal instruments. For example, in one set of interviews, I heard about the leader's behavior that was causing difficulties for her staff, but they also talked about their perceptions of her attitude toward them. This made for a much richer conversation, and more impactful coaching, because these attitudes were affecting her ability to lead, much more than the actual behaviors.

Interviewing the people who work with your leader has some additional benefits. First, it lets these people know that your leader is working with a coach and working to improve their performance and results. A leader who models self-development and introspection can create an environment others will do the same. Second, it lets people know what areas your leader is focused on and gives them the opportunity to suggest additional areas for improvement. This can generate a feeling of respect and empowerment among these people, as they are being asked to provide valuable information that may impact the leader and the organization. Third, it may cause them to reflect on their own performance. Just by interviewing people about the organization's performance, there is an opening created for others to take action because they see that the leader is supportive of changed behavior.

Work with your leader to prepare for the interview or the survey. Discuss the areas where they want to focus and what information would be helpful. Work together to generate open-ended questions that explore how the leader is perceived, what actual behaviors are noticed, and the impact the leader is having—positive and negative.

Some basic questions you can ask are:

- What does this leader need to do well to be successful in this position and to get to the next level?
- What strengths does this leader demonstrate that helps them to be successful?
- What would you like to see this leader do differently? Do more of? Do less of?

After the prepared interview questions, I ask "What haven't I asked that is important for this leader to know?" I've often seen leaders get the most value from these "free form" comments (these are often included in the formal 360-degree survey instruments, too). For example, one leader knew that she was working too hard and not taking care of her physical health, and, she thought those sacrifices were important to help her team succeed. It was only when she read one of these comments that she realized how concerned her employees were about her health. They liked working for her and were worried that she would leave because of burnout or some other effect of being overworked. Once she saw the negative impact of her "sacrifices" on her employees, she was willing to take some time off of work for self-care.

When the interviews are complete, you will need to generate a report of findings that conveys the feedback in a neutral and objective way and preserves the confidentiality of the people who were interviewed. Look for themes and patterns, and specific examples to ground the feedback (especially if you think it will be difficult to hear). Some categories I've used include:

- People describe you as…followed by a list of adjectives that I heard in the interview
- What's expected of you in this position and how to get to the next level?
- Strengths people see
- What people would like to see more of in the future?

By keeping it simple and focused on what's needed for them to achieve their development goals, it makes the messages more meaningful and useful for the coaching to come.

Reviewing the Data

Once the data has been collected, the coach and leader should each have the opportunity to review the information before discussing it. There are some good questions to pose to the leader for them to consider while they review the data, such as:

- What surprises you about this data?
- What patterns do you see?
- Where are your strengths?
- What's most important to address now?

The coach, too, needs to approach the data with some specific questions—and be open to discovering new insights that the data may show. Here are some areas that I look for:

- Consistent messages—from within groups or across groups of people who completed the assessment.
- Conflicting message—do different groups see the leader differently?
- Outliers—if data about individual responses are available, look for the "spread" of responses. Some very high and some very low scores within groups could indicate "in group/out group" distinctions held by the leader.
- Leader's self-perceptions relative to others' perceptions—does the leader consistently over or under rate themselves?
- Clear strengths—what are the areas where everyone (even the leader) sees they have strengths? These are areas that you may want the leader to take full advantage of and "claim" as their own.
- Clear blind spots—similarly, areas that everyone (including the leader) sees as a weakness can point to something the leader may want to address, with the caveat that they should understand the impact of that weakness and consider options for filling that gap in their leadership.

The coach's role is not to draw any conclusions, but to look for new questions to pose to the leader, new avenues to explore, and new insights into the working relationships and environment that can help to focus the leader on how to be more successful.

Most important, however, is to note the areas where you are curious about something or where your intuition tells you there is something interesting to explore with the leader. One leader I worked with had very strong results overall and just a few of his direct reports who said that he didn't listen to them. My intuition told me this was a place to explore, although I had no idea why. When I brought it up, the leader denied that he exhibited this behavior. He always listened to everyone. As he went on protesting, I pointed out that he wasn't listening to me or to what the data (his direct reports) were telling him. He protested some more, and we dropped the subject. In our next session, he told me that I had really hit on something. He didn't *really* listen and he did keep people at a distance and, from there, we began the exploration of why and what were the impacts on his staff and his leadership, and how he might want to change in the future.

In your conversations with the leader about the feedback, it's important to remember your job as coach. You are not expected to have answers, but to create opportunities for self-exploration, learning, and action in the areas that are the most relevant for the leader.

Let them know that you've looked at and thought about the data. Give them an overview of what you saw. Since most of my leaders focus on the negatives, I start with the positives, telling them where I see their strengths, affirming where others see them as performing well. I give them my overall sense of their leadership. "You are a leader who sets clear direction and holds people to high standards. You're tough and your boss is satisfied with your business results."

Then I ask them for their perceptions and for what they've learned by looking at the data. I ask questions about where I'm curious. "You have two bosses who rate you very differently. What's going on?" The leader has much more insight into the working environment than I do, so I avoid drawing any conclusions before I hear their story about the data.

Then I ask, "What's most important to focus on here?" Moreover, we follow that path. Connecting the feedback to what's most important to the leader at this time— maybe a particularly challenging project or relationship—will give the feedback life beyond the feedback session. I give myself permission to come back to items that I think they are avoiding and that I believe are important. One leader, for example, again had strong scores and one peer score that was consistently lower than the others. When I first pointed this out and asked about it, he admitted that there was one peer with whom he had a very strained relationship. He wasn't willing to look at changing it; he was OK with the way it was. When that relationship came up again in another coaching session, I came back to the feedback and asked about the impact of this strained relationship on his direct reports. How did it affect their ability to do their jobs? What kind of example was he setting about collaboration within the company? After looking at these impacts he saw the importance of improving this relationship and added that to his action plan.

Goal Setting and Action Planning

In leadership coaching, we want our leaders to be moving toward specific results. The 360-degree data can give very specific areas for goal setting. By analyzing the feedback and connecting it to real situations the leader is facing, you can create specific goals for changing behavior and perceptions. The assessment itself can become a mechanism for evaluating results if the assessment can be repeated in six–twelve months.

None of us can change too many things at one time. I ask leaders to choose no more than three areas of focus for their action plan based on the feedback. I ask that they be relevant to their main responsibilities, the organization's goals, or the leader's personal goals. We don't just focus on improving areas where they are weak. I also ask them to look at areas where they can use their strengths more prominently.

The action steps can be "doing" focused, for example "hold meetings with your staff more regularly, particularly the ones who are feeling out of the loop." They can be "being" focused, for example "be present when your direct reports come to your office to talk with you. Give them your full attention so they feel heard and appreciated." They can focus on the leader's inner thoughts and attitudes, for example "turn off the inner critic for a week, and watch the impact you are really having on your people. Learn to appreciate the 'good enough' rather than constantly striving for perfection."

Give your leaders every opportunity to embrace what the assessment data says and be successful at making the shifts and changes that will help them be successful. Understand that receiving feedback is often difficult and our natural tendency is to explain it away, defend ourselves, and look for reasons to maintain the status quo. Be gentle and understanding as you work with this feedback. Moreover, be challenging and hold firm to the belief that you are this leader's coach because they want to change.

Note

1. There are other types of assessments—including tests of skills and abilities, external assessments from just direct reports, and others. The approach to using all of these tools is similar. I focus on these types here to stay focused on the coaching, rather than the assessments themselves.

CHAPTER 17

Coaching and Leading as Stewards for Sustainability

Lloyd Raines

Coaching, like leading, lends itself to endless innovations and evolution. The evolution of leadership has covered a lot of territory—from Theory X, Theory Y, situational, values-driven, emotionally intelligent, and Level V leadership, among others. Likewise, coaching has evolved over time, including performance-based, behavioral, cognitive, systems thinking, neuro-linguistics, emotional intelligence, somatic, and holistic coaching, to name a few prominent ones. One of the beauties of evolutionary biology is that in any of its forms it builds on what is, innovates, experiments, and evolves. It's nature's gift to life—continual awareness, feedback, and learning.

I see in the progression of coaching and leadership a parallel theme. Each in its own way is about stewardship and sustainability. What coaches and leaders do is steward vital resources. To be a steward is to care for and cultivate the things that matter in life and work. What we are here to do with our lives is to be stewards of that which we are given—whether it be as responsible stewards of our bodies, emotions, minds, spirits, families, communities, nations, global human community, wildlife, domesticated critters, or natural resources. When we steward these domains well, we act not only from a sense of self-interest, but also from an *enlightened self-interest*—holding the long view—for individual sustainability as we live nested within and inseparable from the health and well-being of larger life-supporting systems.

Stewardship is a *mental model*: an orientation held toward work and life. It assumes care for the integrity of social life that includes working to ensure dignity, health, mutual accountability, and fair opportunities (including access, development, and rewards). In doing so, lives are nourished in ways that support our resilience and sustainability within the broader world. *Stewardship* is a basic life orientation, and *sustainability* is its goal. In adopting this mental model in my coaching, I've noticed shifts in the ways I observe, listen, and engage in inquiry with leaders. I now see any aspect of coaching as an element or factor in the leader's overall sustainability—as a person, leader, and organizational contributor.

Common sense and self-interest call us to care for what matters in life, and more and more we're seeing how global factors affect local conditions (human and financial costs of war, terrorism, energy prices, pollution, global warming, etc.). When we, as coaches and leaders, connect the local and global, the part and the whole, then our self-interest matures into an enlightened self-interest, bringing us into conversations that are bigger than the personal and organizational. Grasping the interconnectedness of humans, and the open-loop systems of nations and nature, we can engage in the challenges of our times.

Since the late 1990s, books such as *Natural Capitalism* (Hawkins, Lovins, and Lovins), *The Natural Step for Business* (Nattrass and Altomare), *Biomimicry: Innovation Inspired by Nature* (Benyus), *Green to Gold: How Smart Companies Use Environmental Strategy to Innovate, Create Value, and Build Competitive Advantage* (Esty and Winston), and *State of the World 2006* (Worldwatch Institute) have provided business and government leaders with the trends, statistics, guiding principles, and new conceptual maps needed to address the collision path between our economies and the sustainability of the natural world. These principles and maps are familiar to coaches who have studied Meg Wheatley, Peter Senge, Joe Jaworski, Fritjof Capra, E.O. Wilson, and Ellen Sahtouris. Holistic systems thinkers address the broader context of organizational life and leadership, drawing from insights embedded in nature and articulated through chaos and complexity theories.[1]

Just as coaches are evolving toward a more holistic approach, leaders too have moved beyond bottom-line considerations and command and control leadership. Many well-known corporate leaders are stepping forward in the absence of political leadership and assuming stewardship responsibilities that go well beyond compliance with compliance regulations and environmental law. Scores of major companies, including Nike, 3M, GE, Starbucks, and Wal-Mart are moving to double or triple bottom-line (financial, social, and environmental) integrated strategies. They see their enlightened self-interest in care that goes beyond maximizing quarterly shareholder returns.[2]

In coaching and leading, *stewardship* is an active application of love and care through the ways we choose to work and live. Consider the following four interdependent dimensions of stewardship that can be explored with leaders:

- Care for one's self
- Care for others
- Care for work
- Care for nature

Taken together, these four stewardship relationships (figure 17.1) comprise a basic infrastructure of life, offering a simple, yet robust lens for integral coaching.

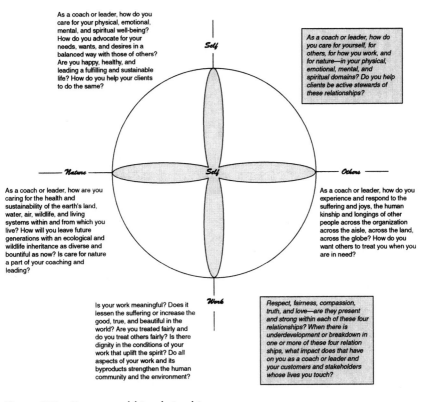

As a coach or leader, how do you care for your physical, emotional, mental, and spiritual well-being? How do you advocate for your needs, wants, and desires in a balanced way with those of others? Are you happy, healthy, and leading a fulfilling and sustainable life? How do you help your clients to do the same?

As a coach or leader, how do you care for yourself, for others, for how you work, and for nature—in your physical, emotional, mental, and spiritual domains? Do you help clients be active stewards of these relationships?

As a coach or leader, how are you caring for the health and sustainability of the earth's land, water, air, wildlife, and living systems within and from which you live? How will you leave future generations with an ecological and wildlife inheritance as diverse and bountiful as now? Is care for nature a part of your coaching and leading?

As a coach or leader, how do you experience and respond to the suffering and joys, the human kinship and longings of other people across the organization across the aisle, across the land, across the globe? How do you want others to treat you when you are in need?

Is your work meaningful? Does it lessen the suffering or increase the good, true, and beautiful in the world? Are you treated fairly and do you treat others fairly? Is there dignity in the conditions of your work that uplift the spirit? Do all aspects of your work and its byproducts strengthen the human community and the environment?

Respect, fairness, compassion, truth, and love—are they present and strong within each of these four relationships? When there is underdevelopment or breakdown in one or more of these four relationships, what impact does that have on you as a coach or leader and your customers and stakeholders whose lives you touch?

Figure 17.1 Four stewardship relationships

Source: © Lloyd Raines, 2004+

Care for One's Self

In the first few sessions of coaching with a new leader, I'm eager to learn about her relationship with herself. Leaders, by and large, are hard drivers—of themselves and others. They tend to work long hours, put the company first, and overlook some basic awareness around self-care. For me, coaching from a holistic perspective begins with the presenting issues while listening and observing to discern connections and disconnections in the leader's awareness. This is a process of raising the leader's awareness about what matters—from the inside out, around what impacts their effectiveness, health, and well-being, and what they do that impacts the effectiveness, health, and well-being of others.

Whatever is being expressed through a leader's language, body, emotions, and spirit is a window through which we begin to learn about his world. Being in the interior of many leaders' worlds is a chance to notice similarities. After a while, coaches see a kind of universality, with leaders having largely similar needs, wants, desires, and challenges. What leaders (and people) have in common, in other words, is much greater than the differences. The wiring of that common anatomy, and the endless variations it spawns, informs the holistic approach to coaching.

For many leaders, their overall health is not an issue until it is. In my initial sessions with a new client I do a comprehensive assessment of their self-care: When is the last time you had a full physical and dental check-up? What is your diet like? How much sleep are you getting? On average how many hours a week are you putting in at work or on work? How are your caffeine and alcohol intake? What is your exercise regimen? What time of the day are you most alert and do you do your best work? How is your general state of mind? How would you describe your mental health? What mood do you find you are in most often? What emotions seem to be the most challenging for you to handle? Are you finding a deeper sense of meaning in your work?

Initially, leaders are caught off-guard by some of these questions, yet soon begin to see the obvious connections between their physical, emotional, mental, and spiritual well-being and their overall leadership fitness. They see where their self-care (or the lack thereof) either adds or drains energy from their *being*, affecting in turn their capacity for *doing* the work of leadership. Each question draws their awareness and focus to the *ecology* of their energy—where and when their energy is high and low, and what variables affect their resilience and sustainability.

To the leader I may ask, How might your energy level, nutrition, and caffeine intake affect your moods and the resilience of your emotions? How does your physical wellness affect your relationship with your family and social relationships? Over the long haul, is your self-care balanced in a way that enables you to sustain in contributing value and investing energy in the work and relationships that most matter?

By asking questions that evoke reflection on the connections between body, emotions, mind, spirit, and relationships with others, leaders can experiment with self-observations or behavioral practices that bring about slight or major shifts in their awareness and self-care. Those shifts can have immediate benefits for his health and well-being. Benefits also include an enhanced resilience when in difficult, tense situations at work and home. If exploring connections and disconnections stopped at the personal level, however, it would be an inadequate picture of the leader's reality.

A leader's care for self includes taking care not only of her physical, emotional, mental, and spiritual health, but also her important relationships—the ones that nurture her health and well-being in her private and professional spheres. Care for oneself shares a permeable boundary with care for others. Reciprocity and mutuality in our relationships help balance and make life meaningful, cultivate empathy and compassion, and transform transactional life into intimate life. This mutual accountability is positive, not a burden.

Self-actualization is in reality inextricably tied to social-realization. Self-realization without social realization warps the ego, making it difficult to manage and self-correct around one's weaknesses and personality shadows. The brilliant contributor who lacks empathy or is unable to listen to or collaborate with others is not likely to sustain over time in an organization, or if he does, will force others to leave in his wake.

Care for Others

Beyond the leader's care for family and friends is her relationship with her organization's employees and stakeholders. Those stakeholders include internal and external customers and stakeholders affected by the organization's actions.

To gain insights into the leader's thinking around care for others, I might ask, Are your decisions and those of your organization respecting the rights and interests of your less visible, less powerful stakeholders? What are the ways you reach out and strategically build trust and confidence with internal customers and stakeholders? Does your organization reflect and benefit from a diverse population? Does your organization help develop leaders at all levels? Do leaders solicit the ideas and feedback of others? Do you actively listen to what is said and dialogue to understand how to strengthen your relationships? Is it safe for employees to speak the truth to power? How do you gauge the morale and mood of your organization's members? Are employees inspired and engaged by the company's vision?

Individual behaviors are nested in and interdependent with many other factors. In a sense, every aspect of the leader is an interdependent system or ecology: their mind, body, emotions, and spirit—all internally and symbiotically connected while being externally dependent on nature's interlocking systems of air, water, land, resources, and wildlife. Our survival and well-being are directly, inextricably tied to our care for nature. Our health and nature's health are one and the same. Humans are sustainable only if nature is sustainable.

Industry leaders at Patagonia, The Body Shop, and UPS have integrated sustainability and social well-being into their core values, strategic plans, and goals. They each integrate financial, social, and environmental health into their core values and strategic efforts. They conduct their businesses with care for the quality of life of people locally and in other countries (their suppliers), their cultures, and their environments. Besides returning a healthy profit to their shareholders, these companies also have engaged their employees' spirits, their sense of being involved with contributing to a better world.[3] The results are obvious—high morale, low turnover, and superior customer service.

As coaches and leaders, some of what we care about is obvious to us, although other things we care about are more hidden and hard to see. We take for granted certain conditions of life that just seem to be "given," although they are not: our health, family, a sustainable environment, a viable economy, our jobs, supportive social relationships, and dignified work.

The flux and flow of life, and coaching, is alive in the jitterbug of polarities between creation and destruction, emergence and dissipation, stability and change, abundance and scarcity, light and shadow, and love and fear. That dynamism also reflects the evolution of the stories we live—how we react to life and fashion the story of who we are as individuals, how we relate to and work with others, the nature of our contributions in our communities, the mood we absorb and feed into our subcultures and into the broader mainstream culture.

A leader I coached several years ago asked me to work with him on developing leadership presence. For most coaches, that desire invites a sustained look at the internal attunement of himself *with* himself (in physical, emotional, mental, and spiritual ways), and then the outward attunement of his connections and affiliations with others. Conducting brief 360-degree feedback sessions with 5 to 10 stakeholders provides data for grounding the coaching conversation and illuminating blind spots.

In addition, I might probe his range of interior experiences when meeting with subordinates, peers, supervisors, and clients. "What are your assumptions about authority, power, and how people are treated?" "Do your feelings, thoughts, and motivations shift substantially when interacting with people from different levels within the organization?" "How do you like to be treated by someone with more organizational authority than you?...with less authority than you?" "What do those different states of awareness and intention have to say to you about your *presence?*" "Which *way of being* is the real you?" "In your best self, who are you?" "Who do you strive to be?" "In your stressed-out self, who are you?" "When do you feel most connected with others and passionate about your work?" "When do you seem to be in a "flow" state—working effortlessly, extremely efficiently, joyfully?"

When a leader is attuned with her internal ecologies, and those of others, she is more likely to be experienced by others as centered, trustworthy, humble, curious, and nonjudgmental. These are simple elements of congruent presence that attract the attention and commitment of followers.

Care for Nature

From the crow's nest, at the highest and broadest levels, we are stewards for the health and well-being of nature. In the last decade, a group of early adopter companies has been designing "green" (environmentally sustainable) prototype organizations. The coaching profession is just beginning to get its legs under it regarding global human and ecological systems as being integral to coaching leaders. And the coaching profession is by no means alone in this gap. The human resource profession and leadership development fields generally have been almost silent on pragmatic ways of connecting from personal awareness to global awareness as late as the end of 2006. At best, coaches, human resource, and organizational development professionals are privately aware of trends and tipping points regarding the gap between the rich and poor, global warming, the deterioration of the environment, the extinction of species in the wilds, and pollution. Yet, for the most part, we do not know what to do with that information or how to incorporate it into our work. These pressing moral challenges in the larger arena are often alien to our workplace conversations. Our world is fragmented to the point that we see these problems as externalities to daily work, the responsibilities of government agencies, social services, nonprofits, and volunteer organizations.

At the same time, there are a growing number of companies and public sector agencies that are creating a comprehensive, green approach. They have found ways to tap into the natural symbiosis of financial, social, and environmental drivers, and they have *chosen* to go beyond the single bottom line to a triple bottom-line commitment. Well-known companies such as 3M, Unilever, Shell, Proctor & Gamble, and a growing number of others have designed for synergy and discovered ways to combine the best for people, prosperity, and the planet.[4] As one example, the

U.S. Environmental Protection Agency created the "3P" focus—people, prosperity, and planet—to spur innovations that support sustainability in the developed and underdeveloped world.[5]

Moreover, coaches have the choice of actively partnering inside that unfolding story or not. This is the great challenge of our era, the alignment of human activities to be in harmony with the natural world.

Leadership coaches, like leaders, choose our particular frames of reference and the range of expressions and connections we look and listen for. Where once coaching was primarily linguistically, psychologically, and behaviorally based, it has expanded in perspective to include the emotions, somatics, and spirit. In addition, of course, it will continue to evolve. From a long-term perspective, "green coaching" may be inevitable. Just as the shift to a green perspective in the business world seems to be approaching a tipping point, bringing sustainability conversations into the business mainstream, something similar will likely happen with leadership coaching. A worldview that was broken into fragments by the scientific and industrial revolutions will regain its wholeness.

Care for Work

We live and work in global interdependence—dressing in clothes made in China, Pakistan, the Philippines; eating breakfast, fruits, and drinking coffee imported from South America; driving to work in our internationally made cars with foreign oil and gas. Once there, we power up our computers made with parts produced worldwide, and we "google" into the global brain for instant information. Since we anchor ourselves in the social world through work and the sharing of products and services produced worldwide, our relationship to work is also a fundamental dimension of stewardship.

When coaches and leaders are attentive stewards at work, we reinforce values of dignity, meaning, and community while also benefiting prosperity and the planet. Those stewardship values inform and guide leaders throughout an organization in strategically using and deploying the organization's resources. For many, work has a hollow ring, knowing at a spiritual level that profits at any cost and growth for itself does not strike a noble chord. It lacks care for the world. A holistic approach to coaching leaders is curious about the leader's sense of fulfillment, dignity, health, and well-being in relation to the work they do, as well as how they affect others.

For leaders, coaches can press them with direct questions that go to their core: "Are you proud of what you are doing?" "In the face of the challenges of the day, are you proud of your organization's vision and stance in the world?" "Does it inspire you?" "Do you feel that your work is making a difference in the quality of life in the world?"

A leader can be attuned with themselves, with others, and with nature—yet, if she is not also attuned with the work she is doing she will not be fully engaged. Because leaders (like people anywhere) are designed for continual growth, work that once was engaging and fully satisfying may be less so after two or three years. Old questions need new answers as leaders continue to scan the horizon of their own lives and of the larger world around them for motivation and meaning. It is common for leaders reaching their high-water marks to look for opportunities that they *really believe in*. Holistic coaching probes a leader's opportunities for introducing into their own leadership work and organization new ideas, principles, and values that could make a difference in the meaningfulness of the work *right now*.

Here's an example of how holistic leadership transformation can happen. At Interface, a billion dollar global company, their CEO Ray Anderson read Paul Hawken's book, *The Ecology of Commerce: A Declaration of Sustainability*, and had an epiphany. Virtually overnight, he became convinced that his company's way of working and producing carpet and office supplies had to change. He immediately committed to transforming his company's oil-based carpet production into completely natural, recyclable carpets. Further, he engaged his entire company of employees in an education around sustainability that was extraordinary.[6]

When Anderson and his employees committed to sustainability goals together, they captured a kind of "lightning in a bottle." Employees love working there because they know they're working for a better world every day—and it inspires them. Leaders who capture a vision that inspires the dedication of their workforce garner the advantage of intrinsic employee motivation along with tapping their collective intelligence. The concepts of stewardship and sustainability have the potential to engage deeper levels of commitment, innovation, and productivity at all levels of organizational life.

When coaches are aware of these cutting edge movements in marketplace and leadership development, coaching conversations can explore more expansive possibilities. By probing, inquiring, and provoking new ways of observing what's possible, or by introducing an article or book at the right moment, coaches can help fundamentally shift a leader's core mental model.

Holistic Coaching and Moral Development

For leaders, leadership coaching is an invitation for *growth by design*. In the ways coaches hold nonjudgmental safe space, listen, inquire, challenge, and trust, we enable leaders to coax from themselves their human potential, wisdom, and courage, *and, in turn, to help them understand how to cultivate that in others*.

Like any profession, coaching is constantly evolving—growing in ways to awaken more breadth and depth in leaders and ourselves—to act responsibly through our actions with a growing moral sensibility. This process moves developmentally upward, in moral and spiritual terms, through stages. In my coaching conversations with leaders, I initially use a three-stage model developed by Carol Gilligan that clients find easily accessible and useful.[7]

At the *first moral level (preconventional)*, we encounter behavior that is *self-interested and selfish*. This looks out for Number One, with little concern for what it means for others. "I am the center of the universe, and I act accordingly."

The *second moral level (conventional)* encounters behavior that expresses *care*. When my circle of concern expands, I see my self-interest as being directly tied up with the self-interests of others in my close-in tribes (based on some particular likeness, belief, or affiliation). "We're in this together—what helps you helps me. The group can count on me and I can count on the group for support." This tribe has an insular feel, with members identifying closely with tribal members and differently with those not of the tribe.

At the *third moral level (postconventional)*, I experience interconnections with people everywhere and with nature and its life forms. This is expressed by behaviors that spring from a sense of *universal or global care*. At this level, the entire global community and ecology are seen in an "I-Thou" relationship. "I'm part of everything and everyone and they are an integral part of me." This stage acknowledges and behaves as if people anywhere are part of one tribe, inseparable, experiencing the joys and suffering of others as akin to their own. *"I hold reverence for and an active stewardship with the ecological commons and the global human community."*

Once I've introduced Gilligan's basic developmental distinctions to a leader, it becomes easier to introduce and contextualize other readings on moral developmental stages. By massaging the linkages between personal self-interest, care for one's community, and global concern, holistic coaching helps stretch boundaries of awareness that may take root immediately or may incubate for many months before being ready to germinate.

Bearing Witness

When coaching, the concept of *bearing witness* entails holding active awareness of the current conditions of joy and sorrow, well-being and suffering, and of stakeholders near and far. I can bear witness to the pain, confusion, and suffering as well as the joy, love, and peacefulness of the leader I'm with. At the same time I can bear witness to what I know is going on in the daily lives of people in other parts of the organization, and at an appropriate moment, introduce that broader awareness to the person in front of me. In addition, at other moments, I may bear witness to the impact of business actions or inactions on the environment, on suppliers or the environment upstream, or consumers and nature downstream.

As leadership coaches, we make choices about the breadth of our frameworks or perspectives, and the developmental levels from which we coach through our listening, distinctions, questions, and provocations. We may coach and bear witness from a level that begins and ends with the leader's *self-interest* (and the coach's self interest, as well). Alternatively, we may coach and bear witness from a perspective of *care* for the leader and their organization's members and customers. Or we may coach and bear witness from a perspective of *global care* for the health and well-being of the global community.

What a holistic framework provides for leadership coaches and leadership coaching is a way to see the actual wholeness of the playing field we enter every time we engage in coaching relationships. By holding a framework that sees the leader within a much broader context, we can be more attentive, careful, and caring about what we listen for and inquire about with leaders. It enables us to have a balanced awareness and approach to supporting the broadest and deepest personal flourishing of a leader in service to the responsibilities and opportunities that accompany their position and ours.

Notes

1. The books, authors, and thinkers referenced in this paragraph are listed, along with some of their seminal works, in the following bibliography.
2. Esty and Winston, *Green to Gold,* 7–29.
3. Anderson, *Mid-Course Correction,* 149–181.
4. See note 2 above, 25, 126, 150–156, 229–233, 314.
5. U.S. Environmental Protection Agency, "P3: People, Prosperity and the Planet Student Design Competition for Sustainability," http://es.epa.gov/ncer/p3/fact_sheet.html (accessed November 13, 2007).
6. See note 4 above, 43–61, 139–181.
7. K. Wilber, *Integral Psychology* (Boston: Shambala, 2000) 45–208.

Bibliography

Anderson, Ray. *Mid-Course Correction.* White River Junction, VT: Chelsea Green, 1998.

Benyus, J. *Biomimicry: Innovation Inspired by Nature.* New York: Perennial, 1997.

Capra, F. *The Hidden Connections (Integrating the Biological, Cognitive, and Social Dimensions of Life into a Science of Sustainability).* New York: Doubleday, 2002.

Cook-Greuter, S. "Making the Case for a Developmental Perspective." *Industrial and Commercial Training* 36, no. 7 (2004): 275–281.

Diamond, J. *Collapse: How Societies Choose to Fail or Succeed.* New York: Penguin Books, 2005.

Esty, Daniel C. and Andrew S. Winston. *Green to Gold: How Smart Companies Use Environmental Strategy to Innovate, Create Value, and Build Competitive Advantage.* New Haven, CT: Yale University Press, 2006.

Gilligan, Carol. *In a Different Voice.* Cambridge, MA: Harvard University Press, 1982.

Hawken, P. *The Ecology of Commerce: A Declaration of Sustainability.* New York: HarperBusiness, 1993.

Hawken, P., A. Lovins, and L. Lovins. "A Roadmap for Natural Capitalism." *Harvard Business Review* (May–June 1999).

———. *Natural Capitalism.* New York: Little, Brown and Company, 1999.

HM Treasury. *Stern Review Report on the Economics of Climate Change.* 2006. http://www.hm-treasury.gov.uk/independent_reviews/stern_review_economics_climate_change/stern_review_report.cfm.

Intergovernmental Panel on Climate Change, Climate Change. 2007. http://www.ipcc.ch/

Jaworski, J. *Synchronicity (The Inner Path of Leadership).* San Francisco, CA: Barrett-Koehler, 1996.

Kegan, R. *In Over Our Heads: The Mental Demands of Modern Life.* Cambridge, MA: Harvard University Press, 1994.

Kohlberg, L. *The Philosophy of Moral Development.* San Francisco, CA: Harper & Row, 1976.

Nattrass, B. and Altomare, M. *The Natural Step for Business.* Gabriola Island, British Columbia: New Society, 1999.

Sahtouris, E. (Summer 2005). "The Biology of Business: New Laws of Nature Reveal a Better Way for Business." *VIA Journal* 3, no. 1 (2005). http://via-visioninaction.org/Sahtouris_BiologyOfBusiness-full_version.pdf

Senge, P. *The Fifth Discipline: The Art and Practice of the Learning Organization.* New York: Currency Doubleday, 1990.

Wheatley, M. *Leadership and the New Science.* San Francisco, CA: Barrett-Koehler, 1992.

Wilson, E.O. *Consilience (The Unity of Knowledge).* New York: Alfred A. Knopf, 1998.

Worldwatch Institute. *State of the World 2006.* New York: W.W. Norton, 2006.

CHAPTER 18

The Thinking Path

Alexander Caillet

This chapter presents a framework called the Thinking Path that has proved useful in leadership coaching. The key idea behind the Thinking Path is that people's conscious and unconscious thought processes (their Thinking) generate emotional/physical states (their Feelings) that in turn drive behaviors (their Actions) that produce outcomes (their Results). Figure 18.1 illustrates the Thinking Path framework.

Coaching with the Thinking Path can yield three outcomes:

1. Clients may recognize that their thinking is linked to their feelings, and that their thinking and feelings are linked to their actions and results.
2. Clients may take responsibility for their actions and the results they produce.
3. Clients may learn to gain more control over their actions and results by intentionally shifting their thinking and their feelings.

This chapter describes the Thinking Path, its theoretical underpinnings, a few case examples, and a set of useable exercises.

Several questions inspired the creation of the Thinking Path:

- How do human beings change?
- What causes sustained change in human beings?
- Why do some individuals succeed in changing their actions and results, and why do others fail?

As a leadership coach, I have always been committed to helping my clients sustain positive change in their behaviors and results. Therefore, I needed to answer these questions for myself.

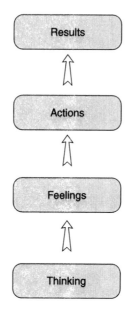

Figure 18.1 Thinking path framework

The answers, I believe, live in an understanding of a deeper mechanism within us: *thinking.* Here is how the chain of causality works:

1. As thinking occurs, feelings arise.
2. Changes in thinking and feelings help redefine the actions that an individual may be inclined to take.
3. When changes in thinking and feelings generate a change in action, changes in results become possible.
4. When a change in thinking is sustained, the probability of a sustained change in actions and results is increased.

The Thinking Path provides a useful framework for coaching by illustrating this chain of causality in a simple, readily comprehensible form. However, as we shall see, the apparent simplicity is grounded in an understanding of the complex interrelationships between the model's four levels.

Case 1: Sales Manager at a Bottling Plant

To better understand each level of the Thinking Path, let us consider a real-life situation.

The CEO of a bottling company toured a plant whose employees were demoralized. The tour proved extremely successful, and the CEO's approval of what he saw generated a visible lift of mood. Once the CEO departed, a sales manager addressed the employees: "The boss really liked what he saw. He said it was the best he had ever seen. But why did you have the order of the products reversed in the coolers? It was embarrassing!" The employees' mood instantly slumped.

Afterward, a colleague asked the sales manager why he dwelled on the negative. He replied, "They won't be motivated toward perfection if you don't keep finding something they did wrong that they need to fix. You always have to find something wrong. Good feelings don't drive productivity and performance."

From Thinking to Results

Most observers would agree that the sales manager's speech constituted an action that produced an undesirable result: lower employee morale. The coach's objective here is to help the sales manager avoid producing such negative results. To achieve this, the coach helps the sales manager become aware of how to change his actions and results by changing their source—his thinking and feelings.

Consider that the origin of the sales manager's actions resides within his thinking. His answer to my colleague's question makes his thinking visible: "You always have to find something wrong. Good feelings don't drive productivity and performance."

Furthermore, my colleague noticed that, just before making his statement the sales manager appeared anxious and impatient. The Thinking Path model suggest that these feelings of anxiety and impatience were a product of the thoughts, both conscious and unconscious, that were running through his mind.

Thinking

Human beings think. We think all the time. It is a central factor in our lives; our experience of reality is shaped by the moment-to-moment flow of our thoughts. One definition of *Thinking* is: *the reception and processing of external and internal data in order to assess and interpret the world within and around us.* Of course, thinking also encompasses the much broader phenomena of human consciousness or awareness. Because of my long study of brain science, however, I am inclined to emphasize the cognitive aspect of thinking, and the mechanical functioning of the brain that underlies it.

It is said that the human body—not only the brain, but also the nervous system and all the sensory apparatus connected to it—processes more than a trillion bits of data every second. These data are received through our senses and are processed, interpreted, and put to use. New data are received, stored, and held as archival memory for later use. Familiar data are matched to the archival memory information to be understood.

The brain's primary function is to receive and store data within its networks and to activate specific networks once the data is presented. From the moment our brain is formed in the fetus, it begins the process of coding the data it receives by creating neural pathways within predisposed areas of the brain. When specific units of data—such as a visual image, a sound, an odor, or a physical sensation—are received repeatedly throughout one's life, specific neural pathways corresponding to these units of data become stronger, creating paths of least resistance within the hardwiring of the neural circuits. From this point on, when data are presented to a human being, the brain responds by activating or "firing" specific neural pathways that correspond to those data. These neural pathways provide a perception of the data, which can then be interpreted and understood. This process occurs continuously in real time, providing us with the ability to make sense of our surroundings.

The beauty of thinking is that we can use what we already know to make sense of confusing and complex data instantly. As we do this, we make decisions and take action. Thinking is what allows us to function and produce results.

Thinking may be described by a variety of concepts. I like to use the scientifically incorrect term *Thought Habits*. "Thought habits" are a simple way for clients to remember the notion that "thinking" includes deeply ingrained values, beliefs, knowledge, perception, assumptions, meaning making, and so on.

From the moment we are conceived in the womb and throughout our lives, we constantly acquire new thought habits because of our ongoing experiences. The more we experience, the more data the brain codes. The more the brain codes, the more thought habits we have. The more thought habits we have, the more we can perceive and interpret. In the end we develop a large storehouse of thought habits that allows us to process and interpret vast amounts of data.

In the case of the sales manager, the thought habit in play was "You always have to find something wrong. Good feelings don't drive productivity and performance."

Feelings

One definition of *Feelings* is *the emotional and physiological manifestation of thought habits*. There is a great deal of debate as to which comes first, thinking or feelings. I believe thinking occurs first and feelings follow. This is supported by research that points to the fact that data is processed first in the brain triggering key organs within the center of the brain that, in turn, launch a set of chemical reactions that occur within the body to create emotional and physiological reactions.

As such, feelings provide the most reliable indicator of the characteristics of the thought habits we are generating. Insecure, chaotic, resentful thought habits generate feelings of anxiety, confusion, and anger; secure, focused, composed thought habits generate feelings of clarity, calmness, and confidence.

Note that the sales manager had observable feelings—anxiety and impatience—before blurting out his statement. As the morning went on, he began to feel anxious that the event was becoming too "compliments focused," and he felt a need to reign in the group. To him, his feelings of anxiety were a normal consequence of the CEO's overly positive remarks. This justified his negative statement to the workers. As he perceived the events unfolding in front of him, he was matching the incoming data to what he had archived in his brain from the past: *"Good feelings don't drive productivity and performance."* He did not realize that his own thought habit was triggering a feeling.

The challenge is that much of the time we do not notice our thinking. By contrast, we *do* feel our feelings. In the moment, our feelings become manifest as emotional and physiological reactions. Therefore, we may believe that our feelings are causing us to act in certain ways—when actually we are being driven, indirectly, by our thought habits.

It is important to understand that it is the *combination* of our moment-to-moment thinking and feelings that create what we experience as reality. Whether or not we have interpreted the data correctly does not matter; our inner experience feels like reality.

The Thinking Path helps clients understand the mechanism that generates what they perceive as reality. This is important because an individual's subjective reality may not reflect the objective situation. Instead, it might be based on thought habits that are questionable, unnecessarily negative, or simply untrue. If a client's reality is based on such inadequate data, he/she may take actions that produce undesirable results.

Case 2: My Consulting Experience

In 2002, I was consulting for a large food company in the Midwest. The client was quite satisfied with the quality of my firm's work and felt that we were adding significant value. As account leader, I was feeling quite satisfied.

One morning, I walked into my client's office at 8:00 a.m., looking forward to another challenging day of work. As I settled into my chair, one of my teammates informed me our client had sent out a "Request for Proposal" to five other consulting firms. It was now 8:02 and I started getting worried. I had thought my client and I had a good relationship and that we were honest with each other—but perhaps I was wrong. By 8:06, I felt anxious and became convinced that my firm was not performing as well for this client as I had thought; I began to doubt whether I had a real partnership with my client. By 8:10, I was fearful and began to question my value as a consultant: I started to imagine that I would not be promoted to partner in my firm that year. I considered resigning from the account. By 8:14, I was drafting my resignation speech in my head. By 8:15, I felt angry. I decided to avoid my client at all costs and spend the morning behind closed doors with my team designing an argument to convince my client that we were the best consulting firm for them.

By 8:20 I was nauseous.

What happened here? What occurred between 8:02 and 8:20? The only data I had received was a single passing comment from one of my teammates. How could I go from feeling good to being nauseous in eighteen minutes?

Once again, we see the impact of thinking. I received data: the simple statement made by my colleague. I processed and interpreted it using thought habits archived in my brain. These old thought habits concerned doubts about my self-worth, and when matched to the data being presented, they generated the feeling of anxiety. This anxiety further fueled my thought habits that generated more feelings; the process spun out of control.

Actions and Results

One definition of *Actions* is *the behaviors we manifest; what we "do."* Our actions, in turn, lead to results. One definition of *Results* is *the observable and measurable outcomes of actions.* Therefore, each action we take produces results, and it is on our actions and results that we ultimately are assessed.

In the case of the sales manager, the action was a statement: *"But why did you have the order of the products reversed in the coolers? It was embarrassing!"* The result he produced was a mood of disempowerment and resignation among the workers. He may not have seen the connection between action and result, but it was unmistakable from the observer's standpoint.

In the case of my consulting experience, the action I envisioned taking was to "avoid my client at all costs and spend the morning behind closed doors with my team designing an argument." Moreover, this action might have yielded the result "to convince my client that we were the best consulting firm"—or not! Fortunately, I did not take that action. Instead, when I realized I was spinning out of control, I used the Thinking Path to pull myself out of my nosedive.

Coaching With the Thinking Path

The power of the Thinking Path lies in its ability to help clients understand what is creating their current state and to define what a better state would look like. It also allows clients to understand that the ultimate source of change is in our thinking.

Coaching with the Thinking Path can yield solid results. However, it needs a little preparation. Here are two "warm-up" exercises that you can conduct with your clients:

Exercise 1: A Current Situation

This exercise will help the client become acquainted with the four levels of the Thinking Path and better understand the relationships between them.

Instructions for the client:

1. Reflect on a current situation you deem positive and that is yielding a good result.
2. Refer to template 18.1: The Current State:
   - Fill in the blanks with a description of your Thinking, Feelings, Actions, and Results in this situation.
   - You may begin at any level and proceed through the other levels using any sequence you wish.
   - You and your coach may use the "current state questions" provided in the following text to engage your reflection.
   - You may also use the "starter" phrases provided above each set of blank lines in template 18.1 to engage your reflection.
   - You may choose to write your responses down in the blank spaces or simply speak them.
3. When you are through, reflect on the following questions with your coach:
   - What do you notice about the relationship between the levels?
   - How does one level impact the other?
   - What is the impact of your thought habits and feelings on your actions and results?

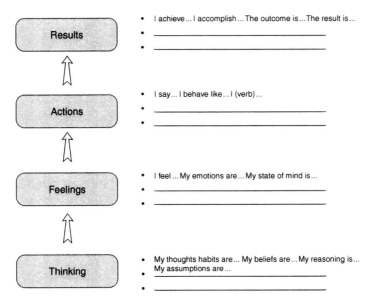

Template 18.1 The current state

To coach the client through the exercise, a series of questions pertaining to each level of the Thinking Path are provided in the following text. These "current state questions" can be used by the coach or the client to direct the client's reflection.

Results

- What is the outcome?
- What is achieved or accomplished?
- What is the end result or end state?
- What is the consequence?

Actions

- What are you doing?
- How are you acting or behaving?
- What are you saying?
- How are you showing up?

Feelings

- How are you feeling?
- What are your emotions?
- What is your state of mind?
- How are you reacting?

Thinking

- What thought habits are running through your mind?
- What are your assumptions?
- What are your beliefs?
- What is your reasoning?
- What are you thinking about?

This preliminary exercise may take from ten to twenty minutes and can reveal a great deal for a client. A typical outcome for the client is that he/she will begin to compartmentalize and label the various pieces of his/her experience. This demystifies thinking and feelings and points to the thought habits he/she is using to generate positive experiences.

Exercise 2: A Time When Change Occurred

This exercise provides the client with an opportunity to assess his/her Thinking Path in the context of a real change event he/she has lived through. It drives home the fact that it was truly a change in thinking that created and sustained the change experienced by the client.

Instructions for the client:

1. Reflect on a situation in the past when you successfully journeyed through change:
   - This can be a personal situation, such as a move, or a professional situation, such as a promotion.
2. Refer to template 18.2: A Time When Change Occurred:
   - The "original state" was the situation you were in before the change and the "new state" was the situation you were in after the change.
   - Fill in the blanks with a description of your Thinking, Feelings, Actions, and Results in both the original and new states for this particular situation.
   - You may begin with the original state or new state and jump back and forth if you wish.
   - You may begin at any level of the Thinking Path within a state and proceed through the other levels using any sequence you wish.
   - You may choose to write your responses down in the blank spaces or simply speak your responses.
3. When you are through, reflect on the following questions:
   - What is the difference in the levels from the original to the new state?
   - What is the role of your thinking/thought habits and feelings in your actions and results in the original and the new states?
   - How did you "become" the new state and how did you sustain the change?

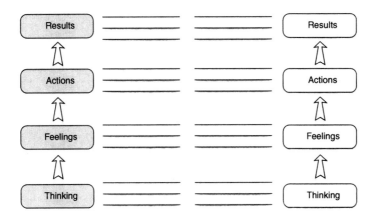

Template 18.2 A time when change occurred

This exercise may take from fifteen to thirty minutes and may reveal a great deal to the client. A typical outcome for the client is that he/she will notice that there actually is a difference in thinking between the two periods and that the change of thinking contributed to the change.

A Thinking Path Coaching Session

Following these two preliminary exercises, most clients are ready for a Thinking Path coaching session. The purpose of this type of coaching is to help the client define his/her current state and desired state, and assess the difference between the two states. Crucially, the client also identifies the thought habits in the desired state that would generate the desired Feelings, Actions, and Results.

The approach is similar to Exercise 1 but it goes farther, adding the definition of a desired state. During the coaching session, the client works through a real issue or challenge. With the guidance of the coach, the client uses the Thinking Path framework to identify his/her Thinking, Feelings, Actions, and Results in the current state. Template 18.1 and the "current state questions" are used for the current state. The client then defines his/her Thinking, Feelings, Actions, and Results in an improved desired state. The client uses template 18.3: The Desired State and the desired state questions for the desired state. Template 18.3 and the "desired state questions" are provided in the following text.

Instructions are similar to those provided in the two preliminary exercises:

Instructions for the client:

1. Refer to template 18.1: The Current State and template 18.3: The Desired State
   - Fill in the blanks with a description of your Thinking, Feelings, Actions, and Results in this situation.

2. You may begin with the current or desired state and jump back and forth if you wish.

3. You may begin at any level of the Thinking Path within both the current and desired states and proceed through the other levels using any sequence you wish.

4. You and your coach may use the "current state questions" provided in Exercise 1 and the "desired state questions" provided in the following text to engage your reflection.

5. You may use the "starter" phrases provided above the blank lines in template 18.1 and template 18.3 if you wish.

6. You may choose to write your responses down in the blank spaces or simply speak your responses.

To coach the client through the desired state, a series of questions pertaining to each level of the Thinking Path are provided in the following text. These "desired state questions" can be used by the coach or the client to direct the client's reflection.

Results

- What would be the outcome?
- What would be achieved or accomplished?
- What would be the result or end state?
- What would be the consequence?

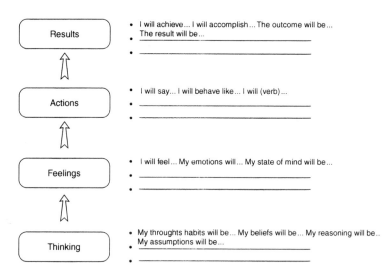

Template 18.3 The desired state

Actions

- What would you be doing?
- How would you be acting or behaving?
- What would you be saying?
- How would you be showing up?

Feelings

- How would you be feeling?
- What would be your emotions?
- What would be your state of mind?
- How would you be reacting?

Thinking

- What thought habits would be running through your mind?
- What would be your assumptions?
- What would be your beliefs?
- What would be your reasoning?
- What would you be thinking about?

A coaching session using the Thinking Path may take thirty minutes to several hours and may occur over the course of several sessions. Figure 18.2 provides an

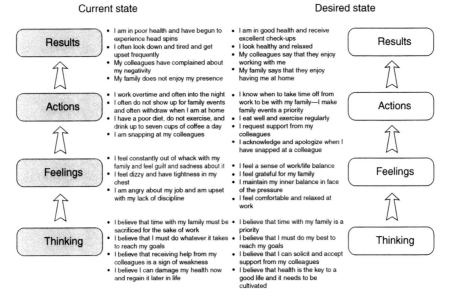

Figure 18.2 The current and desired states

example of an executive who completed both the current and desired states in a coaching session. He found the session challenging but made the discovery that underlying his actions and results were a set of beliefs he had never seen with such clarity.

As stated earlier, coaching with the Thinking Path can yield solid results. Yet it is important to remember that this is only a framework—a tool for understanding. Like any framework, it best serves those who invest in study and practice,—and it will not be appropriate in every situation. Therefore, give yourself time to learn how to use the Thinking Path. Try it on yourself first or with a person in your life who is not a client and who is willing to experiment with you. When you try it for the first time with a client, apply it to an issue or challenge that is not charged with great intensity; you can apply it to such issues later on, after you have gained experience with the model.

When you begin using the Thinking Path with clients, remain alert to the energy in the room. If the mood feels constrained or weakened, be ready to let go of the framework. You may choose to come back to it later or drop it altogether. The key is to remain flexible and to always meet your client where he/she is.

Changing Thinking

Up to this point, the Thinking Path has provided us with an effective approach to understand our current state and define our desired state. However, is this enough to help our clients really change their thought habits? The answer is no. In my experience, a majority of clients need something more to help them change their thought habits in a sustained manner. What is needed is an action plan comprised of a set of goals and practices that transform the desired state into reality.

The coach can help the client build this action plan. The client can generate a set of goals based on the results he/she wants to see in the desired state and can commit to several actions defined in the desired state. For many coaches, this is enough. I believe, however, that it is not. Instead, another set of "practices" aimed directly at the Thinking level of the Thinking Path can ensure that the necessary change in thought habits actually does occur.

Figure 18.3 illustrates this point by expanding on the example of the executive used in figure 18.2. On the left side of figure 18.3, we see the executive's desired state Thinking Path, just as in figure 18.2. On the right side, we see a partial action plan created with his coach. This Action Plan was created by focusing on the Results and Actions levels of his desired state. In my view, it was a good plan but not sufficient. Indeed, the executive had created similar plans in the past, with clear goals as well as a solid set of practices. Every time he did so, however, he implemented the practices for a while and then bounced right back to his current state.

To remedy this, the coach recommended that the executive generate a set of practices from the Thinking level as well, to increase the likelihood of achieving his desired results.

What types of practices exist to help our clients change their thought habits? I put them into two broad categories: those that can be implemented on an ongoing basis and those that can be implemented in the moment.

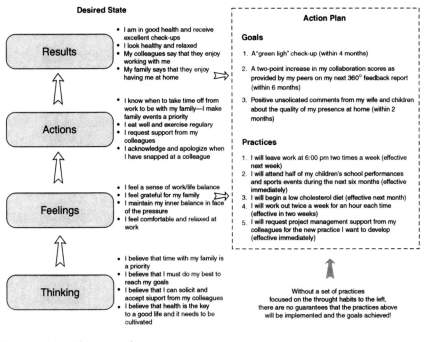

Figure 18.3 The action plan

Changing Thought Habits: An Ongoing Journey

Human beings can acquire new thought habits and even change or eliminate old thought habits. As long as we can still learn, we can change our thought habits. The brain's primary function of receiving and storing data within its networks continues throughout our lives. The brain can create new neural pathways within predisposed areas of the brain based on new data. These new pathways are built next to the old neural pathways, and over time they can become stronger than the old pathways, effectively quieting them down or extinguishing them altogether.

Many types of practices may help clients learn new thought habits. Let's focus on three: Repetition, Education, and Conversation.

Repetition

Repetition involves actively repeating new thought habits, such as mantras. In the case of our executive, he could repeat the thought habit "I believe that time with my family is a priority" until it anchored as an actual pathway within the brain.

A coach might suggest the client quietly repeat the new thought habit several times daily: on waking, at midday, at the end of the work day, and before sleeping.

He/she can continue to do this until the thought habit begins to manifest itself in feeling and action.

Education

I define *education* broadly, to include various forms of engagement with concepts and ideas, such as reading, watching TV and films, listening to experts, and attending courses.

In the case of our executive, he chose to develop the thought habit "I believe that health is the key to a good life and it needs to be cultivated." To support that thought habit, he might read articles on exercise and fitness, watch a documentary on the adverse effects of cholesterol, attend a course on dieting, or consult a nutritionist. Such education practices would serve to reinforce the executive's desired thought habit.

Conversation

Talking about a specific thought habit with others can generate a remarkable amount of learning quickly. Simple conversation may be the most effective way to help thought habits develop neural pathways within the brain. The most effective Thinking Path conversations occur when the client is curious and open, and when he uses inquiry and listening to gain insight from the interlocutor.

Our executive might reinforce his desired thought habit "I believe that I can solicit and accept help from my colleagues" through conversations. He might ask his colleagues about the value of soliciting and accepting help. He might also ask them to share what they believe is the best way to do it. Ideally, he would be open to their suggestions and share his own reactions. He might then commit to one or more practices that were suggested to him. These conversations could increase the likelihood that he would obtain project management support and support his goal of achieving a two-point increase on his next 360-degree feedback report.

If a client combines the three practices of repetition, education, and conversation for a particular thought habit, the power of the approach is exponential. For example, if our executive were to...

1. Engage in a repetitive practice of the thought habit "I believe that I can solicit and accept help from my colleagues";
2. Read a good book on high performance teams; and
3. Conduct conversations on soliciting and accepting support...

...he would surely increase his chances of achieving his goals.

Changing Thought Habits: In the Moment

The practices just described are helpful for clients who want to change their thought habits. However, what happens when clients find themselves in the same old current state experiencing the same old Feelings, Actions, and Results? What can they do in the moment to move to the desired state?

This is a critical aspect of the Thinking Path approach. If a client can learn to change a thought habit in the moment he/she will increase the likelihood of moving into the desired state by him/herself. This self-initiated experience powerfully supports sustained change.

One key thing to remember is that *we cannot easily stop our thought habits from occurring—but we can change thought habits once they have occurred.* The reason is that the brain's neural pathways will always fire when they receive data. This is the way the brain functions, and it is very difficult to interrupt or get "in front" of this process. Once neural pathways have fired, however, we can act.

This is where our clients have the power to change themselves.

There are a myriad of ways to change thought habits in the moment and volumes have been written on this. I suggest an approach that requires four "movements," and this can be easily learned. These four movements are:

1. Awareness
2. Time-out
3. Reflection
4. Choice

Awareness

During the first movement, the client remains aware of his/her feelings. In this way, the client can recognize the feelings identified in his/her current state Thinking Path.

In the case of the executive, these feelings were:

- "feeling 'out of whack' with my family and feeling guilt and sadness about it";
- "feeling dizzy and having tightness in my chest"; and
- "being angry about my job and upset with my lack of discipline."

Time-out

During the second movement, the client stops what he/she is doing in the moment and engages in reflection. This is the hardest of the four movements. Many clients claim they do not have the time to stop or that it would be awkward to take a time-out in the middle of a private or personal situation. Others claim they do not know how to stop or that they do not remember to stop.

To help their clients learn how to take a time-out coaches can

1. Practice calling a time-out during the coaching sessions. At an appropriate moment, the coach literally stops the conversation and points out that he/she has done so. This provides the client with an experience of a "time-out," which he/she can replicate later.
2. Ask the client to give a select few people permission to "stop" him/her when undesirable current-state feelings show up in action.

3. Request that the client write the word "Time-out" or "Stop" down on a number of post-it notes and paste them in key places. This leverages the repetition practice.

Reflection

During the third movement, the client may ask him/herself the following four questions, allowing answers to arise naturally.

1. What am I feeling right now?
2. How am I acting and what are my results given this feeling?
3. What thought habit(s) is driving my feeling?
4. What shall I do about this thought habit(s)?

The questions are powerful because they can stop current-state thinking habits and engage the brain in inquiry. In other words, this simple practice can override the original neural pathways that were generating the old thought habits with another set of neural pathways that require reflection. This creates a moment of clarity within which fresh thinking can occur.

Choice

During this fourth movement, the client selects how he/she will change the identified thought habit. Although many approaches exist, I focus on four: Letting Go, Substituting, Documenting, and Declaring.

With the first choice, *Letting Go*, the client stops focusing on the thought habit and effectively "lets it go." To encourage the client, the coach can remind him/her that thought habits are transient in nature, and that they can be changed once they occur. This means there is no real need to hold on to a thought habit, it will go away as the neural pathways stop firing. Techniques that clients can use to build their ability to let go of thought habits include:

- taking or requesting a break from the situation if at all possible;
- taking or requesting a moment to reflect;
- "sleeping" on it; and
- shifting the focus of their attention by engaging in another activity.

With the second choice, *Substituting*, the client develops the reflex to substitute the current thought habit with another one. The new thought habit may be taken from the thought habits defined in the desired state, or a fresh thought could be generated right there and then. These fresh thought habits can be more positive or constructive in tone thereby changing his/her feelings.

With the third choice, *Documenting*, the client writes down the current state thought habits that he/she is generating in the moment. This widely used technique is also known as jotting or journaling. Documenting is effective because if the client can articulate the thought habit on paper, the thought habit may lose its grip on his/her mind, allowing fresh thinking.

With the fourth choice, *Declaring*, the client shares his/her current state thought habits with others. For this to succeed, the client needs to be willing to share his/her desire to change openly with others. Then, the client must be willing to ask others what they think about the thought habit and what they suggest to change it. This curiosity and inquiry works best when accompanied with openness to new ideas. In the case of our executive, he may, in the moment, share with his wife his original thought habit that time with his family must be sacrificed for the sake of work. She then has the opportunity to help him explore what it would take to adopt his desired belief that time with his family is a priority.

Four movements leading to four choices that when learned and practiced can become an integral part of our clients' lives. These four movements can make the crucial difference when clients find themselves stuck again in their current states.

The Thinking Path Live

In conclusion, let's apply these ideas to my consulting experience at 8:21 a.m.

As you recall, I was angry, nauseous, and ready to avoid my client at all costs and spend the morning behind closed doors with my team. My teammate's original statement triggered a deep thought habit within me called "I am not good enough." This thought habit initiated my negative spiral.

Fortunately, I had been working for quite some time on a new set of self-confident thought habits. I had also been in conversations about these new thought habits with several people and had been repeating them to myself often. I was also aware that I could change thought habits in the moment and knew the four reflection questions.

Therefore, at 8:21 a.m., when I realized my feelings were in the tank, I stopped what I was doing. I left the office and began walking down the long corridors nearby. As I walked, I asked myself the four questions. I quickly realized the actions I was about to take would likely be counterproductive—and I saw one of my key thought habits in action: "I am insecure about my value."

In the moment, I chose to substitute this thought habit with two others I had been working on: "I am doing the best I can" and "I am appreciated for what I do." As I repeated these thought habits I began to focus on my assets. I began to think about my family and friends. I reviewed the successes we had had so far with this client.

Soon my mind began to clear and I felt a sense of relief. I began to explore alternative actions that would yield better results. One needed action became very clear: go see my client, sit down with him, and respectfully ask what was going on. As it occurred to me, this idea seemed much wiser than the plan I had concocted shortly before, while in panic. I marveled at how powerfully I had been gripped once again by my old thought habits.

Within an hour, I was having coffee with my client. Our rapport was as good as ever. I asked my question and, sure enough, learned my client had been speaking with another consulting firm. But the details were surprising and encouraging: The client wanted to bring in the other firm for a very specific, small piece of work for which my firm undeniably did not have the right capabilities. In his mind, this new consulting firm would complement our work, and it would no way impact our relationship with him or with the company.

My client had made the right strategic decision. And I had managed to keep my cool and, as a result, maintain an important personal and professional relationship. I lightened up and the sun came out again.

Bibliography

Captured Light and Lord of the Wind Films. *What the Bleep Do We Know!?* California: Twentieth Century Fox, 2004.

Childre, D. and B. Cryer. *From Chaos to Coherence: The Power Change Performance.* Boulder Creek, CA: Planetary, 2000.

Claxton, G. *Hare Brain Tortoise Mind: Why Intelligence Increases When You Think Less.* Hopewell, NJ: Ecco Press, 1999.

———. *Noises from the Darkroom: The Science and Mystery of the Mind.* London: Harper Collins, 1994.

Csikszentmihalyi, M. *Finding Flow.* New York: Basic, 1997.

Demasio, A.R. *Descartes' Error: Emotion, Reason, and the Human Brain.* New York: Putnam, 1994.

Goleman, D., R. Boyatzis, and A. McKee. *Primal Leadership: Realizing the Power of Emotional Intelligence.* Boston: Harvard Business School Press, 2002.

Greenfield, S.A. *Journey to the Centers of the Mind: Toward a Science of Consciousness.* New York: Freeman, 1995.

Humphries, N. *A History of the Mind: Evolution and the Birth of Consciousness.* New York: Simon and Schuster, 1992.

LeDoux, J. *The Emotional Brain: The Mysterious Underpinnings of Emotional Life.* New York: Simon and Schuster, 1996.

McCraty, R., M, Athinson, and D, Tomasino. *Science of the Heart—Exploring the Role of the Heart in Human Performance.* n.p.: HeartMath Research Center, n.d.

Mills, R. *Realizing Mental Health : Toward a new Psychology of Resiliency.* n.p.: Sulburger & Graham, 1995.

Mills, R., and E. Spittle, *The Wisdom Within.* Edmonton, Canada: Lone Pine, 2001.

O'Neill, M.B. *Executive Coaching with Backbone and Heart.* San Francisco, CA: Jossey-Bass Publishers, 2000.

Ornstein, R., and D. Sobel. *The Healing Brain: Breakthrough Discoveries about How the Brain Keeps Us Healthy.* New York: Simon & Schuster, 1987.

CHAPTER 19

Executive Coaching for Leadership Development: Five Questions to Guide Your Program Design

Sheryl D. Phillips and Frank Ball

Introduction: Executive Coaching as a Leadership Strategy

Executive coaching is an individualized learning process that enables managers to grow as leaders and achieve greater business results.

In contrast with traditional leadership training methods, coaching builds stronger leaders through self-awareness and sustainable changes in behavior. Coaching is a personalized learning process that is accomplished through a series of one-on-one focused coaching conversations; and by having the leader gain feedback, observe his or her actions, and practice new actions/behaviors tied to growth goals. Executive Coaching also helps leaders identify desired business results and the challenges impeding progress toward these goals. In addition to focusing on enhancing the leader's learning, coaching assists the leader in developing strategies to achieve identified business results.

A starting point in coaching individual clients is to help the client focus on what they want in the future that is different from the present and then to work with the client in setting a direction, exploring options, and establishing a structure for action. In this chapter, we will ask the same questions we might ask an individual client for your consideration in developing an organization-wide coaching program: (1) What do you want and why is that important to you? (2) What alternatives do you need to explore? (3) What structure will serve you best in moving forward? (4) Who will be your support? (5) How will you know you've been successful?

What Do You Want and Why Is That Important to You?

To consider how coaching could help make your organization higher performing, consider the following questions:

- What is working well in your organization that you'd like to build on?
- Conversely, what are the recurring obstacles or challenges impacting your organization's effectiveness?
- What do you most need to achieve in the next year? Next five years?
- What do you need from your leaders to get there?
- What is getting in their way of being the leaders you need?

Before initiating the design of an executive coaching program, key stakeholders should be engaged to answer these four critical questions:

1. What do we want to achieve through coaching? What would success look like for us?
2. Is the timing right to introduce it; why or why not?
3. Do we have any existing champions; if not, who needs to be engaged to play that vital role?
4. Do we want to start small or unveil a fully developed formal program?

Exploring these initial questions with a design team or core corporate sponsors will culminate in a defined direction for your coaching program that answers the questions of "what do we want" to achieve with a coaching program and "why is this important" to the organization.

What Alternatives Do You Need to Explore?

Once you have defined what you want to achieve with a coaching program, there are many program structures and program features that should be considered.

Program Structures

Formal Stand-alone Program. In its most straightforward form, coaching can be presented as a stand-alone leadership development offer to managers. At the more formal end of the spectrum, a corporate coaching program may be specifically designed and linked to business strategies and imperatives, defined leadership competencies and possibly specific triggering events (e.g., succession planning, promotion, identification as high potential, etc.). At the less formal end, the coaching is offered to a certain level/levels of managers for their individual leadership growth and development.

Coaching embedded in Leadership Development Programs. An alternative program structure is to make coaching part of a blended Leadership Development Program, in which participants have a classroom training experience coupled with one-on-one sessions with a professional coach. The coaching is intended to embed the training into the real life of the manager.

Ad-hoc coaching. In addition to either a stand-alone or embedded coaching programs as described earlier, coaching can be used as an effective learning tool in a variety of other "ad-hoc" situations. For example, coaching can be effective in supporting the onboarding of newly hired senior executives. Coaching can also be single-topic focused, for example, coaching focused on building the capability for an executive to make effective oral presentations. Another frequently used "ad-hoc coaching" approach is to have a qualified coach debrief 360-degree feedback results with managers and assist them in designing a personal development plan based on that data. Even if no specific follow-on coaching occurs, the support of a coach in clearly understanding the data, what they suggest, and how to engage in development based on that data can be very valuable.

Program Feature Decision Points

This section explores the elements to consider in developing a coaching program for an organization regardless of whether it is a stand-alone program or part of a larger leadership development effort. Keep in mind, there is no one "right" way to design a program. Coaching programs vary by organization and many different designs work effectively. Elements to consider include:

- *Who the coaching will be offered to.* Whether the coaching will be offered to all supervisors and managers or reserved for executive or higher-level leaders is an initial program decision. Available budget, corporate culture, and where coaching is managed in the organization can all drive this decision.
- *Internal or external coaches.* The organization should decide whether to use internal coaches or engage external coaches or a combination of both.
- *Cadre of qualified coaches.* Whether using internal or external coaches, the coaches should be trained, experienced, and qualified as executive coaches. Organizations often use graduation from an ICF-approved coach training institution or possession of an ICF coaching credential as a prerequisite to be included in their cadre of coaches. A bio describing the background and coaching philosophy should be created for each coach. The pool should include coaches with diverse backgrounds.
- *A matching process.* A method to match the client and coach should be created. This method can vary from having coaching bios available for leaders to select coaches to interview, to having a coaching program coordinator interview the leader to assess needs of the client and then match the client with the best coach or coaches.
- *The coaching "package."* At a minimum, include the number of coaching hours, length of coaching engagements, and frequency of the coaching. In many organizations, clients can choose from a limited number of different packages that can vary in length, intensity, and purpose.
- *Defined assessment instruments.* Assessments may vary from formal 360-degree instruments to traditional preference instruments (i.e., MBTI®, FIRO-B®)

to methods for shadowing the leader and gathering feedback in a narrative method from supervisors, subordinates, and peers. Although assessments may vary from client to client, determining which to offer in the program will help create consistency in the program. A basic program decision is whether 360 and other assessments will be mandatory or voluntary on the part of the person being coached.

- *A method to establish goals for the coaching.* This method may be as simple as a form for recording the goals or a more formal method of interviewing the boss and other key stakeholders as to goals for the coaching. Determining whom the goals will be shared with is also an important program element— are the goals strictly between the client and coach or will the goals be shared with the program coordinator and the supervisor of the leader? In addition to those notifications, a decision point is whether individual coaching goals should be tied in some explicit way to the organization's mission or strategic intent.
- *Defined stakeholders and progress reporting.* In a formal program, it is important to decide when, how, and with whom the progress of the coaching will be shared. This decision point is related to the previous one regarding goals for the coaching.
- *A method to evaluate the effectiveness.* How the overall coaching program will be evaluated is a critical element in the design of a leadership coaching program. Evaluation applies to both the individual and organizational impacts. The methods used may be as simple as qualitative feedback from the client and the coach, or as formal as a repeat of assessment instruments, as well as tracking organizational performance goals.
- *Management and materials.* The structure of the coaching program will vary by organization, yet having a clearly defined "home" for management of the program, the coaching cadre, and so on is essential. In addition, an established set of materials will ensure consistency. The materials may vary from simple forms related to the one mentioned earlier to a more formal "coaching manual" with protocols, materials, and resources for participants.

Strategic Decisions

In addition to these program-design elements, additional "strategic" elements to consider include the following:

- *Connection to existing Leadership Development offerings.* Determine whether coaching will be a stand-alone leadership development offer, or whether it will be a part of existing leadership development initiatives, or both.
- *Connection to succession planning.* If the organization has a formal succession planning or high-potential identification process, determine how coaching will be integrated with these efforts.
- *Linkage to critical leadership competencies.* If the organization has defined leadership competencies, these competencies should be used as a core part of the coaching. If competencies do not exist, determine whether leadership

competencies will be developed or existing leadership competencies will be used in the coaching process.

- *Linkage to corporate strategic priorities.* Determine the connection to other strategic priorities and initiatives. For example, in a major reorganization, will coaching be offered to those managers assuming new duties before those not impacted by the reorganization? Or, if a new business imperative requires new ways of operating or leading, determine how this will be incorporated into the coaching.
- *Pilot program.* Organizations often run a limited scope pilot program to determine the best structure of coaching, the right level of person to include as clients, and to test the organization's acceptance of coaching.

What Structure Will Serve You Best in Moving Forward?

Although coaching is an individualized process, the flow of the engagement should have a defined structure (see figure 19.1). We think of this as a defined beginning, middle, and end to the engagement.

Beginning		Middle	End
Up-Front Work	**Program Design**	**The Coaching Itself**	**Closing**
Contracting	• Current state	***During the Session:***	• Pre-/Post-coaching
• Duration	• Goals/Objectives	• Purposeful conversations	comparisons
• Frequency	• Grounded	• Immediate concerns	• Action plan
• Payment	assessments	• Exploring the story	• Next steps
• Agreements	• Format	• Staying in the question	• Evaluation of program
• Other terms	• Timeline	• Models, tools, role-plays,	• Feedback for coach
	• Conditioning	etc.	• Ritual/gifts
Rapport & Trust	• Methodologies	• Congruence of mind,	
Building		body, emotions	
• "Intake"		• Reviewing commitments	
• The Story		• Results of insights;	
		learnings	
Investigating		• Feedback for coach and	
• Presenting		client	
issues		• Re-contracting/new	
• Assessment		agreements	
instruments		• Noticing & offering	
• Interviews		distinctions	
• Workplace			
observations		***Between Sessions:***	
		• Inquiry	
		• Self-observations	
		• Practices	
		• Exercises	
		• Resources (books,	
		poems, videos, etc.)	
		• Structures of Support	
		(day planners, exercise	
		buddies, etc.)	

Figure 19.1   The flow of coaching

Source: ©Frank Ball & Beth Bloomfield

The Beginning

At the beginning of the coaching engagement, the goals for the coaching, logistics for the coaching, any assessments needed to determine current leadership skills, and methods to evaluate the success of the coaching are defined. During the first coaching session, the coach works with the leader to define the outcomes and goals for the coaching relationship, current obstacles or concerns, and what, if any, assessments the client has had or would like to have (i.e., MBTI®, 360-degree feedback, etc.). The coach and client also establish their schedule for coaching and define how they will work together. Depending on the logistics of the coaching engagement, at this stage, the client's boss may also be consulted to see what goals they have for the client or to define desired areas of work. Sometimes HR and/or the coaching program manager will be included in these progress reports as well as the goal setting that precedes the coaching. Although the specific content of a coaching session is confidential, the coach, client, and boss may agree to what information will be provided at critical intervals to the boss. Often, this may include some reporting of progress toward goals. All must be clarified and organization-wide standards established before the coaching begins.

The Middle

A "typical" coaching engagement lasts six months to one year. The coaching sessions may occur in person or over the phone. Coaching sessions may be structured as weekly hour-long sessions, biweekly two-hour sessions, or some other combination as agreed to between the coach and client. The coach also provides support to the leader in-between coaching sessions through e-mail or by phone.

A variety of assessments can be done during the coaching engagement, tied to and to support the leader in achieving his/her goals. Some examples include a formal 360-degree evaluation survey or a narrative 360-degree evaluation in which the coach interviews subordinates, superiors, and/or peers. The coach may also shadow the leader in meetings with his/her team; or may participate in three-way conversations with the client and his/her supervisor. All of these methods allow the client to see things from a new perspective or may illuminate existing "blind spots" to their performance or interaction with others.

During individual coaching sessions: As described previously, coaching is both strategic and just-in-time in nature. During each coaching session, the coach and client spend time on the immediate issues facing the leader and the longer-term objectives or goals defined for the coaching engagement. In between coaching sessions, the coach often suggests readings on the subject of leadership, communication, effective teams, or other subjects relevant to the defined coaching objectives.

Throughout the coaching engagement, the coach supports the leader as action steps are developed and implemented. Coaching is not only about reflection and learning, but it is also about taking new actions. The result of coaching is both vision and action, with the result being purposeful and focused progress.

Between coaching sessions: A tenet of coaching is that people have the wisdom and knowledge within themselves to solve their problems and perform at higher levels. A companion piece of this philosophy is that people "believe their own data" more than they do someone else's data. In this vein, the coach will often encourage self-observations, practices, or other exercises to accelerate the leader's learning and action. For example, the leader who feels that staff never gives him/her the product he/she is asking for may be asked to observe and record the instructions (or request) he or she is giving to staff, specific to clarity, context, and timeframes. After reflecting on this self-gathered "data," the client and coach would work together to design new practices, which eventually might become new behaviors for the leader.

The End

Coaching is not intended to continue indefinitely. Throughout the coaching engagement, the coach and client will review progress toward the originally defined goals, as well as any other areas of work that may have emerged. Check-ins with the client's boss may also occur as established in the up-front agreements. The coaching engagement concludes with evaluation of attainment of development and business goals. In addition, the coach and client may develop strategies for ensuring that the new behaviors are sustainable when unforeseen challenges arise in the future. The coach and client may agree to do occasional check-ins or tune-ups, often on a quarterly basis.

Who Will Be Your Support?

The Necessity of Coaching Champions

It's hard to imagine a successful organizational coaching program without significant sponsorship. In most organizations a champion is necessary to get things going in the first place. Someone has to obtain necessary budgeted funding. This person needs to be senior enough to command the organization's attention and convince the rest of the organization of the value of coaching as a tool for leadership development. Ideally the champions are credible, powerful, and set a strong example as leaders themselves.

The Coaches

The coaches, of course, are also a key partner in any successful organizational program. In selecting and building the cadre of coaches, the organization should consider some of the following key elements:

- *Coaches training.* There are now several formal certification programs for coaching. These programs are intensive and usually last from six to twelve months. Programs that have been credentialed by the International Coach Federation (ICF), the professional association for coaches, can be found on www.coachfederation.org
- *Coaching experience.* Some executive coaches' have been practicing for many years, and they may have developed their coaching practice before the

emergence of coaching as a commonly offered service. These coaches may not have attended a formal training program, but of course may have the skill sets and background to be effective. In general, a client should ask about the coach's background and practice as a coach, including number of years in the coaching profession and number of clients worked with on an ongoing basis. The client should clarify that the coach has a specific coaching practice versus simply advising a client as a part of a consulting engagement.

- *Professional background.* Some external executive coaches are prior managers or executives, which can lend itself to a "been there" understanding of leadership. Likewise, many executive coaches also are organizational development practitioners. This allows them to have particular expertise in group, organizational, change, and system dynamics. Finally, if the sector or industry background of a coach is important to the client, for example, the finance industry or public sector versus private sector, these elements should be considered.
- *Philosophy and style.* Coach style and philosophy can vary as greatly as the coaches providing the service. A client should inquire as to the coach's style to assess the right *balance* between assisting the leader in reflection and action.
- *Methods and tools used.* The assessments, tools, and other resources used by the coach should be discussed. Also, coaching can be done effectively in person or by phone. However, a client with a strong preference should ask the coach about their preferred method.
- *References.* If the coach has not been prescreened by the client's organization, the manager or executive should check up to three client references for the coach.
- *Coach's continual learning.* Asking the coach what he/she does to stay abreast of the latest leadership methods and information, as well as how he/she continues to develop as a coach, will be a good indicator of whether the coach "practices what he/she preaches." A good coach should be able to offer cutting-edge, as well as tried-and-true, distinctions about effective leadership, and he/she should both be a "teacher" and a continual learner.

How Will You Know You've Been Successful?

Ideally, we would like to believe that the results of coaching would speak for themselves. The reality is that most organizations will perform some sort of evaluation of the impact and effectiveness of their coaching programs.

At a minimum this can be a survey completed by the person who was coached asking about the value they obtained, whether they achieved their coaching goals, suggestions to improve the coaching process, and whether they would recommend coaching to others.

In addition, the managers of those coached can be surveyed to determine their satisfaction with the results they see and recommendations they may have to improve the coaching program.

The coaches, too, are often surveyed about coaching outcomes, but because of confidentiality, those surveys often focus more on the administrative and logistics sides of the coaching relationship.

As coaching grows as a leadership intervention, more sophisticated levels of evaluation are being developed. The most critical issue is to find an evaluation method that fits the needs of your organization and does not detract from the anecdotal as well as specific benefits of coaching.

Conclusion

Coaching will continue to grow as a key leadership development method. As you move forward with the design of your organization's program, we offer our thoughts on five key traps to avoid.

Five Deadly Traps

1. Believing coaching is the solution for all leadership shortcomings;
2. Believing the value of coaching is self-evident, and it doesn't require sponsorship;
3. Using coaches to deliver messages and establish accountabilities managers should be doing;
4. Seeing coaching as remedial only and not as a developmental tool;
5. Not creating some level of structure for your program and/or enlisting a solid cadre of professional coaches.

We hope you miss these traps and wish you success on your journey!

CHAPTER 20

Coaching for Leadership Presence

Clarice L. Scriber

Leadership presence is a common concern for aspiring leaders, particularly in today's organizations where technically savvy leaders—even brilliant ones—find themselves climbing the corporate ladder and learn that they are navigating terrain where the stakes are much higher. To succeed at this level, the leader not only must develop a leadership voice with peers, superiors, and subordinates, but also must round sharpen the edges that damage the connection that the leader needs to influence and to lead.

Rewarded for their subject matter expertise, ability to execute, and drive to obtain results, many of the next-generation leaders have neglected the requisite skills that are necessary for success in the executive ranks. Thus, when they get the coveted promotion, they often receive feedback in their initial performance review that comments on a lack of leadership presence. Most are perplexed by the fact that it's not just the work that counts. After all, mastery of their domain was the hallmark of their success. Therefore, they are frequently mystified about how to address the "executive presence" challenge.

The difficulty is that executive "presence" is an elusive concept that arises out of an organization's culture and mores—defined by how the organization sees itself and leaders who have traversed the company's terrain. In Company A, a leader with presence may be one who is authoritative and decisive. In company B, the prototype may be an openness, an ease of engagement, and the capacity to enroll and influence others. In company C, presence may be the leader's ability to think well on his or her feet and to demonstrate grace under fire in stressful times.

Presence is all these things and more. In a larger discussion about leadership, we might explore the underpinnings of leadership, such as strategic focus, integrity, delivery, and accountability. However, for the purposes of this chapter, we examine the qualities

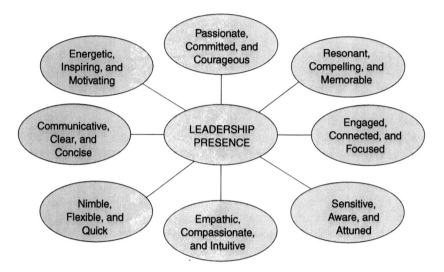

Figure 20.1 Qualities that exhibit leadership presence

that support a leader's effectiveness, ones that we notice and assess when engaging with leaders. See figure 20.1 for qualities that demonstrate a leadership presence.

These qualities are by no way all that a leader must embody, and they are not usually the ones the company measures in the year-end review. The ones shown in figure 20.1 emanate from a leader, one whom we can experience in interaction, in intimate conversations, or in large groups. These qualities support the leader's stance and are among the soft skills that—when missing—can derail a leader. They are frequently among those traits that coaches are asked to help leaders develop.

Client Readiness

When a coach receives the call from a leader to initiate coaching, that coach will want to listen deeply to be able to assess the leader's commitment to doing the kind of work and that may call forward changes that fundamentally speak to a leader's identity. Unlike coaching to build management skills, coaching to change one's way of being in the world involves ego development and a shift in perception of one's essence in relationship with others. That change is transformative. Can the leader commit to regular reflection and self-observation about how he or she is showing up? Can such leaders scrutinize long-held beliefs about how they see themselves and are received in the workplace? Can they engage in a reflective conversation and take on practices that may upend their self-image?

In the initial conversation, both the coach and client will need to answer those crucial questions. Some clients are ready to do this work; others may not be. When the client is ready, the coaching alliance can be exhilarating for both client and coach.

Maxine

Take Maxine for example. A quiet, introverted thinker, Maxine was well-respected and liked by the people who worked with her, particularly by subordinates. She was great at delivery, was generally well-liked, and enjoyed rallying her team to partner on IT projects. Maxine was eager to progress to the next level in her organization. The feedback she received at review time indicated that her boss's peers and other superiors weren't sure she was ready. Although they appreciated her work ethic and ability to perform, they wanted more. In meetings, her colleagues wanted her to speak up more, speak strategically, and engage more robustly in conversations. What was Maxine's point of view, they wondered? How did Maxine think about the work? When there was controversy, where did she stand? Where was her passion?

Until this point in her career, Maxine had been a good lieutenant, largely carrying out the vision of others. Now, the request had changed. Maxine was being asked not only to articulate her vision, but also to do this on a more public stage. She was now being asked to engage in dialogue with others without the benefit of always having the time to think things through in the heat of the discussion. Finally, there was an observation about Maxine's level of energy. No matter what the event, Maxine was always calm and collected. Maxine believed that appearing calm was a strength, especially during a fire drill. However, others viewed it as a lack of passion and conviction on her part.

As I met with her, Maxine proved curious about the feedback and was eager to explore possibilities for building her leadership capacity. "I chose you because I was intrigued by your comments about 'developing my leadership voice,'" she said. At the end of coaching, Maxine was more comfortable speaking up about her vision for the organization; with a great deal of practice and by using visual imagery, she was able to manage her energy to express greater enthusiasm when situations warranted it. Maxine may never be an ebullient leader. She realized that grace under pressure was an asset. Thus, to be authentic, she needed to keep integrity with herself. At the same time, she was able to confidently express her opinion during the conversation, which put her on the road to changing the wallflower perception her colleagues had of her. She took the time to flesh out her point of view, and she practiced speaking about it until it became easier for her to express it.

Jack

My coaching conversations with Maxine had a very different tenor from my conversations with Jack; both were deeply immersed in the tactical approach to leading. Jack is an up-and-coming, 20-something, midlevel executive. He is considered brilliant by peers, as well as by those senior to him. By training, he is an economist. In his organization, he is charged with creating sophisticated analytical models. Energized by his work and by the intellectual conversations that occur when he is engaged with his colleagues, he is oblivious about whether the client is able to keep up with his thinking or the concepts he is trying to convey. He sees himself as an intellectual and equal to those in positions higher in the chain of command, and he does not defer to hierarchy. This quality has set him apart from peers and has helped him to earn the respect of superiors.

Jack does not suffer fools gladly—an assessment his staff, his peers, and his boss have made. His manner is often abrupt, even curt, particularly when he is under pressure. A mentor described him thus: When you encounter Jack and his energy and appearance, you might think, "Oh, a grad student or a professor." He does not look like an up-and-coming leader; what matters most to him is thinking about ideas, solving problems, and getting the work done.

Fortunately for Jack, the company regards him as a "high potential," someone who will climb the ladder more quickly than others because of his knowledge, contribution, and creativity. His sponsors note that he needs to adapt his communications style, his appearance, and his interpersonal style to be less abrasive and more open to others' opinions and ideas.

The reality is that what served Jack well in the past could derail him at the next rung of the career ladder. To help, Jack's boss offered him the opportunity to work with a coach.

Jack's story has a different conclusion from Maxine's. From the start, Jack knew he wanted something more for himself, but in the end, he was not developmentally ready to take on the kind of practice required to change the way he engaged. Although he acknowledged that he was getting in his own way and recognized the efficacy of change, he wanted the coach to give him a template of behaviors he could adapt. Ultimately, it was the work product that intrigued him, not changing his way of working and engaging with others, particularly with peers and subordinates. At this time in his development, Jack was not ready to let go of the person he believes himself to be. The call to an investment in self-reflection was secondary to his tendency to *do* and his reliance on *being* the expert. In time, Jack's development may give way to more connected, collaborative, humble, and engaged leadership with peers and reports.

These two illustrations deal with the readiness of the client to engage in changes that affect how others view them. Early in the coaching alliance, both coach and client should be satisfied that the client is clear about the "why" of the coaching—the larger consideration. Who am I as a leader, and who do I want to become as I shine the light on my presence in this organization?

The Next Step: Unpacking the Institutional Feedback

Once the coach and client-leader agree about a coaching alliance, the next step might be for the coach to engage with the manager or sponsor to further clarify the feedback. Just as the conversation with the client-leader must be utterly candid, so must the one with the boss. Here, the coach can help the supervising manager ground some of the intangibles that arise in feedback that the coach has given to the client. The clearer the feedback, the more specific the manager will be in identifying data that should be addressed in the coaching.

To begin, the coach will want to understand what is at stake and what difference will occur when the leader transforms his or her style. The coach should obtain the following:

- Ask what will happen if the client-leader is not ready or able to make the requisite changes.

- Ask what kind of leader the organization wants.
- Inquire about how the system rewards and supports those who demonstrate the desired leadership qualities.
- Ask about the nature of success and what it looks like to the organization. In other words, press for a concrete picture of what the sponsor or boss is looking for. A total picture is not always easy to acquire, but the manager will often have an idea of what is missing. What is more important for the organization is for the client to have a clear sense of what the sponsor needs to see that will signal the desired leadership qualities. The skillful coach will ask for clear examples and expectations and will ask about the support the client-leader can expect from the manager and from those within the client-leader's sphere of influence.
- Ask for examples of what will signal when the client has demonstrated the "presence" that the organization is looking for. Learn examples of what is missing. Ask about the implicit rules of the organization.
- If the issue involves finding one's leadership voice, ask for concrete descriptors for what particular voice the key sponsor seeks.
- Ask how tolerant the organization is about differences in styles and preferences. Look for examples of leaders in the organization who have succeeded without conforming to organizational preferences.
- Ask how much time the client-leader has to demonstrate change. Remember it takes a long time for a client to let go of a mindset. Leadership presence is more than changing a set of behaviors. Finding one's voice requires scrutiny of one's values within the context of the organization, as well as refining one's ability to articulate and convey those values with clarity. That voice should signify full embodiment and the congruency between action and speech. The developing relationship between leader and coach will need time for the leader to construct a leadership vision, try it on for size, modify it, and master living it.

Finally, a coach should engage with the sponsor to get as much clarity about what is at stake for the client-leader and to discern what the client-leader truly needs to demonstrate to broaden that leadership capacity. Another powerful way to get a read on how the client-leader is doing is to interview peers and other constituents and to see where the leadership is effective and what work needs to occur. Peers and subordinates can provide specific feedback about the client-leader's ability to articulate vision, to influence without authority, and to motivate effectively.

However, when leadership presence is an issue, the most critical feedback often comes from superiors or seasoned peers.

The observations from colleagues can include, but not be limited to, questions that elicit answers to the following:

- Does the leader have a vision that is elegant and easily conveyed?
- Does the leader communicate strategically about matters concerning the organization?
- Does the leader take a stand and articulate a point of view?

- Does the leader manage his or her energy well?
- Does the leader command the room when speaking?
- Does the leader look the part? In some organizations, the right tie and sleeve length, hair cut, and color choice will matter and signal whether a leader is a part of the team or apart from the team.

Although such matters may seem superficial to the client-leader, the question remains: how do these factors affect the leader's ability to connect and to be viewed and accepted as a member of the executive team.

When the coach interviews more than one stakeholder or peer in the client's sphere of influence, that interview can help clarify whether the feedback is an idiosyncratic preference on the part of the boss or whether others hold the same perceptions. It can also bring even more issues to light. Thus, having a conversation with the boss about the boss's challenges and about which leadership issues should be addressed to help expand the client's capacity can be crucial for the client-leader to determine which goals make sense.

How to Coach the Leader

Because of the tender nature of coaching for presence, it is exceptionally critical for the coach to hold the space without judgment and to inspire trust in the client-leader. Then the client will become a more connected, motivational, committed, intentional leader. Making that choice will be life-enhancing if it is meaningful. Having the latitude to make a choice for enhancing one's voice or presence or both when dealing with those with whom the leader works and whom the leader wants to influence is humbling and can be overwhelming.

When you begin with the premise that the leader is competent and whole, the opportunity to broaden his or her capacity can provide an immense opportunity for both leadership and personal growth. Therefore, it is essential for the leader to retain integrity with personal values as the leader changes. Coaching the leader who wants to enhance presence is not commensurate with a makeover. Leadership presence coaching works best when wholesale change is not required. We assume here that the leader is competent to do his or her job. With coaching, the coach and client reimagine and reshape the way the leader relates to others, influences, communicates, or self-manages to have greater effect in his organization.

Working with the client-leader who is challenged with developing or modifying his or her leadership presence requires the coach to be knowledgeable and experienced in adult developmental literature. It helps when the coach is cognizant about how leaders grow and change. The coach must understand emotional intelligence and somatic practices that engender intentionality and awareness. The works of Kegan, Basseches, Torbert, Cook-Grueter, Laske, and others can help the coach become more conversant in the stages of adult development.[1] You may also refer to table 20.1 for questions to ask the client-leader to aid in the transformation.

Contextual distinctions greatly influence this work because the leader is often required to moderate a leadership stance to fit the challenge at hand. This stance requires the leader to be attuned to the organization in a way that is different from

Table 20.1   Questions to aid the client-leader's transformation

To help the client-leader to clearly understand what is at stake and what difference will occur when the leader transforms his or her style, the coach might ask the following questions:

- What will happen if you are not ready or able to make the requisite changes?
- What kind of leader does your organization want? How do you show up?
- What incentives does the system in your organization offer to those who demonstrate the desired leadership qualities?
- What does success look like in your organization? (In other words, press for a concrete picture of what the sponsor or boss is looking for. A total picture is not always easy to acquire, but the boss will often have an idea of what is missing. It is even more important for the organization than it is for the client-leader to have a clear sense of what the sponsor needs to see that will signal the desired leadership qualities. The skillful coach will ask for clear examples and expectations and will ask about the support the client-leader can expect from the manager and from those within the client-leader's sphere of influence.)
- What will happen when you have demonstrated the "presence" that your organization wants?
- What are the implicit rules of your organization?
- What is your organization's tolerance level for differences in styles and preferences?

the way the leader previously perceived it. Thus, coaching occurs in the space between the leader's current locus of control: for instance, how one views oneself within the organization and the power one feels one has to change that perception to what one wants to create when leveraging one's effectiveness. Some such as Jack need to manage their energy, to listen, and to enroll others so they understand his vision. Another leader might need the flip side of the coin: to speak with greater authority and conviction.

To make an authentic change, leaders must buy into the notion that their way of being—their identity in the organization—can be a means of accomplishing more than the current reality. That is, their role is only part of the equation. This concept is often difficult for a leader to fathom, particularly one who depends on hierarchical authority as a primary means of influencing. What may compound the issue is when leaders have relied primarily on their commitment to work and have given scant attention to developing relationships and an astute view of the political aspects of organizational life.

In the initial conversation, the coach strives to discern how the client-leaders are motivated, whether their sense of self is solid, and whether they are developmentally ready to examine how their style affects those with whom they work and who report to them. Does each leader see the value in finding a voice and a strategy for leadership that reflects that stance? Does each view the feedback as an opportunity to leverage personal effectiveness and to work more easily and successfully with colleagues? Does the leader feel put down or supported in such efforts because the coach has been included? Can the leaders imagine themselves as the creator of their destiny, or do they see the organization's request as threatening to their identity?

At the heart of leadership presence is authenticity and a demonstration of genuine respect for oneself and for others. Knowledge, technical ability, experience, and accomplishment are important, but the ability to connect and to be genuinely accessible to others is essential.

When respect is present and consistently demonstrated, it allows others to receive us more easily, and it creates space for a genuine exchange of ideas. As such, the new leader can be more emboldened to articulate personal ideas and to elicit ideas from others. The goal should be to articulate vision, challenge the status quo, contribute to the conversation for future possibilities, move action forward, make a difficult decision public, and lead others. Listening is a key ingredient to this mixture because it keeps the leader in touch with what is going on; it also provides a forum for gathering new ideas from others. Listening keeps the leader in touch with the reality of not having all the answers and with the relief of not having to be the sole repository of information and solutions.

Some Coaching Issues That Involve Presence

As discussed earlier, leadership issues run the gamut—from strategic communication to presence to personal attire and hygiene. In my first work assignment, a supervisor's lack of hygiene provided fodder for frequent conversations among the subordinates, of which I was one. The supervisor's boss was unprepared to address the concern with the supervisor. This problem eroded the morale of the staff because it was difficult to be near this supervisor-leader and because the hygiene problem was a source of derision. A few years after I left my part-time job, I learned that several colleagues had left a package of personal hygiene products in the supervisor's desk. Sadly, no one ever confronted the issue head on. I must admit that—as a college student in my first job assignment—I did not have the skills or courage to call this supervisor-leader aside either.

It takes courage on the part of the coach and the client-leader to embark on this work, particularly with clients whose "gremlin"—an annoying, critical inner voice—is active.

Often clients who are striving to find their leadership voice are new leaders who consider themselves introverts. These individuals are those who prefer time to think before they speak, who find they cannot get a word in when within group settings, or who are at a loss for words when they are questioned about a topic they don't know well. The notion of talking off the top of their head, or speaking extemporaneously, is as uncomfortable as an ill-fitting shoe. Calling forth what they know so they can fashion a "good enough" answer is uncomfortable and sometimes is a scary proposition. Perhaps the biggest challenge is providing a strategic answer that gives context to what they want to convey and that gives relevant detail. A more structured communication style can be helpful for new leaders to gain credibility with their superiors and new peers.

Asking the leader to practice responses on a range of topics before the meeting will signal awareness of the topic, and it will credibly allow the leader to get back to the colleague with more information. Now the new leader can build confidence.

Even more critical is coaching leaders to challenge their assumptions about how they will be viewed if they fashion a response that is not full of details—some of which may not be important to the audience. What's a good enough answer? What do leaders fear will happen if they don't include all details? What's underlying that fear? What might it feel like to shed the data cloak? Whom is the leader trying to impress? What's the worse thing that can happen if the answer is not the very best the leader could give?

To be successful, the leader needs to be discerning about the audience and to craft a message accordingly. Here is where being astute about the culture pays off. What unspoken rules and mores leaders are expected to know and to communicate varies from company to company, and sometimes they vary from department to department depending on who is leading. How much detail a leader might offer in a meeting with subject matter peers or with his or her team will be different from what he or she conveys in a progress update when superiors want to know how the project adds value, when it will be delivered, and what might derail it (i.e., cost overruns or variables that are beyond my control).

Too Bold, Too Much

Now and then, it is a matter of the client ratcheting down his or her way of being rather than intensifying it. One up-and-coming leader received feedback that clients had complained that he spoke too loudly in meetings and was not willing to consider other opinions that he thought unfeasible. This bright, capable leader—who was not American born—realized that his communication style reflected the culture of his native country where word games and one-upmanship were prized. In his current environment, he was seen as a good person, but arrogant, curt, and moody. He was not culturally observant, and his interpersonal style was out of sync with his company. He had missed the subtleties of the corporate culture that rewarded a polished, more sophisticated client approach.

Our coaching helped this leader to shift the way he observed himself in relationship to others, as well as to attend to the practical aspect of making distinctions about his environment: stage voice, conference room voice for most meetings and presentations, and conversational voice for one-on-one interactions. To make it safe for him to practice adapting his voice, he worked at home with his children and wife to create a more intimate style of speaking. Although it was important for this leader not to lose confidence or the edge that was necessary for his success as a consultant, he needed to interact in a style that was not perceived as confrontational by his clients and superiors.

In another situation, the leader's height, garrulous nature, and confidence were off-putting to some colleagues who found his height to be intimidating. This leader became more aware of how others perceived him, particularly when he was engaged in spirited conversation (i.e., when he was trying to make a point or disagreed with someone else's point of view). So it was incumbent on him as a leader and influencer in his organization to manage his energy in a way that made it safe for others to challenge him in conversation and to feel heard by him when they disagreed.

Presence and the Technology Curtain

Of course, issues of presence are not limited to physical and verbal interactions. In today's fast-paced world of ubiquitous technology, the leaders also may be derailed by their written communication, the most lethal of which is e-mail. Etiquette for e-mail often eludes the busy leader who shoots from the hip without considering the e-mail trail being created and the tone of the response. What seems to get lost in the leaders' thinking is congruency about the impression they are sending. Things a leader would never say in a face-to-face meeting can fly off glibly in an e-mail.

One very successful engineer found herself called on the carpet after circulating an e-mail about an idea that came from a company executive. The e-mail had been, she said, in a spirit of calling it as she saw it. She was unwilling to bow to anyone, and she flouted authority whenever she could. This leader also cultivated a reputation for sending scathing e-mails to subordinates. The bottom line was that she had a temper and was frustrated that she found she had to repeat requests to members on her team. In short, they had tuned her out, much as a recalcitrant child does to a parent. Just as she did not have a lot of respect for her superiors, her team did not give her the respect she wanted. The difference was she was upfront about her opinions. Her subordinates were more subtle but were just as destructive. The leader, however, was quite invested in her mission and was committed to excellence. Moreover, what really sparked her contract for change was the physical and personal toll it was taking on her.

In our initial conversation, she was honest about a lifestyle that was unhealthy and emotionally draining. So for the first part of her coaching program, we began with issues of self-care. Once those basic, yet integral, aspects of her being were addressed, both self-management and thinking before responding became easier. It took a while for this leader to change her public identity as a leader who was disparaging of others and mercurial of mood. In the end, colleagues in her sphere of influence reported many fewer difficult e-mails and an enhanced relationship resulting from her calmer interactions—in person and through e-mail. This leader also reported improvements with her personal relationships, as exercise and reflection tempered the reflexive posture she had often taken before our coaching sessions. When we ended coaching, this client-leader was still exploring the balance between support and challenge with her team, but she was not in the same jeopardy in terms of losing her team because of her fits of temper and lack of empathy.

Conclusion

It is imperative for the leader and the coach to be clear about the overarching goal of coaching when presence is the issue. The conversation will need to continue to examine the balance between (1) the organization's request that the leader modify or adapt a personal characteristic and (2) the leader's sense of who he or she is now and wants to become. At the end of the day, the leader needs to retain integrity with his or her core values and sense of self. The goal is not simply about results that the client derives from demonstrating new behaviors. If coaching is successful, the client-leaders will know a great deal more about themselves. In addition to maintaining integrity and values, the leaders and those with whom they interact will be positive about the quality of the engagement, and the leaders will show up congruent and whole. Colleagues will respond with concrete feedback about the work that is delivered, and they will demonstrate genuine respect. This type of development will reflect the difference in influence that the leader manifests. What starts as a daunting journey becomes as satisfying as any coaching engagement when an embodied, more present leader emerges.

Note

1. Kegan, *The Evolving Self: Problem and Process in Human Development;* Idem, *In Over Our Heads: The Mental Demands of Modern Life;* Laske, *Measuring Hidden Dimensions: The Art and Science of Fully Engaging Adults;* Torbert, Cook-Grueter, Fisher, Foldy, Gauthier, Keeley, Rooke, et al., *Action Inquiry: The Secret of Timely and Transforming Leadership.*

Bibliography

Kegan, Robert. *The Evolving Self: Problem and Process in Human Development.* Cambridge, MA: Harvard University Press, 1982.

————. *In Over Our Heads: The Mental Demands of Modern Life.* Cambridge, MA: Harvard University Press, 1994.

Laske, Otto E. *Measuring Hidden Dimensions: The Art and Science of Fully Engaging Adults.* Medford, MA: Interdevelopmental Institute Press, 2006.

Torbert, Bill, Susanne Cook-Grueter, Delmar Fisher, Erica Foldy, Alain Gauthier, Jackie Keeley, David Rooke, et al. *Action Inquiry: The Secret of Timely and Transforming Leadership.* San Francisco, CA: Berrett-Koehler, 2004.

CHAPTER 21

Coaching for Leverage:
Helping Clients to Manage Priorities, Time, Energy, and Resources

Katherine Ebner

The young woman is perched on the edge of her chair in my office. Her face is pale, shoulders slumped. She emanates stress as she describes a crushing list of deadlines and commitments, and I have the sense that she might jump up any minute and run out the door to get back to work. "The worst part," she tells me, looking distraught, "is that I fainted at work last week and again during the weekend. I went to the hospital for blood tests, but they didn't find anything. The doctor said that I have to deal with my stress." As I listened to her, I noticed that, when she finished speaking, she held her breath. I counted silently to see how long she would hold it. After about ten seconds, she spoke. "I don't know what to do. I need this job, but I have no work/life balance." Again she held her breath. "Are you aware that you're holding your breath?" I asked her. "No!" she said, startled. As I described my observation, she began to smile. "Are you telling me that the reason I fainted is that I'm holding my breath?" "Could be," I said. "Would you mind observing this to see if it is happening consistently?" Three days later, she called. "Yes. I'm holding my breath all the time. I have so much going on at work and outside of work that I seem to just keep bracing myself by holding my breath."

This example seems extreme, yet many people who describe their commitments do so in the same kind of breathless rush, running through lists of "to do's," creating mental piles of commitments. As coaches, we meet people like this young woman frequently—high achievers who have gotten far in life by exceeding expectations. Eventually, they achieve a level of challenge that forces them to face up to the limitations of time, energy, and resources. There are too many priorities. Everything is urgent. Nothing can be set aside or removed from the towering stack of "must-do's." At this point, an individual realizes that something is terribly wrong. "I can't go on like this," one of my clients said recently. "Even when I accomplish something important, there are three more things I haven't gotten to. I need help sorting out my priorities and finding some work/life balance."

For the coach, the goal of "work/life balance" may seem at first simply like a call for help with time-planning. Indeed, this is an important skill for leaders to master. However, to truly help a client make a transformational shift in the way she manages herself, the coach must also help the client to look at behavior and attitudes in three other areas: priorities, energy, and resources. In this chapter, we explore concepts and strategies for helping clients to move from a state of being overwhelmed to a healthier way of living and working.

Preliminary Conversation

Before beginning to work with a client who is overwhelmed, the coach and the client must have a preliminary conversation in which the coach invites the client to tell his story and describe his current challenges. During this conversation, the coach listens for:

- the external requirements and standards that the client currently faces, with attention to areas that need the client's immediate attention;
- the client's contribution to the situation, including history, beliefs, and personal standards that may be contributing to the situation;
- the client's emotional, mental, and physical state, which provides information about what is realistic for the client to undertake in the near term, as well as where the client may need to attend to his own needs;
- ideas the client may already have about how to identify top priorities and work for better balance.

This conversation may also give the coach an opportunity to address the mistaken belief—not uncommon among high achievers—that the habit of overwork is one of the key reasons for their success. Many people believe that they risk losing rewards, status, and the support and admiration of others if they do not exhibit this type of "work ethic." Choosing to live a more balanced life feels like the first step *off* the fast track—an invitation to relinquish control of career success. To coach such a client, the coach first must help the client to become aware of the debilitating consequences of overwork—including diminished performance over time, loss of perspective, loss of stamina and health, and the inability to demonstrate self-mastery. Thus, the client's call for coaching on "work/life balance" is an invitation to work with clients, not simply at the level of tactics, but also at the deeper level of self-awareness and self-mastery.

Coaching for Leverage

The concept of "leverage" is well known in business, where it is associated with strategies that achieve equal or better results with less effort and stress. Designed to help the client "work smarter, not harder," the *Leverage Coaching Model* (figure 21.1) looks at the client's life through four interrelated lenses: priorities, time, energy, and resources.

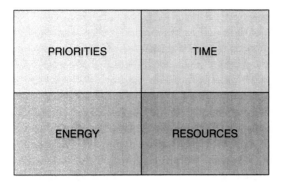

Figure 21.1   Leverage coaching framework

Table 21.1   Priorities interview—Sample questions

- What has heart and meaning for you in your life?
- Who are the most important people in your life? How do they factor into your daily life right now? Are you satisfied with how it is working?
- Identify the priorities in your private life and in your work life.
- Rank the priorities in each category and then explain the ranking.
- What prevents you from focusing on these priorities?
- For each priority, indicate:
  - what is important to you about this priority,
  - what you will have accomplished if you achieve this priority,
  - how your days would be different if you were observing this priority faithfully.
- If you could only do two things in each category, what would they be?
- If you don't allow yourself to set priorities, what will happen?

To gain the full picture of the client's immediate challenges and options, the coach asks the client a series of questions in each quadrant (table 21.1). Typically, the coach will select the four or five questions from each quadrant that seem most appropriate for the client, rather than putting the client through a long questionnaire that may feel like an interrogation.

By developing an understanding of the relationships among these four aspects of the client's life, the coach can readily assess what is foremost in the client's mind and what the internal and external pressures are.

Our priorities are the commitments that we believe deserve our most immediate and constant attention. Busy professionals juggle an astonishing mix of work and life priorities every day. They feel responsible for delivering "results," not only at work, but also in their personal lives. Moreover, as businesses struggle to meet quarterly goals under the scrutiny of shareholders, the pressure on employees at all levels mounts. High achievers internalize the expectations of their employers and add them to their own personal standards and life goals. The result is a continuous sense of urgency and responsibility, with little differentiation between major priorities and minor ones and with little or no time to celebrate accomplishments.

As coaches, we know that the priority list that is most meaningful for the client is one that includes the whole of life. In fact, if client and coach focus only on one arena—work or private life—to the exclusion of the other, it is likely that pressures and priorities in the other arena will derail the client's attempts to deliver on priorities. When we explore priorities with clients, we tap into several levels of commitment and beliefs, from the daily "to do" list to the entire life plan.

The chance to think about all of life can catch a driven professional by surprise. One executive made a startling discovery when she wrote down her priorities during a recent coaching session. In less than 10 minutes, she generated a list of twenty priorities at work. When she worked on listing her priorities for her personal life, however, she became confused. "Are these priorities or goals?" she asked. "Does it matter if I'm not actually doing any of them?" Slowly, she produced a list of priorities for her private life that included time with her husband and with each of her two children, time to practice yoga, and a work schedule that allowed her to be home by 6:00 p.m. to have dinner with her young family. "I'm not doing it, though," she said, thoughtfully. "Every single day I get up at 5:00 a.m. to get to work, so that I can supposedly leave by 5:15 p.m. and have dinner with my family. The truth is, I rarely leave the office before 6:30. The kids are already in bed by the time I get home. My real priority must be work. I am not acting like family is a real priority, even though I say it is." Looking at priorities with a client invites a moment of truth.

A good way to get a clear picture of what someone's priorities actually are is to ask them to track how they are spending time for one week (table 21.2). Since there is a difference between intentions and actual behavior, by collecting the "data," the true priorities become clear. Once the client has done this self-observation, she is usually ready to talk about how to make changes to live in a way that truly reflects her personal values.

For high achievers, one particular barrier that may stand in the way of changing their behavior is a highly developed sense of responsibility to others (company, family, and colleagues), which often causes them to put their own needs last. They believe they are only allowed to give attention to what matters to them after they have satisfied the needs and expectations of their boss, their workplace, and their family. In the coaching conversation, when these clients identify their priorities and

Table 21.2   Time interview—Sample questions

- Describe an ideal day/week.
- What prevents you from having that kind of day/week?
- What deadlines are you facing in the next six weeks?
- How do you budget time for projects and priorities?
- How do you use your calendar to manage your time?
- Look at this week's calendar. Is it realistic?
- Does your calendar reflect your top priorities? If not, how will you find time for important work?
- Is your personal life included in your calendar?
- If you could make three changes in how you expect to spend your time this week, what would they be?

---

actual daily experience, they are often revealing to themselves deeply held beliefs about what success means. Their actual behavior reveals what they are willing to do—and sacrifice—to achieve it.

A client who puts her own needs last is often out of "sync" with her values and suffers not only from overcommitment, but also from trying to achieve success on terms that are important to other people rather than to herself. When prioritization leaves out considerations of the health and well being of the person making the priorities list, that person is working long and hard, with dwindling energy, motivation, and hope. For the client to place herself at the top of the list takes courage and a willingness to make substantive changes in the commitments she makes—and the leaders who do this are held up as "authentic" and as admirable role models for the rest of us.

Executives at all levels of the organization experience problems with saying no to unrealistic workloads. I notice that many of my clients believe that, if they could just manage *time* better, they could succeed more easily. A conversation about how they spend their time reveals the rationale behind the work habits. Some confess to staying late to micromanage the work of others ("I just can't trust anyone else to do the job right.") or to being a perfectionist who procrastinates on complex projects because it seems that "there isn't enough time to do it properly."

As the coach works with the client on time-planning and matching priorities with time allocation, the coach will be able to observe the client's "mode of operating"—what she believes is necessary for her to *do* and to *be* in order to succeed. The coach will also see where the client may be sabotaging herself as a result of unrealistic (or nonexistent) planning.

By attending to time-management early in the coaching process, the client will experience a greater sense of control and focus and will most likely deliver better results in the days ahead. These early wins build credibility for coaching as a helpful learning process and for the coach as someone who can provide real value and benefit for the client.

People focus on mastering many competencies on their way to "the top," but the most successful senior executives—those who have learned to sustain high performance over years and who have a confident, energetic presence—know that the key to success is to pay attention to energy (table 21.3). By doing work that is energizing

Table 21.3   Energy interview—Sample questions

- What gives you energy?
- What drains your energy away?
- What do you love about your work?
- What do you love doing when you aren't at work?
- What are your top work priorities this week?
- Which things on the list do you look forward to?
- Which ones give you a sense of dread? What could you do to increase your enthusiasm and energy for those you dread?
- What is your typical energy level in the morning? Midday? Evening?
- What do you do to refuel your energy? What are your daily habits?
- Do you take care of your health through diet, exercise, and sleep?

and by making time for activities that refuel their energy, these leaders are able to sustain their focus and to thrive.

To discover what is energizing to the client, the coach and client must examine what truly motivates him. We are most motivated to work on challenges that are aligned with our values. Thus, this conversation is a critical part of linking personal values and life vision with priorities.

When the client sees the difference between where he has passion and where he is just tolerating his existence—and understands how passion is linked with energy—he will begin to use as a criterion in managing his responsibilities, "Does this give me energy or take it away?" This key distinction can lead the client to see new possibilities and to let go of old responsibilities, relationships, and habits that are unproductive and unsustainable.

As the coach helps the client appreciate the importance of managing energy to sustain performance, stamina, and health, the client will be able to make heartfelt commitments to improved health and stick with those commitments. He will make adjustments to take care of his health and energy with the new awareness that peak performance requires attention to passion, health, and energy. He also is likely to feel better physically, which increases motivation and well-being in all areas of life. This attention to the physical self often addresses a long-held regret in a busy person, who knows that he needs to change his habits but hitherto has not had a strong enough rationale to commit to it.

Busy people often tell me that "it would take too much time" to delegate work to others or to renegotiate deadlines. Instead, they apply themselves to the tasks at hand, working in isolation to keep all the balls in the air. By overlooking the available resources (table 21.4) or not taking the time to use them effectively, a leader is on a course to fall short of expectations and burn out in the process.

The question "What resources are available right now?" signals to the client that help is available—or at least, it could be. In the Leverage Coaching Model, the concept of "resources" includes:

- *people* who can provide support at work and at home;
- published resources, such as books and articles;
- *experts* or *consultants* who can provide specialized assistance;
- *technologies* that can make work processes more efficient;
- financial resources; and
- competencies, experiences, and skills of the client himself.

As the client's situation is made clear to the coach in the "Resources" portion of the Leverage Interview, the coach can begin to test the client's assessment of the situation, to determine how much support is actually available to the client. Often, the client realizes that he hasn't actually made others aware of his challenges and has not made a clear request for help. The Resources Interview helps the client think more creatively about his current use of resources and about available resources that may have been overlooked.

Occasionally, a client will demonstrate that he is truly alone in having to handle a big responsibility. In this case, coach and client might work together to

Table 21.4 Resources interview—Sample questions

- Make a list of your commitments. For each item, identify your responsibilities and others' responsibilities.
- What special knowledge/information/skills are needed to complete each item? Do you know anyone with these skills who can help you? What would you need to do to get that help?
- Is there anyone on your team who has a passion for one of these projects and would benefit from taking on a bigger piece of it?
- What keeps you from delegating?
- What do you need to request from your family right now to handle this situation?
- If you tackle a project by yourself, can you describe what is likely to happen?

---

frame requests that enable the client to deliver on commitments or to renegotiate expectations.

Paying attention to available resources whenever possible will free up time and energy for the priorities that matter most.

Summary and Strategies for Using the Leverage Coaching Model

After completing the four-part Leverage Interview, the client and coach have a solid, richly detailed body of information and plenty of areas where the client can begin self-observation and practice. Coach and client can continue to work together to design practices and actions that give "leverage" to the client and dramatically improve the way that he functions at work and in life in general.

There are many other applications of the model. Its usefulness relies on the coach's creativity in integrating the activities and ideas from each quadrant.

The following strategies provide examples of how a coach might work with the Leverage Coaching Model. These approaches can be used independently or simultaneously, depending on the client and the situation.

Strategy One: Focus on the Calendar

The purpose of this strategy is to encourage the client to use the calendar to reflect priorities accurately and manage resources efficiently. The coach begins by reviewing the client's priorities with him and then asking him to block out time on the calendar for priority projects and goals. For example, if the client's goal is to sell $1 million in consulting services within the next six months, he needs to map out the steps necessary to achieve that goal and then plan the time needed for each step, blocking out appropriate periods in the calendar to accomplish each.

Focusing on the calendar should get the client thinking well beyond the next month. It is possible, and frequently desirable, to ask the client to plan as far out as twelve or eighteen months. At minimum, the client should look ahead three months to anticipate future deadlines. The calendar should reflect such things as travel plans, important meetings, performance assessments of staff, personal appointments (dentist, doctor, school events, accountant, etc.), management meetings with staff, and vacation plans.

As the client begins to treat the calendar as a helpful tool for achieving priorities, she will begin to experience a sense of relief. The calendar exercise will also show the client when her commitments add up to "impossible," forcing her to a moment of truth about her definition of a successful life.

Strategy Two: Focus on Energy and Passion

Building on the Energy Interview, the coach can provide resources and encouragement to the client to invest in increasing his energy and passion. The first step is to educate the client about the demonstrable difference that passion and energy make in performance. *The Power of Full Engagement: Managing Energy, Not Time, Is the Key to High Performance and Personal Renewal*[1] by Loehr and Schwartz, or the article "The Making of the Corporate Athlete"[2] by the same authors, are outstanding resources for helping the client to understand this link. In these works, the authors share their research on what distinguishes top performing athletes from average athletes, and they apply their findings to the performance of executives in the corporate environment.

Once the client has accepted the idea that managing energy is the key to sustaining performance, coach and client can begin to explore how passion (or lack of it) is affecting performance. As the client begins to observe his energy level and its link with passion, the coach can ask the client to give priority to activities that bring him energy.

The focus on energy also opens the door to a discussion about health and happiness, allowing the coach to talk about the domain of the body. I frequently ask my clients to commit to at least one practice that fosters physical health. Clients quickly sign up for the yoga class or resolve to jog three times per week—activities that they have wanted to do, but previously saw as superfluous rather than essential.

To make room for this new activity, the coach and client must revisit priorities and time-planning, a conversation that strengthens the client's understanding of the relationships among the quadrants of the Leverage Model.

Additionally, the coach can work with the client to identify his life mission, values, and personal needs. This work reveals the client to himself in a way that gives the current challenges a larger, more meaningful context. The mission and values exercises will help the client to understand what his passion really is, while the personal needs exercise will show him what "hooks" distract him from acting with passion and integrity.

Strategy Three: Focus on Reducing Priorities

When someone suffers from overcommitment, reducing the number or scope of priorities is essential.

Once the client has identified personal and professional priorities broadly, the coach can work with her to select those that are most urgent or perhaps are the foundation for achieving other goals. The client is able to find a good starting point for progress by prioritizing the priorities.

The coach's first question might be, "What is on this list that *only* you can do?" encouraging the client to accept the idea that not everything must be "owned" by her. Next, the client could begin to narrow the list by assigning each priority a number in terms of its importance to her well-being. The coach might then suggest that the client set priorities within a specific timeframe (the next week, month; six months, etc.), narrowing the list even more. Suddenly, the path forward is clear and better organized. It is time to identify the tasks related to achieving each priority and slot them into the calendar—including the time needed to enlist the right resources.

At the end of this exercise, the client should have a focused and streamlined picture of what must be accomplished in a defined time period and at least a preliminary plan for accomplishing it.

Conclusion

As it examines four aspects of performance—priorities, time, energy, and resources—the Leverage Coaching Model gives the coach an excellent opportunity to work with the client on three levels—tactical, strategic, and transformational. Of particular value is the inclusion of an energy assessment, which allows the coach to call attention to the crucial relationships among health, energy, and performance. By focusing on the ways in which the client determines priorities, manages time, maintains energy, and uses resources, the Leverage Coaching Model can make a critical difference in whether the client can achieve his goals, stay focused on his priorities, and have a fulfilling private life. A client who understands the relationship between priorities, time, energy, and resources—and can manage these variables effectively—is well on his way to mastering essential skills for leadership and sustainable high performance.

Notes

1. Loehr, Schwartz, *The Power of Full Engagement.*
2. Loehr, Schwartz, "The Making of the Corporate Athlete," *Harvard Business Review*, January 2001.

Bibliography

Covey, Stephen R. *The 7 Habits of Highly Effective People.* New York: Simon and Schuster, 1989.

The Grove Consults International and Joan McIntosh. *Personal Compass: A Workbook for Visioning and Goal Setting.* San Francisco, CA: Grove Consults International.

Heckler, Richard Strozzi. *The Anatomy of Change: A Way to Move through Life's Transitions.* Berkley, CA: North Atlantic Books, 1993.

Loehr, Jim and Tony Schwartz. *The Power of Full Engagement: Managing Energy, Not Time, Is the Key to High Performance and Personal Renewal.* New York: Free Press, 2003.

Watkins, Michael. *The First 90 Days: Critical Success Strategies for New Leaders at All Levels.* Boston: Harvard Business School Press, 2003.

CHAPTER 22

Action Learning: An Approach to Team Coaching

Jennifer Whitcomb

As someone who coaches individuals, you might be intrigued to learn about an approach that uses your existing skills to coach a group or team effectively. Organizations all over the world are using action learning as a group-coaching method to develop teams, enhance leadership skills, solve complex problems, and improve organizational efficiency. Action learning is fast becoming a popular group-coaching method as groups work on real-time challenges and apply learning and action at the same time.

Action-learning Overview

Action learning is a group-coaching approach that uses real people to solve real problems, in real time, to obtain real results. It is a process that brings people together to solve challenges, learn through reflection, and take action. Action-learning groups can work on a single problem or challenge that affects the entire group or on several problems presented by individual group members.

Reg Revans first introduced this approach when working with coal mine managers in the United Kingdom in the 1940s. Miners became involved and energized by solving their own problems and were successful at solving problems at each other's sites. The miners who participated in the action-learning process found their mines' performance increased, compared with the mines that did not participate.

This method emphasizes defining the problem accurately so the actual problem is solved. The group focuses on what it is learning, and how this learning applies to the group's individual members and to the organization. Action learning helps people look at the way they analyze a problem, work together as a team, take action, and get results. Given our rapidly changing work environment, action learning can be considered a just-in-time approach to leadership and team development that individuals may not get in a training program. A training program may not be offered at the right time or provide the relevant content.

Action learning uses many of the same skills that are used in individual coaching: asking powerful questions, creating reflection, enhancing learning, and taking action. With this group-coaching approach you will be able to use and transfer many of the individual coaching skills that you have honed.

The role of the coach is to use the process of listening and asking questions to help the group optimize its performance. An action-learning coach intervenes at various points to help the group improve its process, take action, and capture group learning.

Components of Action Learning

Action learning has six components and two ground rules. The six components are:

1. problem or challenge
2. group or team
3. questions and reflection
4. focus on learning
5. action
6. the coach

For a conceptual view, see figure 22.1.
The two ground rules are these:

1. Statements can be used only in response to questions.
2. The action-learning coach can intervene at any time.

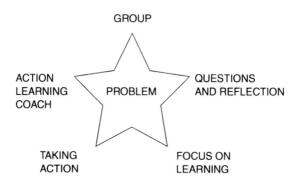

Figure 22.1 Components of action learning

Problem or Challenge

Ideally, the presenting problem should have these qualities:

- It should be urgent.
- It should not be a puzzle.
- It should be complex.
- It should be solvable.
- It should be something that has not been worked on already.

The types of problems, challenges, or opportunities that can be explored include improving a process, creating a new product, cutting costs, increasing business, resolving difficult workplace dynamics, handling leadership challenges, creating a new structure, improving communications, and so forth. For an individual presenting a problem, it can be anything meeting the earlier criteria that are keeping him or her up at night.

A number of people can present individual problems in a session, or one problem can be taken on by the entire group. At an action-learning session offered for executive directors of nonprofits, each executive director came to the session with a problem important to that director. The schedule allowed three people to present their problems during each session. Another organization using action learning for leadership development had two teams work on two different organizational issues.

Group or Team

An action-learning group or team ideally comprises six to eight participants. Groups smaller than six may not generate enough participation, and groups larger than eight may make it difficult for everyone to participate. Bringing diversity to the group through experience, background, age, gender, culture, and organizational level will generate a variety of viewpoints and perspectives.

At least one member of the action-learning group should have the authority to implement solutions discovered during the action-learning sessions.

Questions and Reflection

One of the ground rules in action learning is that statements can only be used in response to questions, thus making questions the major tool in this approach. The group works together by asking questions of each other, and the coach intervenes by asking questions at various points to help facilitate the process.

As with individual coaching, questions can be a powerful tool to gain clarity, build dialogue, create shared understanding, and enhance awareness. Questions help the group focus on the problem to gain clarity, get to the nut of the problem, and avoid the temptation to rush to a solution too soon and potentially solve the wrong problem. Questions help create an opportunity for reflection and for group members to step back and think. By creating this pause, group members can challenge their own assessments, open up perspectives, and possibly think about the problem in a different way. It's very common for the presenting problem to shift and be reframed after the group has started to ask questions. The group is responsible to ask questions either of the problem presenter or of each other. Group members often develop better coaching skills themselves as they begin to ask better questions and to listen more. Asking better questions is a skill that often gets transferred back to the work environment as group members learn the benefit of inquiry.

Focus on Learning

Being engaged in solving a complex problem creates individual, group, and organizational learning. Individuals learn about themselves: how they tackle a problem, how they assess themselves, and how they operate in a group. They may develop and strengthen a leadership competency, enhance awareness of their behavior in a group, or become better at solving problems. One person in an action-learning session realized he was monopolizing the process after the action-learning coach asked, "What are we doing well?" and "How could we be better as a group?" By reflecting on those questions, this person realized he tended to monopolize the process at other points in the workplace and in his personal life. He became more attuned to listening to others, and at work he became more likely to ask questions than to offer his opinion, thus helping improve his work relationships.

The group learns to improve and enhance its functioning. Group members begin to slow down their questioning process by listening more to other questions and building on those questions.

Action

Taking action is a key component in action-learning coaching, as it is with individual coaching. Group members take action by testing and implementing ideas. Taking action can involve doing research, gathering information, designing a process, or trying out a new idea or piece of a process. Individual team or group members take action on the problem between meetings. This is what makes action learning different from other problem-solving methods because the group is responsible for more than providing recommendations or reports. When the group has the authority to take action on its ideas, it remains committed and energized to solve the problem. Taking action provides a great opportunity to learn what action steps work and what needs to be improved. These action steps will form the basis for implementing the solution.

The Coach

As when working with an individual, the action-learning coach is a neutral party who creates the spirit of inquiry, reflection, learning, and action. The action-learning coach does not comment on the content of the session; otherwise, the credibility and neutrality may be lost and the group then may grow too dependent on the coach.

The coach intervenes at various points in the process, when he or she sees an opportunity for the group to learn about its process. One of the ground rules is that the action-learning coach has the authority to intervene at any time. Often the coach will sit a bit removed from the group and move in to intervene.

The Role of the Coach

The action-learning coach acts in four main areas of the process:

1. helping the group define the problem
2. enhancing the group process
3. taking action
4. capturing learning.

Helping the Group Define the Problem

The action-learning coach asks the person presenting the problem to describe the problem in a couple of minutes. If the presenter speaks much longer than that, he or she begins to get into too much detail or begins to solve the problem.

When the problem has been described, the group can begin asking questions about the definition. The time for the coach to intervene is when the group uses statements rather than questions, asks leading questions, asks solution-embedded questions, or when the group seems challenged. The first time the coach intervenes is usually approximately ten minutes into the session. The kinds of questions to ask toward the beginning of a session are:

- How are we doing as a group?
- What is the quality of our questions so far?
- What is the balance between statements and questions?
- How could we be better?
- What questions have been useful so far?

After the group has spent some more time asking questions, the coach may intervene to see whether the group has clarity on the problem. This step often works best when the coach says, "Write down in a couple of sentences what the problem is." This gives each person a moment to pause and reflect, and gives the group an opportunity to see if it is in agreement on the problem definition so far.

Debrief by asking each participant to read his or her statement. If there is one problem presenter, you may ask that person to go last. Ask the group if there is agreement on the problem. Most of the time, the group is either not clear about the specific problem or lacks agreement. Have the group ask questions again; then intervene again by repeating the exercise of writing down the problem statement and reading each statement to the group.

At this point, ask, "Do we have agreement on the problem?" If there is more than one problem for consideration, ask which problem the group would like to focus on.

Enhancing the Group Process

The action-learning coach intervenes when needed to improve the functioning and effectiveness of the group. However, it's just as important to intervene when things are progressing well to keep that momentum going, as it is to intervene when things are not going well. The approach to the interventions with the group is often more appreciative in nature, focusing on making things better and improving its process. For example, the coach will ask, "What's working well?" versus "What's not working well?" When someone in the group says, "That's a great question," it is a good time to intervene to find out what made that a good question so that the group can continue in that line of thought. The action-learning coach can intervene when one person is dominating, when the rate of questions is not allowing for enough reflection time, when the questions are not building on one another, or when the group is not making progress. Here are some questions that the coach can ask:

- How are we doing as a team?
- What would improve our process?
- Are we building on each other's questions?
- What's working well?
- What could we do better?

The interventions are done by asking these very simple questions. It sometimes can be tempting to comment on the process or ask a longer question, but these simple, tried-and-true questions really help the coach and the group.

Taking Action

When the group has agreement on the problem statement, it can move into this phase. The coach needs to make sure that the group has enough time in the session to come up with strategies and action steps. The coach may need to intervene to remind the group of the session's timeline, or he may tell the group to begin developing strategies and action steps.

Group members will begin suggesting strategies and action steps—what to do and how to do it. When one individual presents a problem, the group develops suggested strategies and action steps for that person to consider. When the group is working on a problem affecting the entire group, it needs to come to agreement on what strategies will be helpful, how action will be taken, and who will take responsibility between now and the next meeting.

As in individual coaching, the coach will ask what action steps will be taken as a result of the session. This question may be asked of the individual presenting a problem or of the entire group. This question typically is asked at the end of the session in the phase focused on capturing learning. Each group member will volunteer to take on specific action steps between sessions. The coach typically begins by asking, "What action steps are you going to take as a result of today's session?"

Ideally, each group member will take some responsibility for an action between meetings. Group members need to capture these action steps because the coach will ask what progress has been made on these steps at the next meeting.

Capturing Learning

The coach needs to plan for enough time to capture the group's learning adequately. Reminding the group that he or she will be stopping the process to allow for this will make the coach's job easier. Sometimes it's hard to bring the group to a close when it is making progress, but it's just as important to capture the learning as it is to solve the problem. It's advisable to plan at least fifteen minutes for this step.

Questions can be tailored to the purpose of the action-learning session. If the focus of the sessions is leadership development, then there may be more questions on the requisite skills and qualities of leaders. The action-learning coach needs to choose which questions will be most valuable to the group and will provide the most learning.

If there is one person presenting the problem, then the first three questions will be asked of that individual initially. If the group is working on a problem affecting the whole group, then these questions can be asked of the entire group. Here are questions to capture the lessons learned from the experience:

- What actions are you (we) going to take as a result of today's session?
- Were you/we helped? How?
- What did you learn about yourself?
- What did you learn about the problem?
- What did you learn about problem solving?
- What did you learn about leadership?
- How did we do as a team?
- What did we do well?
- What could we do better?
- What helped us make progress?
- What might we do differently next time?
- How can we transfer today's learning to us personally or to other parts of the organization?

Timing and Logistics of the Action-learning Process

Action-learning groups may meet once or twice a month over a six-month stretch or may meet for longer sessions over a couple of days. Most groups work well for up to a two-hour period. The length of time the group meets may depend on the complexity and the urgency of the problem.

Action learning tends to work best when members can meet face to face; however, many groups are composed of members in diverse locations. When working with groups whose members live in different locations, it's possible to use teleconferencing or videoconferencing; but at least for the first session, the group should meet in one location. When working with a group of executive directors for nonprofits, we hosted the first meeting in a retreat center. At our opening session in the afternoon we introduced the concept of action learning, and we provided an overview and initial practice. The evening offered time for group members to get to know each other. The next morning three people volunteered their problems in forty-five-minute sessions. Half an hour of each session was dedicated to the problem, and fifteen minutes were given to capturing learning. This group met for a period of six months using a balance of face-to-face meetings and teleconferences, with group members rotating the presentation of their problems. We noticed that providing the initial face-to-face meeting and allowing time for the group to get to know each other helped the group bond well. The group was very willing to help individual group members.

Benefits of Using This Coaching Approach

Some benefits resulting from this coaching approach include:

- greater diversity of ideas
- improved employee collaboration and engagement
- solutions to complex problems
- potential cost savings from solving complex problems
- group ownership of the problem
- leadership development
- team building
- transfer of individual coaching skills to group-coaching skills

Conclusion

Action learning may be one form of coaching that you wish to try to expand your portfolio of coaching skills. Many of the skills that you already have will help you with this method of coaching.

Your ability to be a neutral presence is the skill that transfers most easily to group coaching. Your staying objective and neutral helps the group become much more self-sufficient and productive. Another skill that easily transfers to group coaching is the use of powerful questions and reflection. Your familiarity with these kinds of questions will make it easier for you to create space for the group to reflect on both its process and its progress. Another skill that we learn in individual coaching is to facilitate learning and create awareness in our clients. As the action-learning coach intervenes at various points within the process, the group members learn about themselves, problem solving, teamwork, and transfer of learning to other parts of the organization. Of course, the ability to help our clients take action and move forward is another skill that transfers to group coaching. Without this critical step, we would not be able to help our clients learn from the actions they have taken or to help them implement the solution in the organization.

Bibliography

Adams, Marilee G. *Change Your Questions Change Your Life: 7 Powerful Tools for Life and Work.* San Francisco, CA: Berrett-Koehler, 2004.

M.J. Marquardt. *Action Learning in Action: Transforming Problems and People for World-Class Organizational Learning.* Palo Alto, CA: Davies-Black, 1999.

————. "Harnessing the Power of Action Learning." *Training and Development Journal*, June 2004, 26–32.

————. *Leading with Questions: How Leaders Find the Right Solutions by Knowing What to Ask.* San Francisco, CA: Jossey-Bass, 2005.

————. *Optimizing the Power of Action Learning: Solving Problems and Building Leaders in Real Time.* Palo Alto, CA: Davies-Black, 2004.

For more information on Action Learning: The World Institute of Action Learning, www.wial.org

CHAPTER 23

Coaching New Teams

Patricia A. Mathews

Successful teams, whether new or existing, need continuing support from the leader and the organization. A team coach can intensify this support by observing the team's current functioning, assessing the team's strengths and weaknesses, and, in collaboration with the leader, developing a plan for addressing any needed changes. Brand new teams in new situations require extra care and feeding.

There are various "new" team categories. For example, an existing team with a new leader is a team that has already been formed and worked together when a new leader is appointed and enters the mix. If members join an existing team and/ or a new leader is appointed, the hybrid team is actually an existing team gaining new members and/or a new leader. In either case, the end result is a "new" team—different from the original team.

A third example is the brand new team. Here the team is new to the organization and/or its members who may have never worked on a team before. This chapter discusses the specific strategies a team coach can use when working with brand new teams.

The Brand New Team: A Case Study

Meet John Post. He's just been hired as the superintendent of a large public school system. He wants to form a team of senior staff to work together to accomplish great things for the school district. John is new to the area and in the first weeks of his job he observes that there is not a true senior leadership team in place. He spends several weeks observing staff members who serve in administrative roles and determines which staffers should be part of the senior team. After he identifies the members of the team, he decides to hire a team coach to work with him and the team to get them all off to a good start. John interviews me and decides that I would be right for the job.

John and his team are a good example of the benefits of utilizing team coaching with a brand new team. John was committed to leading this team to produce results in a school district where the previous leader had been in place for more than twenty years. Previously, the administrative staff members had never worked together as a team and they did not understand John's expectations of them. He brought a different leadership style to the school district and the potential team members had no experience working as a team or with their new leader.

Workplace teams are not new and have been part of organizational culture for years. What is becoming more apparent is that *how* new teams are managed can make the difference between successful teams and those that fail miserably. John was committed to making his brand new team one of the success stories.

One of the critical distinctions between successful and unsuccessful teams is the role of the leader. Some team leaders act like "bosses" and tell team members what to do and how and when to do it. Others maintain a "hands-off" policy and believe that this approach is best for the team. In our initial conversations, John confided that he was quick to make decisions, was great at vision, urged people to act quickly and that he often floated ideas to team members, but wasn't good at following up on whether team members took action.

We discussed my role as team coach. John wanted help for himself as leader and for the team members to form a cohesive and productive team from disparate individuals. In our initial meeting, we discussed how I might help him with three of the most critical indicators for team success:

1. Focus on performance
2. Define a set of goals
3. Agree on methods to achieve the goals

Initial Contracting and Coaching the Leader

In the case of a brand new team and before meeting with the team members, the team coach spends time with the leader to chart the team course. This includes:

- Team mission and goals
- Roles and responsibilities of team members
- Ground rules for the team

When I met with John initially to help him clarify these important foundational items, I asked him the following:

- Why should this new team exist?
- What does the team have to do to accomplish its purpose?
- What kind of decisions can the team make?
- How will the team make decisions?
- How often and how long will the team meet?
- Where and when will the team meet?

- What have you learned from leading other teams that you want to bring to this one?
- What do you already know about the team members?
- What do you need to know?
- How will you get the information you need?

Once John identified his answers to these questions, he decided to use some of the questions in this vital formative work with his team. In addition, John and I discussed the role of the team coach distinguishing between team coaching and team building. My role in working with his team would include some teaching, consulting, and coaching and would focus on helping the team to work together to achieve their goals, as well as on strengthening John's role as leader. We were clear about the distinctions between team coaching and team building. We were not planning simulations, games, or other means of building his team. We decided on a four-month initial contract with continued team coaching to be contracted after evaluating the first four months.

Team Member Interviews

Once John and I had completed several meetings and he achieved some clarity about the team's purpose, I scheduled an interview with each member of the team. I often do these interviews via telephone, partly because of geographic and schedule concerns, and because team members may feel more comfortable on the telephone. I stress that these interviews are confidential and that the information helps me to understand each member better. I also clearly indicate that the overall results of the interviews will be shared with the leader and the team at our first joint meeting explaining that I give this feedback in the form of general themes, never using direct quotes or indicating which team member contributed the information.

The questions I used for this interview were:

- What do you think will be the strengths of this team and leader?
- What strengths do you personally bring to the team?
- What weaknesses do you think the team and leader might have?
- What areas would you personally need to improve to be a good team member?
- What do you hope will be the results of working with a team coach?
- Is there anything else that I have not asked, by way of background or information gathering, but should know to help me do my job better when I work with you?

I compiled the results of the interviews and shared general feedback with the leader before the first team event.

Using Assessments During the Start-Up Phase of a Team

The next step I take in coaching new teams is to have each team member complete the *Success Insights*[1] team assessment. This statistically valid and reliable instrument uses the DISC model, and it is completed by each team member and the leader via an Internet delivery system. Each team member signs on and completes an assessment. I use it with team leaders and members for several reasons: it identifies their natural style of behavior, it highlights challenges they might have with people of a different style, and it gives me as the team coach a foundational understanding of how to coach the leader and the team. I print all the reports so that they are kept confidential until the first team meeting. I also compile a team report that maps each individual profile on a team wheel.

Applications for this assessment in coaching a new team include identifying team and individual strengths (and comparing them to the interview answers), uncovering stress areas for individuals and potential conflicts between team members, identifying potential blind spots among team members, providing a neutral tool for self-discovery of natural talent and behavior and providing a behavior based tool for assessing behavior shifts.

There are other assessments that are constructive for those teams that have already been working together because they assess the current state of the team, but I find that the *Success Insights* team version is the most beneficial for brand new teams as they have not yet experienced how the team works together. Later in their development as a team, other assessments may be used.

When the team is new, it is helpful for members to complete an assessment that advances each member's understanding of his/her own behavior and how it fits with the rest of the team. This is important during the start-up phase because it helps members understand that their intention (based on their style) may not be showing up in their behavior.

This team assessment contains the following sections:

- Basic characteristics
- Work characteristics
- Value to the team
- Value to the organization
- Effective communication
- Team effectiveness factors
- Perceptions
- Descriptors
- Action plan

Before I met with the entire team, I debriefed John's assessment with him. This step both helped John understand his style and also established the foundation for him to use the results of the instrument when working with the rest of the team. I did not share the results of the individual assessments with the leader.

I coached John to conduct the portion of the team meeting that utilizes the results of the assessment. He would facilitate a conversation about these specific topics:

- Similarities and differences in behavioral style
- How the similarities and differences affect team behavior

The First Team Meeting

Once the background work with the leader and the interviews with the team were complete, John scheduled the first team meeting.

At this meeting, John reintroduced me as the team coach and stated that I would be working with him and with the group both collectively and individually during this meeting and in the coming months. Explaining how the first meeting helps the team to recognize their strengths and to identify objectives for their work together, I shared the general results of the interviews and talked about my role as both coach and occasional facilitator for this first meeting.

I distributed all of the assessments and conducted a brief session about the *Success Insights* assessment to help the team members first understand their individual styles and then to determine their team composition. The value of the assessment is not in the results alone. The true value comes from the feedback conversations, acknowledgement of styles and strengths as well as the follow through on the commitments of just how the team will work together.

First team members read their individual reports. I conducted another short session on understanding behavioral styles and the interpretation of the graphs in the report. Then, in small groups, the team members answered a series of questions, posed by the leader. John and I agreed on these questions before the meeting:

- What 3–5 things from your report should other team members remember to do/not do to best communicate with you?
- What are some of the similarities and differences you are discovering in your group?
- Based on these similarities and differences, how/when do you see conflicts and misunderstandings in communication occurring between team members?
- What are 3–5 words you think other people would use to describe you?
- How would you check these perceptions out to see if they are on target?

John facilitated a conversation among the team members about their answers. I observed how he conducted this part of the meeting and recorded my observations, but I did not intervene during this exchange.

After team members had a chance to work in the initial small group conversation, I did another brief teaching piece—sharing the graphic depicting the team members' behavioral styles so that they could see the style of each member in relationship to each other. I then had them reform into small groups according to their styles.

John resumed leadership of the team. He asked these new groups to discuss the following questions:

- What 6–8 general characteristics do you all have in common?
- List 6–8 things you believe people value about all of you.
- Name 3–5 ways you believe people have difficulty working with all of you.
- Pick one or two of the behaviors in your DISC analysis. How are these behaviors demonstrated at work?

- How have these behaviors made you successful?
- Have any of these behaviors created problems for you or your staff? How?
- How do these behaviors match up with the other team members?

John facilitated a conversation in which team members shared their discoveries with each other. Again, I observed his facilitation. During this portion, I noticed that John was allowing too much side conversation (people were excited about their learning). Requesting permission to coach, I asked John how he thought the meeting was going. He turned the question back to the team, and several members identified that they thought the team was off track. He asked their help in staying on task and proceeded with the meeting.

I could see that some of the team members were surprised by this exchange. Later one of them told me that she was encouraged by John's method of handling the question and the team. Encouraging these conversations between the leader and the team is part of the role of the team coach. For a team to establish the trust that it takes to work together to accomplish their goals, team members, beginning with the leader, must be willing to step up and be vulnerable. Once team members see that the leader is willing to be vulnerable, they are more likely to express their own opinions and consider others' points of view.

Following this conversation, John worked with the team to develop the mission, roles, responsibilities, and ground rules. This phase of team development allowed me to serve in a traditional coaching role, observing the leader and the team members, asking for permission to share observations and asking key questions.

Katzenbach and Smith (1993)[2] define a team as "a small number of people with complimentary skills who are committed to a common purpose, set of performance goals and approach for which they hold themselves mutually accountable." Helping the team get clarity about mission, roles, responsibilities, and ground rules is important formative work for the leader. Teams that operate with a solid understanding of these critical elements produce significantly better results than teams who must find their way without the right foundation.

John worked with the team to establish a set of group norms. The group decided to meet weekly on Monday mornings from 7:30 a.m. and finish by 9 a.m. Norms included the following:

- Start and end meetings on time
- Submit agenda items the Friday before the meeting
- Include the time needed and the expected outcome for each agenda item
- Recap action items at the end of the meeting
- Evaluate the meeting at the end and course correct for the next meeting
- Keep meeting information confidential
- Discuss how to cascade communication to the rest of the organization at the end of each meeting

Each team member agreed to hold each other to these norms. My role as coach was to coach the team to follow through on their commitment to the norms and to each other. I got permission to step in both to have them notice when they were doing this well and when they needed to relook at how they were honoring their norms. The team members became more comfortable with giving each other feedback and realized that by holding back, they were hurting the team and also their teammates.

Continuing Work With the New Team

My ongoing work with a new team consists of attending team meetings, continued coaching with the leader, and coaching individual team members. In this case, after the initial team session, I attended weekly leadership meetings for three months, coached the leader every two weeks, and met with individual team members every month. I was also available between meetings for conversations with the leader and team members. After the initial three months, I attended occasional leadership meetings and continued coaching the leader and several team members.

During the team meetings, I helped John pose well-structured questions rather than offering definitive answers as he initially stated he had a tendency to do. John's style is fast paced, results oriented, and competitive as well as visionary. In the past, he said he lost the support of co-workers when he became impatient and moved ahead with his own agenda. During our individual coaching sessions, John recalled the times he had been successful in team meetings—realizing he had more success as a leader when he enabled the team members to develop their own ideas instead of directing them to his.

A major piece of work for this new team was focusing on their results and not the next "great idea" that the leader (or another team member) came up with. John asked the team members to each identify the most important initiative in his/her department. He then facilitated a group discussion of how each team member would need to contribute to these initiatives for organizational results. Each member committed publicly to what the team needed to achieve and John is in the process of developing a scorecard to review progress against the expected achievements.

Successful teams focus on both task and process. The task of the team is the specific work the team does toward defined objective—the "what" question. The way the individuals work together to complete the work process is the "how" question. To keep success in focus, John has two questions posted on his wall that he asks the team to consider at every meeting:

- Are we working on *what* we should be working on (mission, strategy, goals, and objectives)?
- Are we working *how* we should be working (roles, responsibilities, and following ground rules)?

Conclusion

As the case study shows, team coaches need to shift into consulting, teaching, and facilitation to help the new team understand their behavioral dynamics, maintain open communication, productivity, and effectiveness. The purpose of team coaching, however, doesn't change. As noted by Alexander Caillet (2007),[3] team coaching strives to increase the performance level of a team as it works toward a specific outcome. It strives to promote the individual growth of team members along the way with the intention of creating capacity within the team for sustaining quality and generating excellence.

John's team is certainly not typical of all teams and the coaching approach is not the only model that could be used for a brand new team. There are many approaches to team coaching and many types of teams that may contract for team coaching. Workplace teams enable groups of people to respond to workplace challenges and goals in unique and creative ways, but they can be challenging to manage in the best of circumstances and can easily develop into a quagmire if things go wrong.

Coaching is often used as an effective means of helping new teams draw out the wisdom and experience of each individual while helping them take responsibility for collectively achieving results for the organization. When coaching new teams, it is critically important to coach the leader to create a safe environment for open communication and to support the team members in their own individual development as well as to meet the team's task-related goals. Remember, many leaders are skilled at focusing on task (what), but not on process (how). A masterful coach helps the leader and the team pull together to clarify the goal, develop a plan of action, and overcome the barriers along the way.

Notes

1. Target Training International, Ltd., *TI Success Insights (team assessment program, 2007).*
2. Katzenbach, Jon R. and Douglas K., Smith (March–April 1993), "The Discipline of Teams," *Harvard Business Review,* July 2005, 162.
3. Caillet, Alexander, "Coaching Teams and Groups in Organizations" (manuscript, 2007).

Contributors

Notes on Editors

Christine M. Wahl was a leadership coach long before coaching became a viable and credible discipline in organization development. With more than twenty years of experience, her coaching practice spans numerous industries and is focused on coaching leaders and their teams. Christine is the creator and director of the Georgetown University Leadership Coaching Certificate Program. She holds a BA in psychology and a MA in counseling. She is a certified professional effectiveness coach (New Ventures West) as well as a master certified coach (International Coach Federation). She is active in ICF as an evaluator for coach certification, a frequent contributor to journals, and frequent speaker at coaching and leadership conferences.

Clarice L. Scriber, president and CEO of Clarity Consulting, is a master certified coach (International Coach Federation), who has been a member of the Georgetown faculty since 2001. Clarice earned her coaching certification through the New Ventures West Professional Coaching Course and a certificate in developmental coaching from the Interdevelopmental Institute. She holds a MS in clinical psychology from Loyola College in Maryland; a MA in communications from the Annenberg School of Communications, University of Pennsylvania, and a BA in French from the former Morgan State College.

Beth Bloomfield is the founder and principal of Bloomfield Associates, LLC. Beth is an experienced certified executive coach, strategic consultant, and former senior executive whose clients include leaders in the business, nonprofit, and public sectors. Beth has earned the distinction of professional certified coach (PCC) from the International Coach Federation, and she is also a certified management consultant (CMC), the mark of excellence among management consulting professionals, awarded by the Institute of Management Consultants. Beth graduated from Barnard College and earned a MA from Columbia University. She is an instructor and learning circle coach in the Georgetown University Leadership Coaching Program.

Contributors

Frank Ball has been an independent executive coach and organizational consultant for more than ten years. Before starting his own practice, he was a manager and leader in a number of large organizations for more than two decades. Frank holds a BA in economics from Davidson College, a MS in financial management from George Washington University, and a certificate in organization development from Georgetown University. He completed the yearlong professional coaching course presented by New Ventures West and shorter, more focused courses presented by the Newfield Network, the Strozzi Institute, the Interdevelopmental Institute, and the Gestalt Institute of Cleveland. He has been designated a master certified coach by the International Coach Federation.

Alexander Caillet is cofounder and European managing partner of Accompli, LLC, a global leadership consulting firm. In addition, Alexander is on the faculty of Georgetown University's Leadership Coaching Certificate Program and is an honorary vice president of the Association for Coaching in London. He is a frequent international speaker on the subjects of change, teams, coaching, and leadership. Alexander completed his BS in psychology at the University of Michigan and his MA in organizational psychology at Columbia University.

Randy Chittum is the vice president, leadership development at PSS/World Medical in Jacksonville, Florida. In this role, he coaches executives and other leaders, provides learning opportunities for all leaders, and manages the succession management program. Randy has taught leadership at several universities, including the MBA program at Georgetown University. Randy has a PhD in psychology from the University of Northern Colorado.

Eric de Nijs is an independent executive coach who works in a variety of different Fortune 500 companies and government agencies. He holds a doctorate in human resource development from Western Michigan University and two master's degrees from Bowling Green State University. In addition, he has completed coaching certificate programs from Georgetown University and Corporate Coach University.

Katherine Ebner is the founder and principal of the Nebo Company, a leadership development firm based in Washington, DC. She is also cofounder of a Connecticut-based company dedicated to the professional development of female leaders, called Full Circle Partners, LLC. Katherine earned a BA in English/creative writing from Middlebury College in 1987 and has completed graduate work in English literature at the Bread Loaf School of English. She holds a certificate in leadership coaching from Georgetown University.

Margaret Echols has been assisting individuals, groups, and organizations in taking steps toward transformation for nearly twenty years. Before creating the Development Consortium, Margaret was a senior manager within executive development at PricewaterhouseCoopers. Margaret's academic background includes a MBA from George Washington University with concentrations in international business and organizational behavior and BA and MA degrees in education and administration from the University of Florida. She is a master certified coach

(International Coach Federation), a certified professional effectiveness coach (New Ventures West), and has completed a graduate coaching program with the Newfield Network. Margaret also has extensive training in somatic coaching and is certified as a somatic coach by Strozzi Institute.

Karen Gravenstine is an internal organization effectiveness consultant at AARP in Washington, DC. She specializes in supporting leaders and teams in creating work environments in which committed, competent individuals join together with their unique contributions to achieve a shared vision and mission. Karen is a master certified coach (International Coach Federation), and holds a MA from Catholic University.

Sheila Haji has more than twenty-five years of internal and external experience as a manager, consultant, trainer, and coach. She has spent the past ten years working directly with corporate executives, managers, and teams to enhance their effectiveness in the midst of chaos and change. Before her career as an independent consultant, Sheila spent sixteen years at the former Bell Atlantic Corporation. Sheila completed her undergraduate work at the University of Virginia. She also holds a MS from George Washington University and a MS in human resource development from the American University.

Patricia A. Mathews is a master certified coach (International Coach Federation) and president of Mathews Associates, her leadership and executive coaching and consulting business. She has had more than thirty-six years of health care experience, including clinical, management, and educational roles in acute care, outpatient, and educational settings. Pat is a certified professional behavior analyst and certified professional values analyst. She is a registered nurse and has a MA in health administration from Jersey City State College and a certificate in leadership coaching from Georgetown University.

Sue E. McLeod is the principle of MacReynolds & Company and a senior consultant with Hay Group. She holds a BA in mathematics from Colby College in Waterville, Maine. Sue received her coaching certification from the Coaches Training Institute (CTI) in 2001, and was granted the professional certified coach (PCC) designation from the International Coach Federation in 2003. For more than twenty years, Sue worked for the MITRE Corporation in McLean, Virginia, holding management and change leadership positions on a wide range of consulting projects for the U.S. Federal Government.

Sandy Mobley, founder of the Learning Advantage, has been providing individual and team coaching for more than twenty years. Before starting her company in 1992, Sandy worked as an executive at Hewlett Packard, Watson Wyatt, and McKinsey. Sandy has a MBA from Harvard Business School and MA in mathematics. She is a master certified coach (International Coach Federation), a master somatic coach by Strozzi Institute, and a professional effectiveness coach by New Ventures West.

Sheryl D. Phillips, an executive coach and leadership consultant, has spent twenty years partnering with individual leaders, leadership teams, and the owners of organizational systems to create more effective and whole organizations. Sheryl has a master's degree from the College of William and Mary and a bachelor's degree from Auburn University. She is a certified professional coach by the Newfield Network, a certified somatic coach by the Strozzi Institute, and she has a certificate in organizational learning from George Mason University.

Lloyd Raines is a seasoned executive coach, consultant, and educator. He is principal of Integral Focus, a leadership development consulting and coaching firm. In his early professional years, Lloyd was director of a nonprofit organization in Washington, DC, and then director of an undergraduate honors program in justice studies. He was a founding faculty mentor in the Federal Judicial Center Leadership Program and a founding faculty member of Georgetown University's Leadership Coaching Program, where he continues to teach. Lloyd has a MA in justice for the American University and a BA in psychology from University of Maryland. He is a master certified coach (ICF).

Julie K. Shows is the president and founder of the Coaching Connection, a coaching company that works with leaders, executives, and entrepreneurs. Julie is recognized as a master certified coach, a designation awarded to the most experienced coaches by the International Coach Federation. She has completed coaching certification programs from Georgetown University and Success Unlimited Network. She holds a BA from Miami University in Ohio.

Jennifer Sinek is a master certified coach (International Coach Federation) and management consultant. She has more than fifteen years experience working with individuals, teams, and organizations. Jennifer earned a master's degree in public and private management from Yale University and a bachelor's degree in psychology from Colgate University. She has earned the designation of certified professional effectiveness coach from New Ventures West.

Dave Snapp was a union organizer for more than twenty years before becoming a consultant and coach. As part of his practice, Dave is a core faculty member of the SEIU Institute for Change. He holds a BA from Brown University and a MPH from the University of Michigan. He has completed certificate programs in organization development, change leadership, and leadership coaching at Georgetown University.

Neil Stroul is a professional psychologist, who left the therapy world for organizational consulting and training in 1979. A partner in Kenning Associates, Neil's entire career has been devoted to helping organizations foster a developmental culture. Focusing on leadership coaching during the past ten years has been his most recent discovery about how to help organizations become more developmental.

Jennifer Whitcomb, a professional certified coach (International Coach Federation), is principal of the Trillium Group, a firm focusing on enhancing leadership and organization effectiveness. Jennifer is an executive coach, team coach, and consultant. She has a master's degree in human resource development, and certificates in coaching from the Coaches Training Institute and Newfield Network. She also is a master certified action learning coach. She is a previous director of the Organization Development Certificate Program at Georgetown University.

Index

CPSIA information can be obtained at www.ICGtesting.com
Printed in the USA
LVOW11*1753130813

347695LV00002B/3/P